EUROPEAN CITIES
1890–1930s

For Nick

EUROPEAN CITIES
1890–1930s

HISTORY, CULTURE AND
THE BUILT ENVIRONMENT

Helen Meller

JOHN WILEY & SONS, LTD
Chichester • New York • Weinheim • Brisbane • Singapore • Toronto

OTHER WILEY EDITORIAL OFFICES

John Wiley & Sons, Inc., 605 Third Avenue, New York, NY 10158-0012, USA

WILEY-VCH Verlag GmbH, Pappelallee 3, D-69469 Weinheim, Germany

John Wiley & Sons Australia Ltd, 33 Park Road, Milton, Queensland 4064, Australia

John Wiley & Sons (Asia) Pte Ltd, 2 Clementi Loop #02-01, Jin Xing Distripark, Singapore 129809

John Wiley & Sons (Canada) Ltd, 22 Worcester Road, Rexdale, Ontario M9W 1L1, Canada

LIBRARY OF CONGRESS CATALOGING-IN-PUBLICATION DATA

Meller, Helen Elizabeth.
   European cities 1980–1930s : history, culture, and the built environment / Helen Meller.
     p. cm.
   Includes bibliographical references and index.
  ISBN 0-471-49554-9 (pbk.)
    Cities and towns—Europe—History—20th century. I. Title.

HT131 .M45 2001
307.76'094—dc21

2001017868

BRITISH LIBRARY CATALOGUING IN PUBLICATION DATA

A catalogue record for this book is available from the British Library

ISBN 0-471-49554-9 (paper)

Typeset in 9/12pt Caslon 224 from the author's disks by Mayhew Typesetting, Rhayader, Powys
Printed and bound in Great Britain by Bookcraft (Bath) Ltd, Midsomer Norton

This book is printed on acid-free paper responsibly manufactured from sustainable forestry, in which at
least two trees are planted for each one used for paper production.

CONTENTS

INTRODUCTION

This is a book about the history of European cities in the period 1890–1930. That appears to be a straightforward objective until a few questions are raised. Which European cities will be included? What themes will be highlighted? Why does the chosen period cover the end and the beginning of "normal" time spans in general history books: that is, up to the First World War, or after the War? How does it fit into the literature on the history of European cities that already exists? The literature is vast. Urban history is flourishing in Italy, Spain, Portugal, France, Belgium, the Netherlands, Britain, Germany and the Nordic countries, to mention only those represented in a recent overview of European urban history[1]. The problem here, in communicating the results of this work, remains the hurdle of language. One of the aims of this book is to provide a synthesis of some of this work, on the theme of European civilisation and the quality of urban life, for English speakers[2]. The overall objectives are twofold. First, to provide an insight in sufficient depth of a number of European cities so that it is possible to see the way specific changes, commonly experienced across Europe, influenced particular places[3] Secondly, to use a comparative approach, across cultural boundaries, as a means of revealing the way in which social and cultural differences shaped responses during a period of rapid change and modernisation.

Modernisation is a word that sometimes covers up more than it illuminates. The aim of this book is to explore what it meant in European cities, in terms of the quality of urban life, at a very particular point in time. There were three spectacular challenges in the period 1890–1930. The first was experienced on a national level. There had been, and was still, such constant shift of population from country to town, that many countries were finding, for the first time in their history, the majority of their populations living in towns and cities[4]. This had happened already in Britain by 1851 and in Belgium soon after. In the period 1870–1930, the largest European nation, Germany, was to experience this shift, rather dramatically before the First World War. Eventually France, in the late 1930s, was also to follow. Other European countries still had a majority of population living in rural areas but the underlying trend in population movements was urban, though many migrants, especially the Jews, were taking the final leap to the United States of America[5]. Such movement of people into cities was creating the prospect of mass urbanisation, a new factor in the creation of national identities[6].

The second challenge was international. The period 1890–1930 marks the swansong of European domination of the world economy. The rapid development of a global multilateral economy from 1870, which had taken place without plan but with the aid of European investment, banking, insurance, knowledge and entrepreneurship, had given Europe economic and political domination of the world[7]. The natural corollary of such domination was the supremacy of European culture world-wide. European cities, as the repositories of such culture, were made more self-conscious about their image and identity[8]. Imperial powers, especially Britain and France, nurtured a Europeanised culture in their colonies and colonial cities[9]. Yet at the very apex of this period of European influence, there were signs of counter-economic, cultural and political revolutions of the future. Most important was America's growing economic dominance of the world. The might of America was already apparent in the closing decades of the nineteenth century and became painfully apparent during the Great Depression (1929–32), as a more dependent Europe was pulled into crisis by America's economic problems[10]. In 1917, in the turmoil generated by the First World War, Russia underwent a Communist revolution. It was to prove a mighty attempt to offer an alternative blueprint for the future. Eventually, Soviet cities were to become symbols of the new regime although Eastern Europe is not covered in this book[11]. Choices in the development of the physical environment were given ever stronger political messages.

The third challenge was much more local, immediate and pressing. In Britain, in the early nineteenth century, when cities had grown rapidly, more and more people had crammed themselves into the space defined by the city's boundaries. By the late nineteenth century, these boundaries were extended and further extended. In continental Europe, the problems of expansion were compounded by the fact that most large cities were fortified. Cities, such as Barcelona, were being literally strangled by their lack of space to expand by the mid-nineteenth century. Increasingly, through the latter decades of the century, everywhere fortifications were demolished to allow for development. Yet as cities grew, what constituted urban living was materially affected. Were extensions new cities attached to old cities or were they the means of transforming the whole into something different? The crucial social change in the period 1890–1930 was the creation of an ever larger urban working class. The introduction of factory methods of production into most large industries created a more homogeneous working class which could be more easily organised to achieve industrial power and political influence.

But the medium for translating aims to achieve a better quality of life for the workers into fact: into better housing, better transport, better educational institutions, more parks and open spaces and other leisure facilities, was the city[12]. New ways had to be found of offering all the citizens of European cities more satisfying ways of living and ever more social opportunities. Thus on a local and regional level, on a national and international level, the quality of life in European cities was being severely tested in the years before and after the First World War. It is this which gives a unity to the period covered in this book, though there is no intention of claiming the period has a special unity in other ways. The aim has been to assess one aspect (a constantly changing aspect) of the European urban experience: how people understood and valued the quality of civilisation to be found in their cities and how they tried to adapt their ideas to meet the challenges of present and future. What follows will be an outline of the historical context of the European experience in the period 1890–1930 and the rationale behind the choice of themes and of cities for comparison to be found in this book.

THE GEDDESIAN PERSPECTIVE

First, though, it is necessary to introduce the approach adopted in this book. Generalisations about the "quality of civilisation" in European cities demand a particular perspective[13]. Here, the work of a contemporary figure, the pioneer sociologist and town planner, Sir Patrick Geddes (1854–1932) has been inspirational. He tried, in the very period covered by this book, to develop a general understanding of the past, present and possible future of cities. He was fascinated by the advent of mass urbanisation, by the development of modern technology and the ever more rapid transmission of ideas across national boundaries. He became convinced by his programme of constant study and frequent travelling to cities in Europe and America, that the history and culture of particular places both dictated the way new ideas were absorbed and also gave cities the resilience to change and adapt over successive generations. He set out to try and elucidate the connections between history, culture and the physical environment[14]. This book follows in his footsteps though, it is important to add, not towards the target of promoting a Geddesian theory of progressive evolution. In historical terms, 1890–1930 was a transitional period between a past, when cities just grew and their form and condition were marked heavily by local circumstances, and a future when new bodies of professionals, bounded by national legislation and informed by the international exchange of ideas, would be responsible for the quality of life in cities. The purpose of this book is to capture that historical moment.

In 1915, Patrick Geddes published his only general monograph on cities: *Cities in Evolution*. He had written it before the First World War but its publication, at the point when it was becoming obvious that this was not going to be a short sharp war, was a lone, small, beacon of optimism in the dark days of mass killing and destruction. He wrote:

> The civic awakening and the constructive effort are fully beginning in healthy upgrowth, capable not only of survival but of fuller cultivation also, towards varied flower and fruit – flower in regional and civic literature and history, art, and science: fruit in renewal of towns and cities, small and great[15].

Geddes' career spanned the great transition from the High Victorianism of the nineteenth century to the introduction of modern ideas, culture and technology in the twentieth century. He was a polymath scholar, a professor of Botany, a pioneering British sociologist and geographer, but the passion which absorbed him was a lifelong study of cities and civilisation. What he saw in 1914 was not "the lamps . . . going out all over Europe", the vision of an aristocratic British Foreign Secretary[16]. He saw the war as an aberration, an unnecessary conflict produced by the ignorance of all and sundry about how to deal with the cultural, emotional and political issues of nationalism and class. For Geddes the answer was clear. It lay in the process of urbanisation that had been taking place with increasing intensity in his lifetime.

Geddes' understanding of the process of urbanisation runs like a leitmotiv through this book. This is not because he was always right or even very influential in his own day but because his perspective on city development offers the chance of asking new questions about the relationship between history, culture and the physical environment. At the end of the twentieth century, we are ever more aware that the whole world is now sharing in the process of rapid urbanisation; that economic activity is now global; that modern technology has created yet another revolution in communication, transport and methods of production. The implications of all this on the ground, in the local, regional and national context, are not at all clear[17]. It is easy to assume because of the speed and ease of communication and the globalisation of knowledge, that cities in the advanced world are all becoming similar. Life is roughly the same, bar some climatic differences, if you live in Manchester, Munich or Marseilles. But is it? Are cities mere repositories of a global culture, underpinned by a shared technology? Or do they have not only a chance to interact on their own terms with the exchange of ideas, but also the very act of doing so becomes part of their unending efforts at regeneration and renewal?[18]

There are practical questions about the use of energy sources for sustainable growth and the costs of service infrastructures that have a local and regional as much as a global context[19]. Answers to these latter depend on choice, which in an urban context, is tied up with ideals about the collective good and the well-being of future generations. This is what Geddes, with his belief that cities were organic entities, had already understood. He had grasped that once knowledge and resources had increased and multiplied, how they were used was a matter of morality. As a young man in the 1880s, he had cheekily lectured the leaders of the labour movement in Edinburgh to take a different political route to the future from one determined by the struggle between capital and labour. That was not the crucial issue.

> Capitalists and labourers . . . are very much alike at bottom . . . for both of them life is decidedly a poor affair . . . For both, life is equally blank at present; the capitalist in his big ugly house is no happier than the labourer in his little ugly one; if one has more fatigue, the other has more worry[20].

What was needed was some idealism about the future, based, not on an unobtainable utopia, but on practical, realisable, objectives improving the physical and social environment of cities which would enrich the lives of all men and women, regardless of class.

His sense of mission drove him to devote his life to campaigning for a better future for cities and their inhabitants and made him a pioneer town planner. Modern town planning was the new profession dedicated to improving the quality of the physical environment of cities. Geddes believed that this was a dangerous business. Cities could be damaged as well as improved. He was most anxious about the intervention of the state. National government was an inappropriate level on which to handle the regeneration of the city, which demanded local knowledge and an understanding of the interconnectedness of the social sciences[21]. He believed that the way town planners should envisage their work depended on a unique variable: the cultural context within which they worked, which presupposed an understanding of the economic, social and political factors. As a biologist he was prepared to say loud and clear that the differentiating feature of *homo sapiens* from all other species was greater ability to create more complex cultures which could be handed down from one generation to the next. It was precisely this ability to create civilisations and evolve new patterns of culture which had contributed to increasing knowledge and the means of exploiting it. Furthermore, the power-houses of civilisation had to be cities, where the clash of thought of many men and women led to huge variations and differences, the seed for cultural evolution in the future. Geddes was full of a progressive evolutionism but the elements he chose to write about in *Cities in Evolution* are excellent reference points for the changes European cities were experiencing at the turn of the twentieth century.

His book is written is a strange style and the structure can appear idiosyncratic. However, because of his concern with civilisation and culture on a grand scale, he adopts a general approach. His first contribution (albeit a rather cavalier one since history is reduced to a number of questionable over-simplifications) is to try and distinguish between the different kinds of technology that have had an impact on cities since the Industrial Revolution in the late eighteenth century[22]. He invented a new terminology. The first stage, the period of iron and steam power, he labels the Paleotechnic age. In the Geddesian canon, this was the age when men, women and children were sacrificed on the altar of the steam engine and human life was cheap. Manufacturing cities grew dramatically but were so polluted and over-crowded that their continued growth depended on a constant supply of rural immigrants. This period was followed in the second half of the nineteenth century by the Neotechnic age. New science-based industries, electricity, the internal combustion engine, greater knowledge about the world's resources, all meant a massive change for the still growing populations of Europe. Physical labour was lightened and children progressively removed from the labour force. What was needed now was a more highly skilled, better educated labour force.

Investing in education put a premium on keeping people alive. The public health movement, which swept the cities of Europe in the second half of the century, began to save lives. City boundaries were extended and the great densities of central areas were cleared as modern mass transit systems were built and the physical limitation of the walk to work broken. Geddes wanted to go from the possibilities of his Neotechnic age to what he called the "Eutechnic" age[23]. He believed European cities were on the verge of an age dedicated to the nurture of the common people for the first time in modern history. Technical innovations could be directed now towards improving the quality of life of all people: their work, their health, their leisure. He was thinking not in terms of the political will, or the resources that such a change would need. For him, the effort was to imagine it first, so that it might become a possibility. The experience of mass urbanisation was so new that no one had any clear ideas of the social and physical consequences. In inimitable fashion, Geddes even coined a word for the prospect of the endless, formless, urban expansion that this conjured up: conurbation[24]. He had seen areas such as the Lancashire textile towns where the boundaries of one town had extended to meet the boundaries of the next. The crucial factor in all this building was the quality of homes and the provision of open space. Geddes devoted chapters in his book to homes and housing and was full of admiration for German cities where the process of expansion and the building of homes had been managed better than anywhere else in the world.

Geddes' concern about the quality of life on the periphery of cities was matched by equal concern about city centres, though here his priorities change. He saw historic centres as vital components in the creation of civic identities, something he calls the "civic spirit" which is much more than just an interesting relic of the past. Civic identities played an important role in stimulating ideals, generating a competitive spirit between cities for social objectives and, always an important urban experience, in the constant process of urban renewal. Geddes' own earliest practical work had been in the Old Town of Edinburgh where he worked on a voluntary basis to conserve and renew the built environment of the Royal Mile and its surrounding area[25]. He was not thinking about tourism in the future though he was not unaware of the possibilities. What concerned him most was that this beautiful townscape contained the physical evidence of Scotland's past as an independent nation. He wanted it to be a reference point for future generations of Scottish people, a desire which has been realised a century later with Scottish devolution.

In his work in Edinburgh, his many other social and educational activities and his future as an international prophet of the town-planning movement, Geddes had developed an excellent understanding of contemporary European cities and the challenges they faced. This was recognised by contemporaries at the last international congress before the First World War on cities and municipal life, held in Ghent in 1913, when Geddes' famous Cities and Town Planning Exhibition was awarded the Gold Medal[26]. If Geddes saw the First World War as an aberration, his death in 1932 , at the age of 78, spared him the spectacle of the rise of Fascism in Germany and the human catastrophe of the Second World War. That war was also an urban catastrophe, as the cities of Europe, especially the great cities of

Germany and Britain, were destroyed by massive bombing raids. Yet half a century after the Second World War, the ghost of Geddes might still find some grounds for optimism. The cities that were destroyed have risen again from their ashes. For all of them, their former history and culture were important reference points in their reconstruction and regeneration, even when there was no attempt to rebuild exactly what had been there before. In the 1990s, the rebuilding of Berlin provided the last and possibly greatest challenge for a European city in the twentieth century[27]. The actual dismantling of the Berlin Wall, built through the city in 1962 as a physical symbol of the antagonism of the Eastern and Western blocs, and the rehabilitation of historic areas and buildings, created a highly charged emotional atmosphere that Geddes would have understood. The clash between politics and market forces, between sentiment and reason, between history, the future and the need for vision, stand out in startling clarity. It offers the strongest possible evidence of the role of history and culture in shaping the urban environment.

THE HISTORICAL CONTEXT OF THE EUROPEAN URBAN EXPERIENCE, 1890–1930

The unique, however, always has to be balanced against shared experiences. While this book is devoted to exploring some of the ways in which history and culture have shaped the physical environment of cities, it is necessary to look at the historical context of the period 1890–1930 that influenced them all. What was particular about European urbanisation in this period? What kinds of challenges did cities face at this time? What kind of understanding was necessary to promote effective answers? The answers to these questions come from two directions: from the economic and social history of Europe and from the political and admin-istrative structures of nation–states.

The connecting link was an environmentally based public health movement which was pan-European and developed professional expertise in dealing with the health hazards of urbanisation. This was to lead to the formation of a modern town planning movement which was not only pan-European but global in the exchange of ideas[28]. The period 1890–1930, in particular, was the formative era of an inter-national town planning movement which was to peak in the immediate aftermath of the Second World War. It was a time when the relationship between society and its environment, in all its complexities, was explored. It was a "honeymoon" period when the intoxication of the prospect of future possibilities could run ahead of problems of implementation. Just imagining the future of a modern city, however, at this time, was the broadest possible challenge.

At the great Centennial Exhibition in Paris in 1900, Patrick Geddes ran a special International Summer School, to explain the modern world to anyone who was interested, using the national pavilions and huge range of exhibits as illustrations of his discourse[29]. What he was trying to do was to help people understand the process of urbanisation which seemed to be so overwhelming, so unstoppable, and so relatively recent. In 1800, only one city in Europe had reached a population of 1 million, and that was London. By 1900, London had 6.5m; and three other capital cities in Western and Central Europe were well over 1 million: Paris had 2.7m, Berlin, 1.889m, and Vienna 1.6m. This represented an increase since 1800, for London of 490%; Paris 367%; Berlin 998%; and Vienna, 578%. The experience of capital cities was at the extreme in the process of European urbanisation. For this reason (and because there are many more studies of capital cities)[30] they have been mostly excluded from this book. However, European capitals did not have a monopoly in the matter of giant scale[31]. There were, by 1900, nine other city areas with a population of more than 1m in the world. In America, there was New York, Chicago and Philadelpia; in Russia, St Petersburg and Moscow; and in Britain, pioneer country of mass urbanisation, there was Manchester and Birmingham and the giant port and industrial city of Scotland, Glasgow[32]. But that was not all. Just below these great cities, there was another layer, destined soon to reach the million mark.

In Germany, there was the great port of Hamburg which had reached 1 million by 1914. There were the cities of the Ruhr, so densely developed that one merged into the next creating vast urban areas (Patrick Geddes' conurbations). Munich, Cologne and Leipzig all were growing rapidly in the wake of increasing industrialisation. Budapest, the booming capital of Hungary was soon to reach 1 million. In Spain there was a strange struggle. The capital city, Madrid, had failed to industrialise very extensively during the nineteenth century and Barcelona, regional capital of the suppressed nation of Catalunya, a port and an industrial city, challenged the Spanish capital in size. In the first two decades of the twentieth century, Barcelona beat Madrid into second place, before the natural impetus for growth of the capital city was reasserted[33]. In France, with a less buoyant population growth, massive scale was harder to achieve[34]. Marseilles and Lyons fought for the place of the country's second city, actually falsifying statistical returns in the cause! Lyons was just larger but between the world wars, Marseilles gained the coveted position though neither city reached 1 million before 1930. Four of the cities studied in this book are drawn from this second tier: Hamburg and Marseilles, Munich and Barcelona. These were cities where imagining the future was a pressing concern.

Scale, though, was not the only thing demanding a new understanding of cities at the turn of the century. The decades either side of the Great War mark a turning point in patterns of growth. The era of headlong, dramatic growth in European cities was over. Cities were still growing and absorbing ever greater proportions of the populations of all the nation–states. Yet the desperate demographic pressures of the mid-nineteenth century years had abated. The massive, uncontrolled population growth which had swept Europe from west to east was over[35]. Beginning in the most highly industrialised and urbanised regions of Europe, fertility rates were falling. The check in population growth was not because of disease, disaster or famine, the terrible population checks identified by the Rev Thomas Malthus in

Britain in the late eighteenth century. It was through choice. People in ever more significant numbers, were choosing to have fewer children from the 1870s onwards. Before the First World War, the decline was most marked in the higher socio-economic classes, apart from France where it had been universal for the entire nineteenth century. After the war, it was a common European experience[36].

Of course in the period 1890–1930, there was also a demographic disaster. The First World War and the influenza epidemic in its aftermath killed an estimated 22 million people in Europe excluding Russia. Yet this disaster did not interrupt the flow of people into the cities. In Central and Eastern Europe, immediately after the war, the flow was increased by refugees made unemployed and vulnerable by the break-up of the great Empires, especially the Austro-Hungarian Empire, which had been highly cosmopolitan. Poles, Czechs, Hungarians and Slavs and many other nationalities sought sanctuary and safety within the newly drawn boundaries of their nation–states, set up under the Treaty of Versailles. The great cities of the Dual Monarchy, Vienna and Budapest, were checked in their growth and faced with enormous problems of readjustment and even contraction. Vienna suddenly ceased to be a great Imperial capital and became the capital of a small, mostly rural, Austrian state. Budapest found itself the capital city of a country a mere third of its former size. In the 1920s, these cities faced a huge transformation in their roles. The effort this required of imagining their new futures, makes them fascinating cases for study. How they, and the Czech capital Prague, fared in these extraordinary circumstances, forms a chapter of this book[37].

For most European cities, however, regardless of the war, the period 1890–1930 remained one of growth. The motor driving this process was the same as it had been throughout the nineteenth century: industrialisation. Lewis Mumford, in his early work, *The Culture of Cities*, devotes a whole chapter to describing the modern industrial city, to be found wherever industry flourished, as the "universal Coketown"[38]. The name, invented by Charles Dickens in his novel *Hard Times*, after one trip to Preston in Lancashire in the 1840s, is expropriated to deliver a swingeing attack on the environmental conditions of modern cities. The problem is that "universal Coketown" did not exist. All growing cities were industrialised but how they responded to the inherent environmental hazards depended very much on their earlier history. One of the more astonishing facts about European cities, given the extent of industrialisation, was that so few of them were totally new. New towns were mainly to be found on coal fields or where other vital raw materials, particularly iron ore, had been found. Anywhere where the two were in close proximity was destined to become the site for giant industrial cities in the nine-teenth century. The classic example is the Ruhr basin. Formerly a mainly rural area, the Ruhr became Germany's industrial heartland. Mining and industrial settlements grew rapidly, sometimes without regulations governing street widths, a public health infrastructure or the institutions of a civilised society. But not always. Oberhausen, a new town, grew in an orderly fashion, controlled from the outset by a determined and well informed elite[39].

The speed of urban growth in the Ruhr basin was dramatic and astonished contemporaries. The example often quoted is that of Essen, a little country town of 9000 inhabitants in 1850, which increased by 628 per cent to 55 000 inhabitants in 1875 and then, in a mere 25 years, leapt to 200 000, a further increase of almost 400 per cent by 1900. This was totally alarming. Yet by the 1890s, Essen was beginning to play an influential role in producing ideas about what was to happen next in the Ruhr basin as a whole. Coal and iron were still buoyant so the problem was not yet deindustrialisation. The challenge was to recognise that the towns of the Ruhr basin were part of a region which faced common environmental and social issues. This was highlighted by the problem of securing an adequate water supply. In 1899, the Ruhrtalsperrenverein was formed. This was an association of dam supervisors and it was the first organisation to develop a regional alliance between municipalities and industrial organisations on the grounds of a common objective: the provision of water. In this dawning of a new regional perspective, Essen was to make a special contribution. Robert Schmidt, a man concerned about the physical environment of the region, was asked to serve on Essen city council in 1907. He began to develop his ideas in a systematic way and, in 1912, wrote an influential memorandum for the council, outlining an approach which looked at the future of the city and the region together. With this document, he pioneered a whole new concept of urban regional planning for the Ruhr[40]. It was a response generated by the historical experience of city and region over the previous half century.

In the newly industrialised and urbanised areas, environmental issues were given the starkest exposure. This was not always the case with the older European cities and towns caught up with the process of industrialisation. Much depended on what kind of city they had been before and which industries developed within the city and its hinterland or region. The crucial historical factor here was variety. In Britain, where many towns and cities experienced considerable degrees of industrialisation in the first half of the nineteenth century, a Select Committee on the Health of Towns in 1840 attempted to classify all the different types of towns which existed. It identified the metropolis, manufacturing towns, populous seaports, great watering places and inland country towns, "not the seat of any particular manufacture"[41]. If seaside resorts are added to this list, then it remains a serviceable categorisation for European countries, regardless of national boundaries. Not all towns and cities in Europe experienced industrialisation. Some remained outside the main railway communication systems, servicing their agricultural hinterland. But the process of industrialisation, especially from the 1870s, swept across North-west Europe, making many established towns and cities the nodal points of new economic networks[42]. By the period 1890–1930, even seaside resorts, some of the fastest growing towns in the late nineteenth century, found they needed to create a wider economic base to keep their larger populations employed throughout the year. How Blackpool and Nice, two resorts with diametrically opposed images of themselves, faced the challenge of this future forms the subject of Chapter 5[43].

All towns and cities caught up in the process of growth and industrialisation at the beginning of the twentieth century, faced new challenges. Nation–states, especially France and Germany before the First World War, had imposed tariffs and embargoes on trade to try and protect their indigenous industries. But the process of modern industrialisation refused to be contained within national boundaries. Sidney Pollard's work has shown how it spread from region to region[44]. As each region became caught up in the new market conditions of the global economy, there were greater degrees of economic specialisation. Each region was forced to use its particular advantages to be competitive. Cities found themselves embroiled in international competition, a process which changed perceptions about their functions and their futures. Many were to use international exhibitions to raise their economic profile and maximise their success in international markets. The history of international exhibitions and their impact on cities is explored in several chapters of this book. Here it is enough to emphasise the way in which the process of industrialisation was leading many European cities to take stock of themselves and to put greater effort into defining and achieving goals for their future.

The goals were both economic and social. Promoting local industries and tradesmen were important objectives but equally important were social institutions and the pleasantness of the urban environment, indicators of the quality of life in the city. In the period 1890–1930, there was a remarkable shift in expectations of what constituted a civilised urban existence[45]. By the end of the nineteenth century, the basic requirements for sustaining human life had been achieved. Cities had ceased to have higher death rates than birth rates, relying on immigration to maintain growth. Clean water supplies, adequate drainage, the cleansing, paving and lighting of streets, regulations against the adulteration of food and drink, all were largely in place throughout Europe. International exhibitions, with their thousands of visitors, depended on this fact. But over and above the basic provision was a matter of choice. Visitors required hotels and restaurants. They also required entertainment. The city was on show in terms of what it could offer: parks and open spaces, museums, art galleries and libraries, theatres and concert halls, a vibrant cultural life at every social level[46]. What constituted a civilised life or indeed, European civilisation, was being self-consciously upgraded and made more widely available to all citizens.

In the early twentieth century there were to be some dramatic changes in the experience of urban living. They were brought about by competitive market forces and the rising aspirations of the urban working classes. New technology was important. Major exhibits at the international exhibitions, for example, were now dedicated to demonstrating all the possible uses of electricity for light and motive power. Electric trams and electric trains dominated pavilions. They were to transform the use of space in the city in conjunction with the invention which was to have the greatest impact on every single European city: the internal combustion engine[47]. From the 1890s, however, technology was not only transforming transport and manufacturing, it was also being applied to entertainment and culture. Asa Briggs has suggested that the cluster of inventions of the last quarter of the nineteenth century

> were as basic to new ways of life in the twentieth century as were the inventions of the last quarter of the eighteenth century in textiles, iron and power, to the new industrial patterns of the nineteenth century. The difference between them is that the eighteenth century inventions transformed the material standard of living and the nineteenth century inventions, the forms of culture[48].

The implementation of technology for cultural purposes, while market driven, was still subject to choice. To offer an illustration where public image outweighed economic considerations, there is the example of the very first underground railway in any continental European city which was built in Budapest in 1896. Its purpose was to take visitors from the city centre to Heroes Square, the focal point of the millennium celebrations of the city's foundation in 896 AD.

The relationship between technology and choice was symbiotic. In both the public and the private sphere of urban living, how technology was implemented and developed depended on cultural factors. In all European cities, however, in the early twentieth century, for the first time, the choices of the many, rather than an elite few, took precedence. The growth of mass spectator sport and mass entertainment in the form of the cinema were two instances of this. In the former, the electric tram system played a crucial role in helping thousands of spectators to arrive before a football match and disperse afterwards in the most efficient manner and electric floodlights enabled matches to be played regardless of natural light[49]. In the latter instance, the growth of film industries in France, America, Britain and Germany brought new international perspectives to ever wider audiences. The years between 1890 and 1930 marked a transitional period when the old cultural forms still flourished, especially the bourgeois-dominated cultural institutions in the city, while the new forms of mass entertainment were becoming established. The most ubiquitous form of urban culture, the culture of the street, was also changing. The face-to-face culture of the nineteenth century, dependent on high densities of people living in relatively small physical areas, was gradually disappearing as more people were able, due to modern means of transport, to move to the suburbs. The cultural life of cities was on a cusp, between the old and the new[50].

Perhaps the greatest change of all was the growing expectation of many less affluent citizens that they too could have some of the privacy, the individual lifestyles and comforts formerly enjoyed only by the rich. The crucial factor here was the demand for decent low cost housing. When the young Walter Gropius, architect and future director of the Bauhaus, was in the trenches, fighting a futile war, this was what he dreamed about[51]. Architects, instead of devoting their energies to fulfilling the whims of wealthy patrons, would use their skills to benefit the masses. Design skills would be used to sustain quality while lowering costs. Technology would be used to mass-produce housing units and their contents. This was a future for cities and citizens which the experience of war made more likely. There had been a groundswell of activities promoting healthier homes for the working classes in most European cities, on a greater or smaller scale, in the half century or so before the First World War[52]. But the war expedited change and the involvement of the state in the housing market. In economic terms, the war placed a greater burden on public authorities. Urban rents had been frozen by government decree in the belligerent countries as the war effort stimulated price inflation and depressed the standard of living of the urban working classes. In these circumstances, it was no longer profitable for private landlords to shoulder the costs of housing development. Nation–states and cities were thus faced with the problem, at the end of the war, of meeting the demand for new, better and cheaper housing.

Responses to this challenge were determined by politics, both national and local. Where political parties sought power with the support of the people, new housing was top of the political agenda. Where political freedoms were crushed, there was still greater concern for the health and welfare of the poorer classes as a justification of dictatorial rule[53]. In both cases, cities were in the front line in terms of delivering practical outcomes. How they did so turned out to be as much a matter of the quality of local and regional administration as a question of politics. Between 1890 and 1930, cities everywhere were beginning to grapple with the challenges of providing a higher quality of infrastructure and developing the technical expertise to deliver it. The First World War merely speeded up the process. It did not change conditions already clearly apparent before the war. Poverty of people and public institutions continued to test the extent to which the rich were ready to endorse a redistribution of some resources from rich to poor. In Germany, post-war hyperinflation stopped the great municipalities in their tracks[54]. There simply was little public funding for capital developments. For a while, it was the cities of the occupied Rhineland, such as Mainz and Cologne with its new young *Oberbürgermeister*, Dr Adenauer, who were able to take the lead in imagining their futures. They were particularly open to American and British ideas of urban development. The demolished fortifications of Cologne were to be replaced by parks and open spaces, creating an early attempt to "green" a city centre and make a sustainable city plan.

As hyperinflation was conquered with the help of the American Dawes Plan, other large German cities speeded up their attempts to recreate themselves in new ways. Cities such as Hamburg, Frankfurt and Dusseldorf undertook massive building schemes[55]. Frankfurt went as far as calling the newly developed areas, *Das Neue Frankfurt*, a new city dedicated to a totally different modern quality of life, though its new citizens were not drawn from the poorest classes. In Belgium and the Netherlands, objectives were mixed. In the former, emphasis was placed on recreating what had been lost during the war, especially the historic buildings of the city centres; in the latter, there were more urban housing schemes, created for example, by the New School of Architecture in Amsterdam[56]. For both, there was a strong desire to reward war veterans returning home by building new homes for them of the highest quality. It gave a boost to the ideal of the garden city, invented by Ebenezer Howard in England at the end of the nineteenth century, which was to become one of the most potent ideals for the future modern city of the people at this time. As a way of imagining a future, this ideal was transmogrified by political context and geographical region. How this happened forms the subject of another chapter in this book[57].

In France, emphasis was on the reconstruction of the devastated areas. The poor flocked to Paris where they were to find accommodation in the growing shanty towns on the very outskirts of the city, beyond the jurisdiction of urban authorities. Henri Sellier, Mayor of Suresnes, in the Paris conurbation, and a supporter of the *cité-jardin*, a Gallic interpretation of the garden city, dedicated his efforts to improving the lot of the working classes in his domain. Henri Sellier was a socialist and trade unionist who believed that all citizens should enjoy the same rights and facilities[58]. Such enlightened ideas were not to be found everywhere. Yet all industrialised nations had a greater vested interest now in creating a better educated, better fed and healthier workforce. The growth of new industries and the war itself had emphasised the fact that people were the most important of national resources. In the period 1890–1930, everywhere in Europe, the public health movement had been gaining a new focus. Mortality rates had been brought down for all age groups except for infants by measures against dirt, pollution and the poor quality of public services such as water supply. To get infant mortality down required the intrusion of the state into the private sphere, into the home. Educating mothers to care for their babies in life-enhancing ways concentrated attention on nutrition, health, exercise, knowledge[59]. Remarkably, in view of continuing poverty and the impact of the deprivations caused by the war, the fight against infant mortality was won. In its wake came the cult of health: for babies, children, young people and women. Modern fashions created new styles of healthier loose clothing, children were introduced to gymnastics and sport, campaigns for less overcrowding and healthier homes were constantly reinforced. All over Europe, cities, especially large cities, found themselves at the forefront in national attempts to regulate modern living.

It was in this context that the modern international town planning movement emerged and European nations began to pass legislation relating to the future control of the urban environment. This development is an important theme of this book but the subject is approached somewhat differently to the mainstream histories of town planning[60]. These have tended to concentrate on the growth of professional expertise, the great practitioners, and their ideas and their achievements in particular national contexts under the relentless pressure of technological innovation. In the chapters that follow, the work of pioneers of modern planning is subsumed within the history of particular cities. Sometimes the expansion of a particular city is the work of a particular pioneer, for example, the work of Ildefons Cerdà in Barcelona. Most often, the ideas of planners were introduced in cities by other people who interpreted their ideas according to the particular historical context of the city in which they happened to be working. Munich and the ideas of Camillo Sitte provide an example here[61]. The intention is to show that town planning was only part of a response to the challenge of modernisation of European cities and its achievements were determined by the cultural context of each city. In the period 1890–1930, issues relating to social welfare, public health and education, the quality of the urban environment and ideals of the future were not carefully differentiated. Questions about the role of urban government and the nature of citizenship were being posed, not answered.

Large cities were thus left, poised between the growing body of legislation emanating from national governments especially relating to public health, housing and transport, and the political commitment of local government organisations and private citizens. Since cities are complex, collective entities, outcomes were never straightforward. Social identities, political identities, personal identities, all played a part. Sometimes resistance to urban development was as important as the implementation of new legislation. There was a huge range of responses to urban change. The three leading European nations, Britain, Germany and France had totally different political cultures in this respect, which continued unabated in the period 1890–1930. The fate of British cities was tied up with the democratisation of local government over the nineteenth century, and the route this offered to Nonconformist businessmen to be recruited into mainstream national life. The growth of administrative structures depended on an ad hoc basis, on the quality of local leadership and the scale of the problems the city faced. Help in solving these, especially poverty and squalor, relied on a well-organised and flourishing voluntary sector, supported largely by women who worked out of a sense of civic duty and compassion. It is probably no accident that utopian ideas on the future of modern cities tended to emanate from Britain, especially in the two decades before the First World War[62].

France, on the other hand, had been the most highly urbanised country in the eighteenth century under the *ancien régime* and there was an established urban structure waiting for Napoleon's centralising administrative tendencies. Legislation regulating the physical environment of cities was more or less in place by the mid-nineteenth century, just at the point when Baron Haussmann and others were transforming Paris and creating the model of the modern European capital. The French approach to town planning has much to do with urban design. Mayors of cities, especially large cities, were professional politicians with an eye on the national stage which often led to a lack of interest in urban planning which was not a hot political issue[63]. One of them, Jules Siegfried (1837–1922), Mayor of Le Havre from 1878 to 1886, was unusual in trying to introduce a concern about the social consequences of urbanisation into mainstream politics. With personal experience of the textile town of Mulhouse which had pioneered housing associations to provide higher standards of accommodation for the workers, he had tried to do the same in Le Havre. When he reached Paris in the 1890s, he continued to promote the cause, founding the Musée Sociale as a support organisation. It was a member of this organisation, Marcel Poète, the chief librarian of the Bibliothèque Historique de Paris, who founded the École des Hautes Études Urbaine and influenced a whole generation of architects and politicians in facing the challenges thrown up by "l'urbanisme"[64].

Yet the two strongest visual models of the future emanating from France in the period 1890–1930 were the work of architects and urban designers, Tony Garnier and Le Corbusier. Both of these men produced highly sophisticated design concepts, Garnier publishing *La Cité industrielle* in 1901 to little acclaim at the time and Le Corbusier publishing his series of uncommissioned, large-scale urban plans such as *La Ville contemporaine de trois millions d'habitants* (1922) which culminated in 1935 with *La Ville radieuse*. This was based on an aborted plan for Moscow carried out in 1930 but stripped of its geographical location. Le Corbusier had tried to persuade the Russians to demolish their city before implementing his plans. He wrote in his report:

> It is impossible to imagine a combination of past, present and future in one city; and in the Soviet Union, more than anywhere else, it is a question of two eras facing opposite directions and sharing no common qualities. Everything in Moscow must be redone after everything has been destroyed[65].

These visions of a civilisation of the machine age, locked into a relationship with nature but not with history or society provoked huge resistance in the decades before the Second World War. The Congrès Internationaux d'Architecture Moderne (founded in 1928 and meeting every two or three years), in which Le Corbusier (and Gropius) played a major role, were used to promote an a-historical vision of the city of the future in which urban functions – housing, employment, recreation and traffic – were entirely separated. What was missing was an understanding of the complexities of urban society, what Geddes called "the social machine" which, in his view, of the "organic" city, was what kept the whole process of constant evolutionary change on course[66]. The French were magnificent designers and in the male-dominated world of architects and planners, which grew more powerful as cities grew in scale, their ideas, especially those of Le Corbusier, were to have world-wide influence.

Yet in the formative period of modernisation, in the early decades of the twentieth century, it was the Germans who dominated and impressed. This was because, for historical reasons, German cities had large well-established administrations and professional, often dedicated Mayors who helped to formulate and guide cities' responses to growth and change. Throughout the nineteenth century, the focus had been on controlling extension plans, an activity which was encouraged by the formation of the German State in 1871. Legislation placed the responsibility for the regulation of city extensions firmly on the shoulders of the municipalities, who responded by taking up their duties with considerable vigour[67]. When the American social reformer, F.C. Howe, came to Europe on another fact-finding tour just before the First World War, he published his results as a volume entitled *European Cities at Work*[68]. His first chapter was devoted to "The Birth of the German City" because, as he says, "I know of no cities in the modern world which compare with those which have arisen in Germany during the past twenty years"[69]. An English historian of Germany, William Harbutt Dawson, joined the ranks of many British commentators including Thomas Coglan Horsfall and R.H. Tawney, to give paeans of praise for municipal life and government in Germany (the title he gave to his book, published in 1913).

German cities had, for years, been acquiring land for development and then overseeing the development. Over the past four decades, they had developed municipal services of gas, water and electricity. They provided social welfare and they encouraged and supported the cultural life of the city. By 1914, no English city, not even Birmingham or Manchester, could match that record. There was less scope for modern German architect-planners to ignore totally the established urban environment. Walter Gropius, as first Director of the Bauhaus and doyen of modernists, was expelled along with his School from Weimar in the early 1920s as the bourgeois objected to what he was doing to art education. In Dessau, he and his colleagues got together to offer revolutionary designs for an estate of working-class housing. But their major influence was to be in the transformation of everyday life through the design of objects which could be mass-produced.

Large cities like Hamburg and Frankfurt employed modernist architects to plan their future developments but there was no question that these should supersede the old established city. The two were symbiotic, each feeding off the other. The quality and craftsmanship of German design were to produce modern architects of world class such as Mies van der Rohe. But even he was not able to get many commissions during the 1920s. At this time, the role of planners and architects in the modernisation of European cities was still muted. In German cities, it was the politicians and civic administrators who influenced the quality of urban life. The history of particular cities in Europe, and their attempts to develop a new social imagination in the light of rapid technological and industrial change, have less to do with architects and planners, whether British, French, German or any other nationality, and more to do with the way goals and objectives emerged from the overlap of politics, industrialisation and culture to be found in all large cities. Planning, city-building, community-building, problems of change and sustainability draw on many different elements. At base there are the hopes and aims of people. For the historian, the task is to explore how these were interpreted in particular cities in ways which were not only influential at the time but have continued to resonate across the twentieth century, as cities have been forced to reinvent and regenerate themselves. This is the challenge which has determined the shape of this book.

The Comparative Method and the Organisation of this Book

Finally, in this Introduction, it is necessary to look at the historical method which has been used. Obviously the choice of cities for study has been a somewhat arbitrary matter, dictated by space and the personal knowledge of the author. However, within such constraints an attempt has been made to fulfil a number of criteria. The first relates to the process of modernisation in the period 1890–1930. Social and cultural change at this time was influenced by the globalisation of communication. Thus in every chapter, an attempt has been made to keep the context of the local and regional, national and international in juxtaposition with one another. Europe was still the centre of a European-dominated world economy and cultural diffusion followed in its path. How it did so, though, is a largely uncharted path. The response of cities to change fills in a small part of this historical "lacuna". The next matter to determine was which cities were crucial in this process. What was the best method of analysing historical diversity? The answer has been to develop comparative studies of towns and cities which were related in the vital matter of function or type but were historically and culturally very different. Thus there are chapters devoted to regional cities, capital cities in a new context (the capital cities of Central Europe after the Great War) port cities, industrial cities and seaside resorts. Crucially though, in each case, the cities which are compared belong to different political, national, social and cultural traditions, reflecting the diversity of the European urban experience.

In Chapter 1, the first two cities to be compared are Barcelona and Munich, two "regional" capitals that were transformed in the early twentieth century. Outside capital cities, which had an overtly nationalistic agenda, cities that were classed as regional centres had the strongest, independent, vested interest in developing their economic and cultural identities. Christopher Harvie has written engagingly of the rise of regional Europe over the past two centuries. In the 1980s, the idea of a "Europe of the Regions" took off and with it, the new politics of devolved policy-making[70]. The concept of a region is ill defined. Is it a geographic, economic or ethnic unit? The only constant is that, whichever it is, it will contain a major city which will be seen as the regional centre. Barcelona and Munich are regional centres, regardless of the criteria used. In the period 1890–1930, their populations either doubled or more than doubled, immigrants came from further afield than the immediate hinterlands of the cities and both cities continued to industrialise quickly. Much of their historical past was thus disappearing. Yet they both strove to identify continuities as well as embracing their futures. Identities and aspirations were recast in the new context as part of the process of adaptation and sustaining the cities' abilities to face new challenges. For both cities, the period 1890–1930 was one of dramatic change which tested those abilities to the limit.

Chapter 2 is devoted to a different challenge: the challenge of dislocation and even contraction. Vienna, Budapest and Prague in the aftermath of the First World

Figure 1 *Location of case studies used in this book (modern international boundaries)* [Map drawn by Chris Lewis]

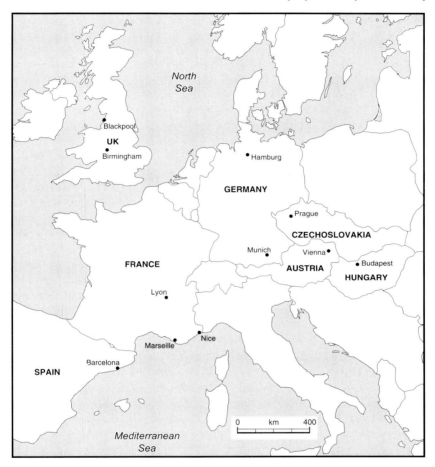

War found themselves in an unprecedented position for great modern cities. Their economic and political structures were wiped out. They had to start afresh, left with the legacy of their built environment, to meet the aspirations of their inhabitants. This was more immediately pressing than their positions as capitals of new nation–states and issues of nationalism. In each of these cases, the modernisation of the built environment was not just a matter of absorbing new technologies: of communication, of transport, of building materials. There was a questioning of what was valuable and what should be preserved as well as what was appropriate for the future. It was a particularly difficult context from which to view the future. What each city could achieve was also limited by the level of administration, expertise and resources available. A comparison and contrast of what they actually did in the 1920s offer a fascinating insight into the interplay of these forces.

Satisfying social aspirations of those formerly outside the mainstream of the political and social life of a city demanded new strategies. There was fresh interest in utopian experiments of the past and a growing exchange of ideas on an international basis of how the city of the future might look. Chapter 3 is devoted to an exploration of how one of the dominant ideas of this period, the idea of the garden city was understood and interpreted in a European context. The garden city was the invention of Ebenezer Howard, an English social reformer and visionary. The book which outlined his ideas was published in 1898, entitled: *Tomorrow, a Peaceful Path to Real Reform*[71]. The title was no idle boast. Howard believed that he had come to understand the challenge of modern urbanisation. He recognised that it was unstoppable and he pitted his wits to invent a method of preventing the clogging up of established cities to the point of their destruction by population pressures. The garden city was the answer. New smaller towns could be built on greenfield sites away from established cities. The garden city could be economically, socially and culturally independent, though modern technology, in terms of communications and transport, meant that it was not unconnected with the larger city of its region. It could guarantee its population the benefits of sun, light and air. Low housing densities, functional zoning and the maintenance of agricultural land in and around the garden city meant that it offered its inhabitants all the advantages of both living in the country and living in the city.

That was the English version. In the process of transmission, much of the content was missed. What was left was an ideal of a new lifestyle for the workers, a potent image in a war-torn and politically turbulent Europe. The chapter concludes with a case study of Zlín in Czechoslovakia in the 1930s, a modern reinterpretation of the nineteenth-century garden city ideal. The international debate about how the workers, how everyone should live in cities in the future, bred a new self-consciousness about the quality of urban civilisation. In terms of global communication, port cities were well placed to receive and transmit ideas about European civilisation and Chapter 4 is devoted to two of Europe's largest ports, Hamburg and Marseilles. They were at the rock face, receiving overseas visitors and providing the first stopping place for immigrants. In the period 1890–1930, these two great port cities of Germany and France were also the second cities of their nations. What did civilisation mean in these cities? What forms did it take? How was it transmitted? What influence did these ideas have on the future built environment as both cities expanded dramatically in scale and industrial activities, as well as fulfilling their functions as ports? These are the questions that this chapter sets out to explore. In many ways, there were astonishing differences in their perceptions of themselves as outstanding examples of European urban civilisation. The process of modernisation, in both economic and social terms, took place very much within the framework of these differing images, with considerable consequences both for their inhabitants and the future development of these cities.

If European civilisation was on trial in this period of economic conflict and war, so were the towns and cities which offered the rewards for capitalist industrial enterprise. These were the towns devoted to leisure and pleasure, that based their economic survival on offering the means for pleasure and consumption to both the leisured classes and the workers. In the nineteenth century, the bourgeoisie had long favoured the spa towns. But at the beginning of the twentieth century, when new technology began increasingly to be applied to entertainment, the seaside resorts were able to capitalise on the image of being more "modern". Indeed, in terms of lifestyle changes, they were at the forefront in defining new ways of seeking enjoyment which depended, not on class so much as money. The period 1890–1930 was a testing time for seaside resorts because they were so dependent on fashion and culturally determined priorities. Chapter 5 is devoted to two resorts, Blackpool and Nice, which approached the challenge of social and cultural change from diametrically opposite starting points. Blackpool, the mecca of the Lancashire proletariat, the inhabitants especially of the many textile towns, had in its favour the fact that holidays for the workers were to become a vital plank in raising standards of living generally in the period. Yet not all Blackpool's visitors were working class. Blackpool, as a holiday resort, had always depended on more affluent visitors. What it faced in the period 1890–1930 was the problem of coping with growth and sustaining its popularity.

This was exactly the same challenge facing Nice. Originally the haunt of European aristocracy who wintered in Nice to escape the tribulations of the climates in their own countries, Nice was faced with a dramatic change in demand, during and after the war. The European aristocracy disappeared and like Blackpool, the town had to reinvent itself for the next generation, only in the case of Nice, it was also a new clientele. It was helped by the cult of sunbathing and seabathing which became much more fashionable after the war as part of the modern cult of physical health and outdoor living. It ceased to be only a winter resort and attracted summer visitors by offering new events. Some of these were related to new technology. Nice was one of the places which pioneered car races along its esplanade. Nice, like Blackpool, continued to invent new images of itself as the place where the most "up-to-date" pleasures were available, the place with the truly modern lifestyle. Its transformation was complete when in 1936, as the French workers won their fight for paid holidays, the first train left Paris, packed with workers, destined for Nice. Throughout the period 1890–1930, Nice had also been developing as a port and an industrial city, in its role as regional centre. Such development threatened the quality of its environment, one of its greatest attractions for visitors. Nice and Blackpool, as seaside resorts, provide outstanding examples of urban environments which were created to attract and please visitors. Their wholehearted attempts to embrace modern trends and current fashions were a way of satisfying social aspirations. The control of their future and their physical plans were not just a matter of legislation, there were strong economic vested interests. The future of their physical environment was driven by market forces.

The final chapter in the book is devoted to a comparison of a built environment in which culture and politics, rather than economics, were the strongest influences determining future plans. One of the most important of all of the changes to the physical environment of most European cities was the building of areas of working-class housing on urban peripheries. The provision of working-class housing is touched on in a number of chapters. Here, however, the intention is to compare two developments, Kingstanding in Birmingham and Villeurbanne near Lyons. These two developments were both built in 1934 yet the physical environments produced offered two starkly contrasting interpretations of modern living. Kingstanding and Villeurbanne are not famous places. By 1934, the pioneering days in the provision of working-class housing were over. The Nazis had come to power in Germany. There had been a civil war in Austria. The great experiments in meeting the demand for huge quantities of low cost housing by adopting new designs, building materials and methods of construction, such as the work of Ernst May in Frankfurt had been abruptly terminated. That image of modernity did not suit the propaganda machine of the Nazis. May had gone to Russia, hoping that the communists would be more sympathetic to his work. He was building, not just housing, but a whole new way of modern living. His complex at Romerstadt, built in the 1920s, not only looked dramatically "modern" with its huge scale (1200 units) and long rows of low rise building. It also contained community amenities including shops, daycare centres, communal laundries and shared garden areas. May, however, found the Russians less than interested in his plans and he joined the great diaspora of modernist architects seeking work all over the world.

So 1934 was not a particularly auspicious year for building a brave new world. Yet in England and France, the two second cities, Birmingham and Lyons, both remained concerned about housing. The chapter explores why what was built in these places was so different, when both were trying to give form to an ideal of urban living, within the resources available. The different cultural and political contexts within which Kingstanding and Villeurbanne were developed were given permanent form in bricks and mortar. Both developments contributed towards a total transformation of the built environment of their respective major cities. The fact that they were built at all was due to the main theme of this book: the ways in which large cities responded to meeting the aspirations of their inhabitants during a period of rapid social and political change. Also, 1934 was the year that Catherine Bauer, the American housing reformer, wrote her influential mono-graph, *Modern Housing*, which was based on her study of workers' housing in Europe over the previous two years. She had seen the great apartments of Vienna, the experimental housing in Frankfurt and Berlin and examples of the work of many leading architects. She wanted to bring the best European ideas on future housing to an American audience. She quickly recognised that it would require a social, political and cultural commitment which was just not possible to engineer in the totally different historical context of American society[72]. The achievement of Kingstanding and Villeurbanne must thus be seen as products of a European tradition which did much to foster socially sensitive ways of helping cities respond to their futures. The aim of this book is to explore key aspects of this European urban tradition.

NOTES

1. R Rodger (ed) (1993) *European Urban History: prospect and retrospect* Leicester, Leicester University Press.
2. Astonishingly, the most widely used comparative history of European cities remains L Mumford (1961) *The City in History: its origins, its transformations, and its prospects* London, Secker and Warburg, though there is now L Benevolo (1993) *The European City* Oxford, Blackwell (simultaneously also published in Italian, German, Spanish and French).
3. This is to take a diametrically opposite approach to that of some historical geographers who, for their own valid reasons, try to find the common elements in the European city. See D Burtenshaw, M Bateman and G Ashworth (1991) *The European City: a western perspective* London, David Fulton Publishers; and to a lesser extent, P White (1984) *The Western European City: a social geography* London, Longman. For an overview of the geographical approach which keeps the individual and the general in perspective, see TR Slater "Urban morphology in 1990: developments in international cooperation" in TR Slater (ed) (1990) *The Built Form of Western Cities: essays for MRG Conzen on the occasion of his eightieth birthday* Leicester, Leicester University Press.
4. AF Weber (1899 repr. 1963) *The Growth of Cities in the Nineteenth Century* Ithaca, New York, Cornell University Press; PM Hohenburg and L Hollen Lees (1985) *The Making of Urban Europe 1000–1950* Cambridge, Mass., Harvard University Press.
5. AJ Fielding (1989) "Migration and the Growth and Decline of Cities in Western Europe" in R Lawton (ed) *The Rise and Fall of Great Cities* London, Belhaven Press.
6. EE Lampard (1976 edn) "The Urbanising World" in HJ Dyos and M Wolff (eds) *The Victorian City: images and reality* Vol I London, Routledge and Kegan Paul.
7. J Foreman Peck (1995 2nd edn) *A History of the World Economy: international economic relations since 1850* London, Harvester Wheatsheaf.
8. CE Schorske (1966 edn) "The Idea of the City in European Thought" in O Handlin and J Burchard (eds) *The Historian and the City* Cambridge, Mass., MIT Press, 95–114.
9. RK Home (1997) *Of Planting and Planning: the making of British colonial cities* London, E & FN Spon.
10. CP Kindleberger (1986) *The World in Depression 1929–39* Berkeley, CA, University of California Press.
11. DR Brewer (1990) *The Russian City between Tradition and Modernity 1850–1900* Berkeley, CA, University of California Press; SV Bittner (1998) "Green Cities and Orderly Streets: Space and Culture in Moscow 1928–33" *Journal of Urban History*, 25, 1, 22–56.
12. For Britain, see AJ Sutcliffe (1982) "The Growth of Public Intervention in the British Urban Environment during the Nineteenth Century: A Structural Approach" in JH

Johnson and CG Pooley (eds) *The Structure of Nineteenth Century Cities* London, Croom Helm.

13. For definitions of "civilisation" in the context of the city, see KE Boulding (1966) "The Death of the City: A Frightened Look at Postcivilisation" in Handlin and Burchard.

14. HE Meller (1990) *Patrick Geddes: social evolutionist and city planner* London, Routledge; P Boardman (1978) *The Worlds of Patrick Geddes: biologist, town planner, re-educator, peace-warrior* London, Routledge and Kegan Paul.

15. P Geddes (1915) *Cities in Evolution: an introduction to the town planning movement and to the study of civics* London, Williams and Norgate, preface v.

16. The foreign secretary was Sir Edward Grey, Viscount Grey of Falloden. The famous quotation concludes "We shall not see them lit again in our lifetime". EJ Hobsbawm (1994) *The Age of Extremes: the short twentieth century, 1914–1991* London, Michael Joseph, 22.

17. A von Saldern (1999) "Identities, Communities and Policies – Cities on the Threshold of a New Era" in B Blanke and R Smith (eds) *Cities in Transition: new challenges, new responsibilities* London, Macmillan, 67–78.

18. AD King (ed) (1991) *Culture, Globalisation and the World System: contemporary conditions for the representation of identity* Basingstoke, Macmillan. This is the more general issue rather than the one relating to a new world order of cities in a global economy, see S Sassen (1991) *The Global City: New York, London, Tokyo* Princeton, NJ, Princeton University Press.

19. KR Kunzman (1997) "The Future of the City Region in Europe" in K Bosma and H Hellinga (eds) *Mastering the City* Vol I, Rotterdam, NAI Publishers/The Hague, EFL Publications, 16–29.

20. P Geddes (1886) "On the Conditions of Progress of Capitalist and the Labourer" *The "Claims of Labour" Lectures*, no. 3, Edinburgh, Co-operative Printing Co., 34–5.

21. P Geddes (1886) "On the Conditions", 24.

22. P Geddes (1915) *Cities in Evolution*, 60–83.

23. He developed this idea further in his lectures at the first meeting of the British Sociological Society in 1904. P Geddes (1904) "Civics as Applied Sociology" published in *Sociological Papers 1904* London, Macmillan. Reprinted in HE Meller (ed) (1979) *The Ideal City* Leicester, Leicester University Press, 75–103.

24. P Geddes (1915) *Cities in Evolution*, 46–9.

25. P Geddes (1915) *Cities in Evolution*, 13.

26. P Geddes (1915) *Cities in Evolution*, 259–70.

27. U von Petz (1996) "Berlin after 1989: the renewal of a capital" *Proceedings of the 7th International Planning History Conference*, Thessaloniki, School of Architecture, 540–9; B Ladd (1997) *The Ghosts of Berlin: confronting German history in the urban landscape*, Chicago, Chicago University Press.

28. A Sutcliffe (1981) *Towards the Planned City: Germany, Britain, The United States and France 1780–1914* Oxford, Blackwell; K Bosma and H Hellinga *Mastering the City*.

29. P Geddes (1900) "Man and his Environment – a study from the Paris Exposition" *International Monthly II*, August, 169–95; P Geddes (1900) "The Closing Exhibition – Paris 1900" *Contemporary Review* November, 649–67.

30. Recent and full bibliographies can be found in T Hall (1997 English edn) *Planning Europe's Capital Cities: aspects of nineteenth century urban development* London, E & FN Spon.

31. T Barker and A Sutcliffe (eds) (1993) *Megalopolis: the giant city in history* London, Macmillan.

32. Sutcliffe (1981) *Towards the Planned City*, 2.

33. David-Sven Reher "Ciudades, processos de urbanización y sistemas urbanos en la

Península Ibérica 1550–1991" in M Guàrdia, F-J Monclús, JL Oyón (eds) (1994) *Atlas Histórico de ciudades europeas* Barcelona, Salvat Editores, 17.

34. J-L Pinol (1996) "Un système urbain vieux de vingt-cinq siècles" in J-L Pinol (ed) *Atlas Historique des Villes de France* Paris, Hachette Livre, département Hachette, 13.

35. For statistics on population and urban growth in Europe, see J de Vries (1984) *European Urbanisation 1500–1800* Cambridge, Mass., Harvard University Press; PM Hoenburg and L Hollen Lees (1985) *The Making of Urban Europe 1000–1950* Cambridge, Mass., Harvard University Press; AF Weber (1899) *The Growth of Cities in the Nineteenth Century: a study in statistics* New York, Columbia University Press.

36. J Gillis, L Tilly and D Levine (1992) *The European Experience of Declining Fertility 1850–1970* Oxford, Blackwell.

37. See Chapter 2.

38. This was the second volume in his four volume "Renewal of Life" series. The first was *Technics and Civilisation* New York, Harcourt Brace, 1934; the last two, same publisher, were *The Condition of Man* 1944 and *The Conduct of Life* 1951.

39. B Ladd (1990) *Urban Planning and Civic Order in Germany 1860–1914* Cambridge, Mass., Harvard University Press, 13.

40. U von Petz (1997) "The German Metropolitan Region. The Ruhr Basin: toward a new spatial policy" in Bosma and Hellinga (eds) *Mastering the City*, 57; U von Petz (1999) "Robert Schmidt and the public park policy in the Ruhr district 1900–1930" *Planning Perspectives* 14, 2, 163–82.

41. Quoted from W Ashworth (1954) *The Genesis of Modern British Town Planning: a study in the economic and social history of the nineteenth and twentieth centuries* London, Routledge and Kegan Paul, 15.

42. P O'Brien (1983) *The Railways and Economic Development of Western Europe 1830–1914* London, Macmillan.

43. See Chapter 5.

44. S Pollard (1981) *The Integration of the European Economy since 1815* London, University Association for Contemporary European Studies.

45. CG Pooley (ed) (1992) *Housing Strategies in Europe, 1880–1930* Leicester, Leicester University Press, 326–38.

46. HE Meller (1976) *Leisure and the Changing City, 1870–1914* London, Routledge and Kegan Paul, Chapter 5.

47. The earliest sociological studies of the city emanating from the University of Chicago focused on mobility as the pulse of community. See EW Burgess (1925) "The Growth of the City: an introduction to a research project" in R Park et al. (eds) *The City* Chicago, University of Chicago Press.

48. A Briggs (1960) "Mass Entertainment: the origins of a modern industry" 29th Joseph Fisher Lecture in Commerce, University of Adelaide, 11.

49. See John Bale's work on the evolution of sports stadiums: J Bale (1993) *Sport, Space and the City* London, Routledge, Chapter 2.

50. A recent study exploring this cultural perspective in a particular city, is T Kaplan (1992) *Red City, Blue Period: social movements in Picasso's Barcelona* Berkeley, CA, University of California Press.

51. É Forgács (1991) *The Bauhaus Idea and Bauhaus Politics* Budapest, CEU Press, 10.

52. CG Pooley (1992) "Introduction" in CG Pooley (ed) *Housing Strategies in Europe*, 1–10.

53. This will be discussed in more detail in Chapter 2.

54. For contemporary comment on the experience of hyperinflation see S Pollard and C Holmes (1973) *Documents of European Economic History* Vol III London, Edward Arnold, 257–94.

55. A Schildt and A Sywottek (eds) (1988) *Massenwohnung und Eigenheim. Wohnungsbau und Wohnen in der Großstadt seit dem Ersten Weltkrieg* Frankfurt a. M/New York, Campus.

56. E Hoogenstraaten, D Stadig and H Michel (eds) (1992) *Sociale Woningsbouw Amsterdam (the Amsterdam Social Housing) Atlas* Amsterdam, Amsterdamse Federatie van Woningconporatie. From the First World War, Amsterdam's Muncipal Corporation and public housing authorities began building and purchasing the housing stock of the city so that by 1992, one in every two buildings in the city was in public ownership.

57. See Chapter 2.

58. B Marrey (ed) (1998) *Henri Sellier: "Une Cité pour tous"* Selection of Sellier's published writing from the early twentieth century to 1943 Paris, Éditions du Linteau.

59. G Bock and P Thane (eds) (1991) *Maternity and Gender Policies: women and the rise of the European welfare states, 1880s–1950s* London, Routledge.

60. For example, A Sutcliffe (1981) *Towards the Planned City*; P Hall (1996 new edn) *Cities of Tomorrow: an intellectual history of urban planning and design in the twentieth century* Oxford, Blackwell.

61. This is discussed further in Chapter 1.

62. HE Meller (1997) *Towns, Plans and Society in Modern Britain* Cambridge, Cambridge University Press, 25–45.

63. PY Saunier (1999) "Changing the City: urban international information and the Lyon municipality 1900–1940" *Planning Perspectives* 14, 1, 19–48.

64. D Calabi (1997) *Parigi anni venti: Marcel Poète e le origini della storia urbana* Venice, Marsilio.

65. Quoted in Bosma and Hellinga, *Mastering the City* Vol II, 92.

66. HE Meller (1990) *Patrick Geddes*, 59.

67. German cities were also encouraged to undertake the provision of services such as water, sanitation and gas supply from the 1870s, transforming municipal administrations. B Ladd (1990) *Urban Planning*, 7–77.

68. DT Rodgers (1998) *Atlantic Crossings: social politics in a progressive age* Cambridge, Mass., Harvard University Press, 68–9.

69. FC Howe (1913) *European Cities at Work* London, T Fisher Unwin, 3.

70. C Harvie (1993) *The Rise of Regional Europe* London, Routledge.

71. E Howard (1898) *Tomorrow: a peaceful path to real reform* London, Swann Sonnenschein; revised and republished in 1902 as *Garden Cities of Tomorrow* London, Swann Sonnenschein.

72. G Radford (1996) *Modern Housing for America: policy struggles in the New Deal Era* Chicago, Chicago University Press, 59–84; DT Rodgers (1998) *Atlantic Crossings*, 394–6.

CHAPTER 1

BARCELONA AND MUNICH, 1890–1930: CITY PLANNING, MODERNISATION AND CIVIC IDENTITIES

At certain points in the history of cities, if they are fortunate, a combination of factors produces something special. Barcelona and Munich both enjoyed this experience in the period 1890–1930. They were very different cities indeed, yet both provided the context for an outpouring of cultural creativity in the arts: in architecture, painting, music, theatre, literature and poetry which marked pinnacles of achievement in European civilisation. Picasso moved from his hometown of Malaga to gain further experience, training and a livelihood in Barcelona where he lived from 1895–1904[1]. From 1896 to 1914, the Russian painter, Kandinsky had followed the same path as many other Eastern and Central European artists to Munich, famous for its artistic community throughout the world[2]. It was unusual for two regional centres to have, arguably, two of the greatest twentieth-century artists working in them. Yet at the same time as these cultural achievements, both these cities were changing very rapidly in terms of land area, population growth and industrial structure. They needed "modernising" in terms of their administration, infrastructure, transport system, and housing. Both cities were to experience the onset of modern town planning by the leading practitioners of their day: in Barcelona, Ildefons Cerdà; in Munich, the influence of Camillo Sitte[3]. What this chapter aims to do, by comparing these two very different cities, is to explore the relationships between the onset of modern city planning, the demands of modernisation and social and cultural change.

Each city had created a context, by both serendipity and design, in which great cultural creativity could flourish. But it required a new self-consciousness and commitment to sustain it in the face of urban growth and social and political change. In twentieth century terms, these two cities could be called modern, regional centres but they could not be more different in their history and traditions, in their efforts to sustain their identities as they grew. Both had around 500 000 inhabitants in 1900 and by the early 1930s, both had achieved the status of "world" cities, if such a status is conferred by gaining a population of 1 000 000. By 1900, there were already 13 agglomerations in Europe and North America that had reached this figure[4]. Munich was the third largest city in Germany after Berlin and Hamburg. Barcelona was only just a few hundreds behind the Spanish capital city Madrid, in an otherwise highly rural country. Growth on this scale, though not the fastest in Europe, was enough to raise questions about the need to modernise while controlling change so that the "character" of the city was not destroyed. One of the most important parameters in this was the relationship between the city and its national context. Barcelona saw itself as a capital city of a nation, the Catalans, repressed by the power of the tyrannical Spanish State[5]. Munich had been the capital city of Bavaria which, until the First World War, remained a princely state within a federal structure with an emotional hostility to Berlin and the Prussians[6].

These rivalries spilled over into the economic sphere. Throughout the nineteenth century, the industrialists and entrepreneurs in Barcelona had fought to keep themselves and their city abreast of technological progress in manufacturing and transport. They had had to fight because of double disadvantages: Spain was not well endowed with the essential commodities for the first phase of modern industrialisation, coal and iron[7]. Furthermore, the national government of Madrid was not intent on overcoming these problems for political reasons[8]. These latter dictated that the interests of the Spanish ruling class lay in sustaining the administrative and legal framework of a non-industrial state. This left the entrepreneurs of Barcelona often operating outside the mainstream of national political culture. In Munich, the "outsider" status stemmed from a very different context[9]. Germany was, after unification in 1870, to become the greatest economy in the world after the USA. Cities on the Ruhr coalfields sprang up like mushrooms but also the well-established cities in other provinces such as Frankfurt am Main, Cologne and Dusseldorf were growing rapidly. While Berlin's phenomenal growth dominated, the new German State had many large cities which, by the first decade of the twentieth century, would contain the majority of the German population[10].

In the face of this transformation, Munich set out to be a symbol of continuity with the past. Writing in 1904, a journalist, Theodor Goering, suggested that "whereas energy and intelligence predominated in the north, Germany's 'spiritual side' (*Gemütsseite*) emerged more clearly in the south"[11]. There may be arguments about this characterisation but it was clear in Munich that if Berlin was to be the political centre, then Munich should set its sights on being the cultural centre of the nation. This did not mean that it was not an industrial city. As early as 1854, when Munich was still ruled independently by its royal family, King Ludwig I had reacted quickly to the challenge thrown down by London with its Great Exhibition of 1851, demonstrating British economic and supposedly artistic supremacy. Ludwig provided the means for a German Industrial Exhibition. In direct imitation of the Crystal Palace, he built the Glaspalast which was to remain the largest exhibition hall in Germany until Berlin acquired the Landesausstellungspalast, built in 1886. Yet Munich's industries at this time were not those based on coal and iron. They were the industries of a large city set in the midst of a prosperous rural hinterland: brewing, bleach mills, tanneries, dyeworks, and leadworks[12].

As an indication of its cultural status, it had one of the most famous printing industries in the world. The city also had the largest market for works of art in

Germany. The Glaspalast became, not an exhibition hall for industry but for art. The Munich branch of the German General Art Association (founded in 1856), mounted regular art exhibitions which attracted buyers from all over the world, especially America. The first was in 1858, commemorating two significant anniversaries: the fiftieth anniversary of the Munich Academy of Art and the 700th anniversary of the city itself[13]. The image of Munich as a city of art was well established. Just after the Secession in 1895, there were 1180 painters and sculptors in Munich, 13% of the total in Germany and still a few more than were to be found in Berlin (at that time four times larger than Munich)[14]. Yet this image depended on a myopic vision. As the city grew, greater Munich was dependent on industry. By 1900, the city had already become the largest industrial centre of South Germany, surpassing Nuremberg. By the First World War, its engineering industries had been vastly expanded by war production and during the 1920s, there was no doubt about the city's reliance on new science-based industries: engineering, chemical works, the manufacture of cars.

In Barcelona, too, there was a gradual transformation in its industrial structure. Obviously its position as a port was vital but in the first half of the nineteenth century, it had pioneered a modern steam-powered textile industry and heavy engineering[15]. By the turn of the twentieth century, continued growth of the city's economy depended on the development of new science-based industries: electricity, car building and light engineering. These developments had far-reaching social and cultural consequences. In both cities, the hope of work provided the magnet to draw people, mainly unskilled and with rudimentary education, from the rural hinterland to the city. The work on offer in the science-based industries of the second phase of industrialisation, however, demanded a new kind of workforce. There was a demand for literacy, skills, advanced training. City governments thus needed to invest in people just as much as a new infrastructure for the city in the process of modernisation. Public health measures, education and housing all had to be increased and standards raised. In this context, Barcelona was greatly disadvantaged in comparison with Munich since the latter city had enjoyed stable, efficient and far-sighted government throughout the nineteenth century. The challenge for Barcelona was to catch up, and, for Munich, to find a way forward in a rapidly changing political environment.

For the immigrants swelling the numbers of urban dwellers, work may have been the major reason for their migration, but they also hoped that life in the city would be more exciting. Especially since the development of the railways, the poor had poured into the city on feast days and holidays to seek amusements and entertainment. Both Barcelona and Munich had strong cultural traditions from a pre-industrial past, some related to the Catholic Church, others to national culture and politics[16]. There was a vibrant popular culture to be found in the streets and cafés of both cities. An important part of the cultural creativity in these cities in the period 1890–1930 stemmed from the clash of "high" cultures and the strength of popular culture. In Munich both the well-established secular and religious

Figure 1.1 *Street market, Arc del Teatro,*
Barcelona 1932 [By permission of Arxiu
Fotogràfic, Arxiu Històric de la Ciutat, Barcelona]

Figure 1.2 Women mending the fishing nets, Barcelona, 1934 [By permission of Arxiu Fotogràfic, Arxiu Històric de la Ciutat, Barcelona]

festivals remained. The famous *Bierkellers* and the beer festival, the Oktoberfest, continued to flourish as did the winter games and festivities played at Fasching each year before Lent. In Barcelona, Catalan songs and dances helped to integrate the immigrants while the Catholic processions on particular holidays continued to take their traditional forms and traditional routes through the city.

Peasant arts and crafts, fairground theatres, puppet shows, café bars, circus performers, prostitutes and entertainers provided both an inspiration to modern artists and an environment in which they could pursue their avant-garde ideas. In Barcelona, in his "blue period" (the stylistic convention he had adopted in Paris), Picasso painted striking images of people: entertainers, circus performers, the men, women and children he saw in the course of his daily life in the city[17]. Kandinsky drew inspiration not only from the vibrant cultural life of Munich but also from the idyllic Bavarian countryside. He was inspired not only by nature but also by the work of the village artists and craftsmen, especially the practice of painting on glass[18]. Both artists were totally alive to the richness of their surroundings. It was a richness based on the face-to-face nature of social and cultural life and the retention of a great variety of traditional skills nurtured in both Catalunya and Bavaria. It was the skills of local craftsmen that were vital to the success of the architectural projects in Barcelona which were so important in creating the city's new identity at the turn of the century. In Munich, the building ambitions of the ruling family, the Wittelbachs, throughout the century had sustained a larger number of highly skilled craftsmen than elsewhere. Theodor Fischer, the architect who became the first director of Munich's City Extension Office, mounted Arts and Crafts exhibitions in Munich and was a founder member of the German Werkbund in 1906 which aimed to sustain and encourage the continuation and development of craft skills.

Societies like the Werkbund are often founded at the point when economic changes threaten the very existence of those things they wish to preserve. Similarly, the particular context of the social life enjoyed by Picasso and Kandinsky was itself coming under threat. There were no societies to protect popular entertainers, they were subject to the harsh determination of market forces. Yet their livelihood was being threatened as different patterns of leisure and recreation began to emerge. In place of the traditional, spontaneous social life of the street, with its unstructured leisure patterns, the ever greater demand for regular, organised rational entertainment was appearing. Working conditions in the new science-based industries demanded new kinds of workers who were better educated, more regular in their working hours and, if in regular employment, were able to sustain a modest improvement in their material conditions. They wanted new leisure facilities in the city. Parks and open spaces, swimming pools and gymnasia were part of the new apparatus of healthy, rational recreation. Organised sport became a possibility. While the bourgeois had dominated many sporting activities in the 1890s, by the early twentieth century, a passion for sport was spreading rapidly among the working classes. Playing football or, more often,

Figure 1.3 *Street cleaners in Barcelona c.1929*
[By permission of Arxiu Fotogràfic, Arxiu Històric
de la Ciutat, Barcelona]

Figure 1.4 *Dancing at Montjuïc in the 1920s, Barcelona* [By permission of Arxiu Fotogràfic, Arxiu Històric de la Ciutat, Barcelona]

watching others play it became a major urban leisure activity. The identities of Barcelona and Munich were becoming formed not just around industrial prowess or artistic achievements but on success in sporting competitions. Social and cultural changes were taking place as fast as the cities were growing.

In these circumstances, the special "character" of a city becomes an elusive phenomenon. In the period 1890–1930, the clash between the historical customs and traditions of these cities and the activities expressing the hopes and fears of the present and the future reached a new intensity in the face of rapid economic change and large-scale growth. Such clashes were expressed politically, resulting in considerable violence as the disadvantaged fought for their rights. Both cities witnessed massive strikes, merciless repression, political assassinations, and, in Munich in the aftermath of war, revolution. The First World War cut like a knife through existing cultural compromises, both for a participant city like Munich and Barcelona, which became rich as a neutral city but whose citizens suffered from a massive currency inflation which reduced the value of real wages. Yet both before and after the War, both cities were concerned about their social identities and planned and promoted them to the outside world. Partly this was due to concern over the economic future of these cities. Partly it was also about making claims about their past and future aspirations. All cities, especially those such as Munich and Barcelona which were expanding rapidly, needed a guide in the constant process of urban regeneration. What was available to them was the particular image created of their city's individuality. It was the strongest emotional guide to their future.

THE INTRODUCTION OF MODERN TOWN PLANNING IN BARCELONA AND MUNICH

Of course, the image of the past did not always encourage continuity. Here, once again, Munich and Barcelona followed very different paths. For all European cities, the crucial moment of expansion came with the decision to pull down the city walls and remove their fortifications[19]. The experience of Barcelona and Munich were very different in this respect. Munich had dispensed with its walls long before the nineteenth century, protected by the River Isar on one side and the Bavarian army on the other. The ruling family, the Wittelbachs (made royal in 1805 by a grateful Napoleon), wanted space to lay out their city in the Grand Manner. Looking to Italy, their closest neighbours to the south, the Wittelbachs adopted classical Italian axial planning: impressive, monumental and requiring a great deal of space. Barcelona, on the other hand, was firmly confined within its strait-jacket of city walls until the middle of the nineteenth century. It did not matter that the city was pioneering industrial development as well as being a thriving port. The walls remained and nothing could be done about it until there was an edict from Madrid. Overcrowding, pollution and public health hazards had reached an extreme level. In 1855, there was the first General Strike in the city and at last, Madrid decided to act, though reluctantly.

The civil governor-general of Catalunya was located in Barcelona as was the military commander, with the troops necessary to enforce law and order. The destruction of the fortifications would mean the destruction of the eighteenth-century troop garrison which hemmed the city in on its eastern side. The extension of the city was thus a matter of high drama, a physical symbol of change, a bone of contention between a repressive government and irrepressible citizens. It is extraordinary that the man destined to plan the extension of the city, Ildefons Cerdà I Sunyer (1815–1876), began as a nominee of Madrid and ended as a dedicated Catalan, set to free his city. In the business of handing cultural legacies to the next generation of modern planners, Cerdà's contribution to Barcelona was every bit as important as the Wittelbachs' to Munich. Curiously, it was the image and intention of the original planners, which were of great significance to the future. The difference between the two cities is startling. Cerdà was committed to using modern knowledge and technology in the liberation of the people; the Wittelbachs were creating a Residenzstadt, the capital city of an established kingdom. Modern technology took second place to the perception of the quality of life in which comfort was measured in terms of the number of servants in the household and court ritual was still symbolically historical. The Upper House of the Diet was the Imperial Council of the Crown of Bavaria and on state occasions, the etiquette was Spanish-Burgundian[20].

With its town extension plan, Barcelona was, in effect, creating a new city; Munich, with its annexations and extension plans, was merely controlling the orderly development of the city. Barcelona depended on the outstanding contributions of gifted individuals, working in a hostile environment under pressure from shortage of time and resources; Munich was managed by teams of professionals, encouraged to pursue the implementation of best practice and backed up by generous resources. What these differences meant for the citizens of these cities can best be illustrated by reference to public health activities in the nineteenth century, which became the cornerstone of modern town planning. In Munich, note had been taken of Hamburg's efforts to install a water-borne sewage system after the great fire of 1842 in the city. Hamburg had used the opportunity to replan its city centre with a new infrastructure. The English engineer responsible for the Hamburg plan, William Lindley, was invited to Munich to advise on the construction of such a system as a way of cleaning up the city. Munich city council also wished to encourage the people to be clean and, unusually, alongside a few other German cities such as Nuremburg, Frankfurt and Leipzig, the city invested in building large numbers of small baths and washhouses throughout the city. The norm elsewhere was to build large showpiece establishments which were beyond the reach of most citizens.

By the mid-1850s, when the extra pollution from an expanding steam-powered industrial sector was making public health conditions in Barcelona ever more diabolical, in Munich, a pioneering chemist and hygienist, Max Joseph von Pettenkofer (1818–1901) was researching the connections between pollution and public health. Pettenkofer gained an international reputation for his work on the causes of cholera which he published in 1855. He used the disease-ridden conditions of the old city centre of Munich as his laboratory for the study of epidemiology and other aspects of public health. He set up the first hygienic institute in Germany in 1879 and through the publication of his work in national journals and in the local press, he was to make Munich one of the healthiest cities in Europe by the last quarter of the century[21]. He was a great exponent of fresh air, pure water, proper clothing and housing, and adequate sewage disposal. As a chemist in the forefront of his profession, however, Pettenkofer did not confine himself to public health. He was ready to use his knowledge on any current problems found in the city: from the best ways of restoring oil paintings in the city Art Gallery to improving the quality of Portland cement. His career provides an illustration of one aspect of Munich's "modernisation" in the light of modern science and technology: the application of new knowledge to improve old practices. In Munich, public health advances were implemented to improve conditions and to sustain traditional lifestyles.

In contrast, Cerdà's plan for the Eixample, the new town of Barcelona, which he worked on in the 1850s, was designed to be a complete break with the past. For him, the implications of modern science and technology were that they offered a new beginning. Von Pettenkofer, the chemist, wanted to deal with old problems in new ways; Cerdà, the civil engineer, wanted to build a new environment in which not only did the old problems not exist, there was also a new social order. Improvements in public health were central to the Eixample but they were not the guiding principle. That stemmed from Cerdà's extraordinary vision for the city to which he was to commit his whole life. The son of a rural landowner in Catalunya, Cerdà had gained entry after training, to the prestigious Cuerpo de Ingenieros (Society of Engineers) in 1841. This society, which was very exclusive, could guarantee high salaries to its members as it was the civil arm of the State in matters of modern engineering. Cerdà, however, became more and more interested in the social consequences of modernisation. In a manner reminiscent of the French mining engineer, Frédéric Le Play, who had similar interests at around the same time, the social consequences began to dominate his thinking. In France, Le Play published his pioneering work *Les Ouvriers Européens* in 1855; he introduced the idea of conducting social surveys to create a proper understanding of conditions; and helped to found the La Société d'Economie Sociale to study methods of social reform in 1856[22].

In Spain, Cerdà was far more constrained. He developed his ideas on the future of Barcelona between 1855 and 1859. At the earlier date, he had been commissioned by the government to carry out a topographical study of the outlying area around the city while the city architects had been commissioned to do the same for the city itself. His activities focused his mind on the future expansion of the city and he decided to resign from the Cuerpo de Ingenieros (an unprecedented action for anyone who had gained admittance) and to devote himself to the prospect of working on a plan for the future of the city. He went into politics to try and bring concern over environmental factors into political life[23]. He was elected as a representative to the Cortes and in 1854, became a trustee of the Barcelona City Council, but his success with his mission was minimal. In 1859, the Madrid government, through its Ministry of Works organised a public competition for the best future plan for the city. Most entries were channelled through Barcelona City Council but Cerdà sent his directly to Madrid without any extensive local consultation. This brought him his greatest personal success, because his plan was accepted but the price he paid was hostility from the bourgeois of Barcelona who objected to arbitrary action concerning the future of their city being taken over their heads. They opposed Cerdà's plan and continued their opposition for at least two decades. However, the power of Madrid overruled their objections and work began on demolishing the walls and laying out the new extension which was to be eight times the size of the old city. Regardless of local opposition, Cerdà was buoyed up by the belief that what he was doing was going to change the lives of the people of Barcelona forever. His total commitment to this project had sustained him in the researches he made at his own expense in 1855 into the conditions of the Barcelona working classes. Such commitment kept him going in the condition of total isolation and lack of support in which he carried out work on his plan. Although a Catalan, his plan represented the power of Madrid over local choice and he was made to suffer.

There was one brief moment when he gained some support. Between 1868 and 1874, the Spanish government were without a monarch and in 1873, a new Republican constitution was drawn up. It led to the very brief First Republic, when Spain tried democratic government, which only lasted a few months before a political coup which restored the monarchy. Yet for that short time, the political environment had been transformed. The Council of Barcelona assumed the functions of a Catalan government. There was the prospect of a new administrative structure for the whole region of Catalunya and its capital city. Barcelona became far more positive about its future and its extension plan. Cerdà was elected Vice-President of the Council and, for the first time, felt himself to be at the centre of an attempt to transform the old feudal Spain into a modern Iberia of free men through politics and science. In 1867, he had completed a major theoretical work in two volumes: *Teoría general de la urbanización y aplicación de sus principios y doctrinas a la reforma y ensanche de Barcelona*[24]. He felt free to think of a new future for Barcelona that modern technology made possible if only the cultural "baggage" of the past could be shed. He was conscious that in doing this, he was rebelling against two of the strongest cultural influences of Spanish society of his time: the love of history and the hatred of modernity. To do this required the most intense emotional commitment and Cerdà used the language of an infatuated husband contemplating his bride when he wrote, in the introduction to his major work on the theory of urbanisation, "I am going to introduce the reader to the study of a virgin, intact, completely new subject"[25].

The subject was urbanisation[26]. He was going to marry his skills as an engineer with a moral vision. Cerdà defined his understanding of urbanisation as follows:

> this concept describes the series of measures aimed at arranging buildings and regulating their functions, as well as the body of principles, doctrines and rules to be applied so that the buildings and their arrangements, instead of oppressing, weakening and corrupting the physical, moral and intellectual capacities of man in society, promote their development as well as his individual well being and contribute to increasing collective happiness[27].

The old city of Barcelona was a product of history, but one which Cerdà wanted to reject. It expressed the history of man's oppression by man. To extend the historical city meant perpetuating the oppression it symbolised. What was needed, Cerdà suggested, "was a new form of city which could grow historically but which responded to a new, just society. It had to take habitability, privacy and man's social relations as its basis and use technical and scientific progress to translate these needs into an urban structure." Unfortunately for him, the Restoration of the monarchy in 1874 cut off the political structures of the Republic. The Council of Barcelona was disbanded and Cerdà resigned from politics and left the city, only to die in exile in 1876.

His plan, however, lived on. It was built up of a chessboard of squares[28]. He believed that steam trains, currently the most modern form of transport, should determine both the shape of cities and the speed of communication at every level. Every square he planned (and he was to work with a gridiron pattern) had tracks for railways which networked the city. The plan was cut through by major diagonal avenues, north–south and north-east–south-west. These crossed with a third diagonal in the approximate centre of the new city in a large square. Two factors were important: the movement of traffic and people, and the privacy and pleasantness of their homes. Cerdà allowed wide openings at the corner of each square to accommodate the railtracks. He believed that only two sides of each square should be built on to ensure the maximum of light and air into homes and to preserve large areas of open space for gardens and recreation. He wanted the squares to support balanced communities and every 25 blocks was to have its own social and religious centre. Every four districts would have a market, every eight a city park and every 16, a hospital located on the city's periphery. Population densities were to be less than a third of the old city. Cerdà's plan was a blueprint for an ideal city and needless to say, his social vision was not implemented. Neither were the railway tracks across the new city. But the gridiron pattern remained, though once again, Cerdà's hope of building on only two sides of each square was overruled by the forces of capitalist property development. But one thing did remain. The citizens of Barcelona found they had a new city. It only

Figure 1.5 *Barcelona showing historic core and Cerdà's extension plan* [Map drawn by Chris Lewis]

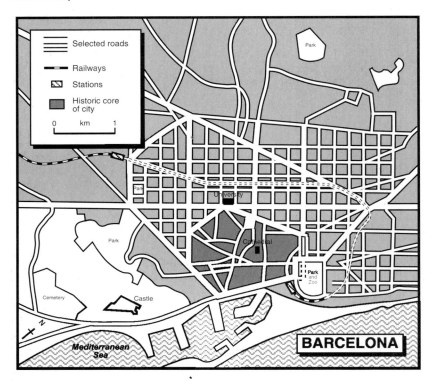

slowly took form as the vagaries of economic fortune and the property market went in fits and starts over the next half-century. What Cerdà had done was to give the city a form for its future expansion which was controlled, dynamic and capable of generating a new self-consciousness about modern Barcelona.

The introduction of modern planning in Munich was, of course, completely different. For a start, there was very little drama. The practice of modern town planning in Germany had emerged in a piecemeal fashion since unification and the rapid growth of German towns and cities[29]. It was a product of careful legislation mostly generated by municipal authorities themselves. Initially there was no German social philosopher with engineering skills. Problems of public health and orderliness were the touchstone of German urban planning. Mostly it was a matter of developing extensions to existing cities to relieve inner city congestion and to solve public health hazards[30]. Richard Baumeister (1833–1917), engineer and municipal administrator had produced the first German textbook devoted specifically to town

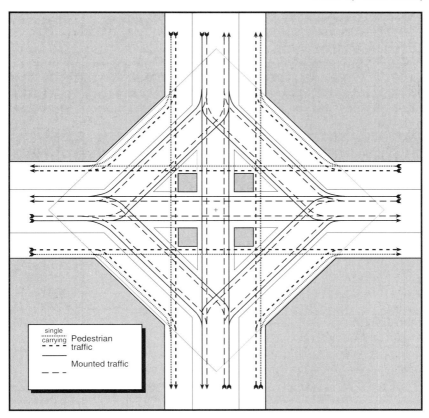

Figure 1.6 *Detail of traffic circulation at junction of square in Cerdà's extension plan, 1863* [Map drawn by Chris Lewis]

single
carrying   Pedestrian
·········   traffic
- - - -

Mounted traffic
- - -

planning in 1876. This book, *Stadterweiterungen in technischer, wissenschaftlicher und baupolizeilicher Beziehung*, was a practical manual which gave details of how to plan the infrastructure of a new area with drains, sewers, water supply, roads and rail tracks, densities of housing, etc. It was meant to be used by the municipal engineers faced with the problem of dealing with rapid urban growth. There was no vision of social justice or an ideal city of the future. But the very fact that German municipalities, by and large, had control over their own development did introduce a competitiveness between cities, each vying to demonstrate how well they could deal with the modern problems of growth.

The grand capital of the Austro-Hungarian empire, Vienna, had started the practice of holding a public competition for its extension plan in 1856, when the reconstruction of Haussmann's Paris was at its height and Imperial Vienna did not wish to be left behind as a city not abreast with the modern age. The former fortifications of Vienna were dismantled to provide space for the impressive Ringstrasse, producing a great wave of architectural excitement as commissions were put in hand for new buildings for the Imperial Parliament, the University, the Art Gallery and many other culturally significant buildings[31]. Provincial capitals in Germany picked up on the idea of competitions for city extension. This was not because they wished (or could afford) to emulate Vienna but because the whole question of town extensions and questions of public health had become controversial and the Viennese solution of "competition and plan" seemed a good model to individual city mayors.

It was a question of autonomy. A debate had flared up in the national Deutscher Verein für öffentliche Gesundheitspflege (German Public Health Association founded in 1873 in Frankfurt) about the role of the state and the cities in implementing new public health legislation. The largest faction led by Franz Adickes, the progressive and professional Mayor of Frankfurt from 1891 to 1912, argued that each city should be left to regulate itself since cities were committed to their own development and would handle the many and varied problems of urban extensions most effectively if left to do so[32]. To support his arguments, Adickes had Joseph Stübben (1845–1936), the architect planner who had won the competition for the extension of Cologne in 1881 and was then employed to carry it out. Stübben himself, with this track record, and the publication of his book, *Handbuch der Architektur Pt IV* in 1890, was to become one of the key figures in the introduction of modern town planning in Germany[33]. He saw planning as an orderly method of controlling and directing expansion according to principles of design and public health. He was particularly concerned with the modernisation of German cities and planning for modern methods of transportation.

The city of Munich came rather late to all these developments. It had demolished its fortifications far earlier than many other German cities and the Wittelbachs had established the orderly development of the city long before it began to expand rapidly. But by the end of the 1880s, it was obvious that Munich would need a plan for the future and in 1891, a competition was held. The timing was to place Munich at the centre of the greatest debate shaking the fledgling profession of German town planners. The debate had been stimulated by the ideas of Camillo Sitte (1843–1903), Austrian architect and the author of a work which was to change the practice of planning in Germany and all over the world, *Der Städtebau*, first published in 1889[34]. Sitte was an architect planner with a social vision[35]. He had been stimulated to write *Der Städtebau* by witnessing the building of the Ringstrasse in Vienna. His vision sprang from his appreciation that cities were the product of civilisation, that the modern city needed to grow from the old. The strength of each city depended on its individuality and the intimate and constantly changing relationship of city and citizens. As an architect, he saw this relationship in terms of an aesthetic approach to town planning which put practical concerns of public health and traffic circulation in their proper place. As he wrote in Appendix II of his influential work,

> City planning represents the fusion of all the technical and creative arts into a great and integrated whole; city planning is the monumental expression of civic spirit, it is the soil that nurtures true patriotism. City planning regularises traffic, it provides healthy and comfortable living conditions for modern man who has for the most part become a city dweller: it has to arrange the most favourable placement of industry and business, and it should foster the reconciliation of class differences[36].

Camillo Sitte was one of the judges for the Munich competition. The elderly Richard Baumeister was another and one of the four finalists they chose, Karl Henrici (1842–1927), had worked with Joseph Stübben in Cologne. So the full force of established practice and modern ideas were brought to bear on the Munich competition. Was city planning a science or an art? If it was an art, choices had to be made on subjective criteria. What should be preserved? What should be introduced? Whose sense of the city was to prevail? The case of Munich and its extension plan did not provide any clear answers but it gave an excellent opportunity for the arguments to be rehearsed[37]. Baumeister and Sitte were, in many respects, at the opposite poles in their approach, one the engineer full of technicalities of implementing a modern approach to planning, the other, dedicated to a visual aesthetic which was culturally as well as artistically important. The prize-winner, Henrici, a professor of architecture from the Technical University at Aachen and a fervent supporter of Sitte's ideas, had an argument with his former colleague Stübben (with whom he had worked in Cologne) who criticised his Munich plan in the pages of the architectural press, *Deutsche Bauzeitung*, published in Berlin[38]. Henrici was deeply impressed by the historical process whereby the current city of Munich had grown from its medieval past to its stately present[39]. His plan gently tried to extend the city by gradual accretion to preserve its essential character. Stübben suggested that Henrici's plan was very artistic but the lines were too hesitant and hazardous for the traffic circulation of a great city.

Gradually Sitte's ideas, though not Henrici's plan, began to prevail. The Munich competition entries were used in exhibitions for the next couple of decades and were included in the great town planning exhibition in Berlin in 1910. Sitte went from strength to strength. He was asked to be a juror on further city competitions in Mainz, Hamburg and Hannover. His book was translated into French (badly) and reached the English planner architects in that form[40]. The German original went through many editions and became the guiding text for architects setting out on the road to convert themselves into town planners in many different countries. Stübben graciously put some amendments in his own textbook on planning to accommodate some of Sitte's ideas. Munich's future, however, was not to be left in the hands of Karl Henrici. The post of director of the city extension office was given to the architect, Theodor Fischer (1862–1938). He was the first choice of Rettig, currently Munich's City Architect, who, in the past, had been the oldest

Figure 1.7 *Portrait of Theodor Fischer (1862–1938)* [By permission of Professor Dr Winfried Nerdinger]

architect in the team to build the Berlin Reichstag, while Fischer had been the youngest. Rettig badly wanted the City Extension Officer to be an architect[41]. Fischer, however, did not have dictatorial powers. He set himself the task of getting city planning fully established in Munich. He worked towards establishing a kind of intermediary role between private enterprise, the providers of essential services and the local authority to ensure that everything complied to some kind of plan. He was also closely in touch with the cultural circles in the city and had contacts with Jugendstil artists, Eckmann, Endell and Obrist of the Munich Secession. City planning, art, architect and civic spirit had forged a new relationship.

FROM PAST TO FUTURE: BARCELONA AND THE PROCESS OF "MODERNISATION"

For an extraordinary period, from the fall of the first Spanish Republic in 1874 until the *coup d'état* of Primo de Rivera in 1923, Barcelona was to shape and be shaped by the intensities of religious and political struggles. Cerdà had dreamt of a new beginning when he had planned the extension as a new city but not in his wildest dreams could he have imagined the outcomes achieved by the passionate commitment of the first two generations of citizens whose lives encompassed the old city and the building of the new. Barcelona, capital of the wealthiest province of Spain, with ambitions to be the greatest port in the Mediterranean (though it was still second to Marseilles) was subject to economic boom and bust, social turmoil and internecine strife. There was a huge desire on the part of the urban bourgeoisie, both industrialists and professionals, to modernise the city come what may. The leaders of the labour movement were committed with equal passion to achieving parity for the workers with their European counterparts. They all had to operate in a hostile and repressive political environment. This merely seemed to harden their resolve. What inspired them, though in differing degrees, was a rebirth of Catalan nationalism.

This was a social and cultural nationalism in which such elements as a shared language sustained a sense of civic and personal identity. It needs to be seen in the context of the Romantic nationalism sweeping across Europe in the second half of the nineteenth century, often in tandem with rapid economic change[42]. There was a search for the roots of an old culture which could be reinterpreted in the present. It provided the context for the great flowering of cultural creativity which took place in the city as it was modernised[43]. In Barcelona, there was an impatient desire to reinterpret the past in terms, not of the present, but of the future. In the brief days of the First Republic, Catalan nationalism had seemed to be a common cause for workers and bourgeoisie. But soon after this, in the late 1870s, the city began to enjoy an accelerating pace of economic growth and a shared Catalan culture could not bridge the conflicting interests of capital and labour. The labour movement was absorbed in organising and educating the masses of immigrants who poured into the city from the Catalan countryside or the neighbouring states. By 1910, only 66% of the city's population was Catalan. By the 1920s, the first major flood of immigrants had arrived from even further away, from the Andalucian south. Thus the issue of Catalan culture did not figure large among organised labour. Only the spirit of it did and the songs and dances continued to produce a lively popular culture. Among the Barcelona labour leaders there was also another strong Catalan trait – the desire to be at the forefront of the European labour movement. They made special efforts to keep in touch with their European counterparts and to ensure that the workers in Barcelona were aware of what was happening elsewhere in the struggles to achieve the liberation and new identities for the working classes[44]. This did not lead to a sense of shared cultural identity with the Catalan bourgeoisie!

But for the city's bourgeoisie, the cause of Catalan culture was completely different. Since political control was in the hands of the state, cultural activities offered a chance to develop a sense of a shared culture and the all-important opportunities for regular meetings. It was a route to some kind of freedom. As artists and musicians rediscovered a Catalan identity, the cause of Catalan culture became like a bush fire, flaring up first here and there until the whole landscape seemed ablaze. Music, poetry, art and architecture, literature and journals were all caught up in this. The high point of this cultural outpouring would appear to have been the decade from the International Exhibition of 1888 and a few years either side of this[45]. The young Picasso, in the city from 1895 to 1904 would have experienced the full force of this dynamic cultural milieu. The fact that this *renaixença* occurred at the same time as the city's expansion was extremely fortunate for the city. It released the talents of a group of outstanding architects who produced a new architecture, based on modern technical expertise, stylistically grounded in a reinterpretation of Catalan culture, which was to be defined as *Modernisme*.

In fact, it could be argued that the prospect of the Eixample was the factor which stimulated this outcome. The challenge of creating a new city spawned the architectural style, Barcelona's unique version of the modern Romantic Movement which had created Art Nouveau in Paris and elsewhere, and the Jugendstil of Vienna and Munich. Catalans, working with the disadvantage of their provincial status, were yet able to put their city on a par with the cultural capitals of the world. Partly this was due to the receptiveness of key individuals to what was happening in Europe; partly it was to do with the talent that was available; partly it was the unique political context of the city. Catalan talent stayed in Barcelona because of the willingness of the industrialists to support it. This combination of factors created a freedom of expression for often rebellious youth which, at the same time, produced work with an impersonal social message.

An illustration of how these factors combined can be taken from the case of the "father" of the "young bloods" who were to build the Eixample. Elies Rogent i Amat (1821–1897) began his studies of architecture in the 1840s. As a rebellious young student himself, he symbolically tore up the architectural textbook offering academic classicism which was the basis for his course and set out for Paris, Berlin and Munich to see what "modern" architects were doing[46]. He particularly fell in love with the German style, *Rundbogenstil*, which had rounded arches reminiscent of the Catalan ancient Romanesque and yet the buildings in this style incorporated all modern technical requirements. The new buildings for the University of Munich, constructed over a lengthy period from 1816–1852, deeply influenced him. Much later in 1860, when new buildings were required for the University of Barcelona, in consultation with Cerdà himself, it was decided to build in the Eixample[47]. Rogent was commissioned to do it. He took the Munich *Rundbogenstil* and redeveloped it with Catalan connotations. A new School of Architecture was added to the University in 1875 and Rogent was appointed as the first Head[48]. He still eschewed the classical model and encouraged an individualistic eclecticism, with an emphasis on finding new ways to solve problems. His school was the powerhouse which produced the young architects who took Barcelona to the forefront of architecture by the end of the nineteenth century.

The history of city planning, modernisation and culture in Barcelona at this time was tied up with the struggle for political power. Leading architects, alongside other professionals such as the financier Francesc Cambó and the lawyer, Prat de la Riba, both of whom were to become leading conservative politicians finally achieved some success with the establishment of a Catalan Lliga Regionalista in 1901, capable of winning elections[49]. One of the key concerns which brought them together was the fact that the disbanding of the Council of Barcelona by the Restoration government had left the city with a weak municipal council. It was not even allowed to set its own taxes. The great period of building in the Eixample and the flowering of a vigorously reinvented Catalan culture took place in the 27 long years before there was some restitution of rights. This meant that, unlike German cities, Barcelona's city council could not develop its own regulation, even of extension plans, beyond the Eixample. Industrial suburbs grew up beyond the city's boundaries in Gràcia, Sant Martí, Sants and Sant Andreu, to name the largest. The city council was left to make gestures. One such was the truly magnificent effort to mount an International Exhibition in the city despite all these difficulties. The decision was taken in 1885. Since 1880, numerous well-appointed and ambitious provincial European cities had chosen to hold International Exhibitions to promote themselves and their industries. In 1881, it had been Frankfurt, 1882 Bordeaux, 1883 Amsterdam, 1884 Nice[50]. Why not Barcelona?

A Universal Exhibition in Spain could not take place anywhere else than in Barcelona since even Madrid was not a manufacturing centre. The industrialists were happy to support the idea. But at the crucial moment, there was a downswing in the city's economic fortunes and some of the private backers of the enterprise went bankrupt. The Mayor, Francesc Rius i Taulet, took a bold decision. The project should go ahead and the municipality would borrow the money for it[51]. Finance was not the only problem. The key feature of urban growth that led to the development of planning control was public health. In Barcelona, provisions for public health were primitive. Outbreaks of cholera were rife. In 1885 itself, there had been an outbreak which had occasioned 3765 deaths. The Exhibition would attract hundreds of thousands of visitors. It would be a disaster if there was a cholera outbreak. In the city's hour of need, the municipality found another outstanding Catalan public servant and engineer, Pere Garcia Fària. He set out an answer to the huge challenge of providing a drainage system of the subsoil of the entire city. In his report of 1886, he laid the foundations of Barcelona's future in terms of modern standards of public health[52]. Because of these problems, there was both a tight schedule to meet when the date for the Exhibition was set for 1888 and a huge desire to display Catalan pride and confidence.

The site chosen for the Fair was that formerly occupied by the fort, scene of Catalan humiliations in the past. When the fort was pulled down, it was made into a park, Barcelona's only park. Elies Rogent was asked to design the layout. He appointed many different architects to build the various pavilions. The huge new Hotel project and the Café-Restaurant, he gave to Lluís Domènech i Montaner (1850–1923); the triumphal arch, to Josep Vilaseca (1848–1910). Both the latter architects built in brick as a strong reference to Catalan culture[53]. The Hotel had to be built in three months. Domènech used a modular system of repetitive units which was totally modern in conception. His Café-Restaurant also used modern engineering methods which expedited the time taken for construction and solved load-bearing problems in new ways. The link between modern technology and a revitalised Catalan culture had been inaugurated. Domènech's career expanded as an architect, but also as an academic, appointed for two periods to head the School

Figure 1.8 *Café-Restaurant, 1888 Exhibition, architect Lluís Domènech i Montaner (1850–1923)* [Author's photo]

Figure 1.9 *Arc del Triomf, 1888 Exhibition, architect Josep Vilaseca i Casanovas (1848–1910)* [Author's photo]

of Architecture and also as a politician. He became a member of the Lliga Regionalista in 1901 and was one of the four Catalans elected to be MPs in Madrid. He was to break with the conservative Lliga as his heart was always in a revitalised Catalunya where modern technology could be harnessed for the good of all. With his partner, Antoni Gallissà, he founded an Arts and Crafts workshop in 1889, stimulated by the ideas of Ruskin and Morris[54].

Symbolically, it was located in the Café-Restaurant, the only building (apart from the triumphal arch) to remain after the Exhibition and one considered to be the pioneering work in the *Modernisme* style. It was also recognition of the skills of the Catalan craftsmen who made such a contribution to the outstanding architectural achievements of all Catalan architects. Domènech's best student, Josep Puig i Cadafalch (1867–1956), who took the *Modernisme* style towards the *Noucentisme*, devoted considerable effort to promoting Catalan Arts and Crafts. His championing of these skills made them internationally known and in 1903, a young Walter Gropius made the trip to Barcelona to see their work[55]. Domènech utilised all these skills to the full in his work and also that of the exceptional civil engineers working in the city. His two greatest works demonstrate this clearly. His Hospital de Sant Pau (1902–10) was built on four of Cerdà's squares. Domènech turned the buildings by 45 degrees so that the wards would catch the maximum of sunshine and air. He created huge problems for the building engineers, including subterranean passages between different sections. His masterpiece though, is the Palau de la Música Catalana (1905–8)[56]. Besides the engineering needs of good acoustics, this building displays the huge skills of the Catalan craftsmen in ceramics and many other skills. Such was the quality of their skills and imagination, the *Modernisme* architects were able to provide a modern identity for Catalanism which at certain points, overrode the bitter conflicts of class. They were able to inspire a sense of belonging to the new city among all.

The unique and awe-inspiring work of the greatest genius of the movement, Antoni Gaudí i Cornet (1852–1926), was dedicated to an all-enveloping social and moral purpose from choice, though most of his major works were funded by bourgeois patrons[57]. The earliest and also the latest of his greatest works, the unfinished cathedral, the Sagrada Familia, begun in 1882 and taken over by Gaudí in 1883 and to which he devoted himself totally from 1911 until his untimely death in 1926, was located on the edge of the Eixample adjacent to a poor area. It was intended to serve the local community and the elementary school was one of the parts which was actually finished. The Sagrada Familia was an extraordinary icon, outside the mainstream of the city's political and religious life (since it was paid for by subscriptions collected by Josep Bocabella who had founded a branch of the Association of Saint Joseph, a modern lay Catholic cult)[58]. But Gaudí's extraordinary talent could only have been supported in the context of the huge outburst of cultural creativity which took place in the city. There was a happy coincidence of economic wealth, opportunity, and talent which produced a dazzling result. It was an outcome which was aspired to often but rarely planned.

Figure 1.10 *Corner of façade of the Palau de la Música Catalana (1905–8)* [By permission of the Biblioteca, Palau de la Música Catalana]

Figure 1.11 *Plan of the Palau de la Música Catalana showing narrow site* [By permission of the Biblioteca, Palau de la Música Catalana]

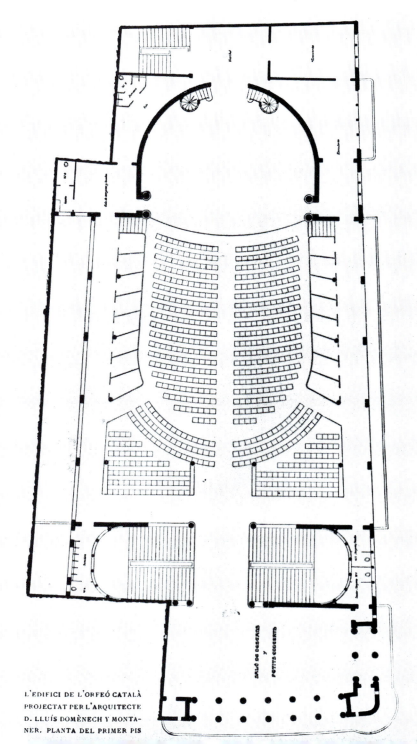

L'EDIFICI DE L'ORFEÓ CATALÀ
PROJECTAT PER L'ARQUITECTE
D. LLUÍS DOMÈNECH Y MONTA-
NER. PLANTA DEL PRIMER PIS

The Lliga Regionalista, elected to power in 1901, made it a top priority to remedy this[59]. Under the conservative leadership of Prat de la Riba (1870–1917), their main efforts were directed towards consolidation of local administration and the institutionalisation of cultural activities from education to leisure under local authority control. Being conservative, he envisioned these institutions in a strictly class-segregated, hierarchical way. At a stroke it was to cut the heart out of the egalitarian Romanticism which had sustained the first developers of Barcelona's future. There was no chance now of Catalan class equality under the auspices of a shared culture, though maybe that had always been a very faint hope. Alejandro Lerroux (1864–1949) had made his career as the undisputed leader of the Radical Republicans in the city by exploiting the cultural gap between the working classes and the self-satisfied bourgeoisie. He built up a network of alternative social clubs to sustain a revolutionary working-class culture. He gained the informal title, somewhat strange for a dedicated republican, of "Emperor of the Paralelo", the street which had grown as the centre of entertainment as the Eixample developed[60]. Here could be found all types of entertainment from theatres, cafés, restaurants and taverns. It was the informal social and political centre of the city. Lerroux's power continued until the First World War though he lost much support after the terrible events of "Tragic Week" in 1909.

Meanwhile, the Lliga Regionalista continued to try, under Prat's leadership, to work for Catalan autonomy within the Spanish State. His representative in Madrid was the millionaire financier and banker, Francesc Cambó (1870–1947), who was an astute politician. Yet there were electoral reverses, conflicts and debates and, in 1909, the shocking events called "Tragic Week" when the city fell into the grip of popular violence, mostly directed towards anti-clericalism and the city's many nunneries. The Lliga survived to go on and achieve its greatest coup – the formation of a political regional organisation in 1913, the Mancomunitat. This organisation was intended to co-ordinate the activities of municipal councils in towns across Catalunya. It produced a sense of regional identity, with Barcelona in a totally dominant position. Prat was the first President of this organisation and he was succeeded, shortly before his death, by Puig i Cadafalch, in 1917. Puig was a figure who spanned the old *Modernisme* period and the new *Noucentisme*. He had been a student of Domènech, 17 years his senior. Despite working on many buildings in the Eixample (including the Casa Martí in 1895–6 that was to house on its ground floor a few years later, the famous artists' café, "Els Quatre Gats" on the ground floor, often visited by Picasso[61]), Puig grew to hate Cerdà's plan.

He also hated the *Modernisme* style. He longed for the current European fashion for the monumental and grand, and was instrumental in introducing a new style, *Noucentisme* which was far more restrained, classical in inspiration and with a tendency towards the monumental. Otto Wagner, the Viennese architect, had published his essay on "Modern Architecture" in 1896, which espoused a refined classicism on a grand scale[62]. When a new main street, the Via Laietana, was completed in 1908 to connect the docks with the Eixample, it was done in

Haussman style, cutting arbitrarily through the built environment of the old city. The first building of note to be constructed near it was Domènech's masterpiece, the Palau de la Música Catalana. The final piece was to be a Palau Comunicacions. It was one of a series of Central Post Offices erected in all Spain's important cities. It was built in the *Noucentisme* style by Josep Goday, one of the stars of Puig's favoured style which he believed brought Barcelona closer to what was happening elsewhere and away from the parochialism of *Modernisme*[63]. Puig, meanwhile, as a town councillor was intent on practical measures to keep Barcelona abreast with what was happening elsewhere.

In 1897, the outlying industrial areas of Barcelona were incorporated into the city. Puig pressed for a new extension plan to be drawn up which would give a coherence to this further extension. A competition was held in 1903 and first prize was awarded to the French architect, Léon Jaussely (1875–1932)[64]. Jaussely planned a grand, winding boulevard connecting the outer suburbs and enclosing great areas of parkland. It was a complete contrast with Cerdà's tight but flexible grid. It was also not a Spanish plan. Barcelona was not ready to learn from Madrid and follow the ideas of Arturo Soria y Mata (1844–1920). The latter had been involved in the development of the Madrid tramways and this experience had encouraged him between 1882 and 1913 to work on plans of a "Linear City" extension for Madrid based on a tramway system of mass transit[65]. As ever, resources were too meagre to implement the Jaussely plan. Puig made his first unsuccessful bid for another Exhibition in 1905 in the hope that this would force the adoption of Jaussely's plan. The preferred form of transport for the rich was becoming the motor car. With foreign capital, the Hispano-Suiza Co had set up in Barcelona in 1904 initially to create an electrical generating plant, but it soon branched out into engineering and began to build automobiles. This development had lent extra attractiveness to Jaussely's aborted plan. An influx of foreign capital in the city was transforming its industrial base but there was little public investment in the fabric of the city until after the war. During the First World War Spain's neutral status was to bring prospects of unparalleled profits to Barcelona's entrepreneurs.

The war ushered in turbulent times for the city. While business was booming, a currency inflation caused by war dislocations and demands was not handled well by the Bank of Spain[66]. Consequently, Barcelona workers found their wages decreasing in real value while at the same time, hordes of poorer people from other regions of Spain continued to pour into the city in search of work. Little was done, though, to help the people to adjust to new conditions. The new industries, electrical engineering, precision machine tools, the chemical industries, needed a literate and highly educated workforce. Suddenly there was a new wave of private initiatives to provide schools and by 1916, a new public one, bringing more resources to the cause. It was a remarkable *volte face* made possible by the advent of the Mancomunitat, which, by 1917, was being led by Puig. What was most remarkable, though, was the determination to use the most modern educational techniques and to build the most modern schools. There was a revolution in educational methods backed up by the designs for the schools, many of them by Josep Goday[67]. At the infant level, there was a wholehearted adoption of the Pestalozzi techniques. Secondary schools were grouped around a large communal hall, eliminating the necessity for corridors and offering more light, space and air.

But this "method" of modernisation in Barcelona which, over the past half century, had seemed to perfect a tradition of starting from behind and moving to the very forefront was brought to an abrupt end in 1923. The onset of the dictatorship of Primo de Rivera brought an end to the Mancomunitat of Catalunya in 1925 and to Barcelona's relative autonomy. Not all the industrialists and businessmen of the city were sorry. The labour movement had gained greater power among the workers and since 1917, there had been a violent and intense struggle. The fact that there had been 283 murders between 1917 and 1923, by the hired assassins of the bosses, or in retaliation by the workers of the extreme groups, was one of the factors which caused the middle classes to tolerate the new dictatorship. The injustice of the dictatorial ban on the Catalan language, Catalan songs and dances was the price to pay for continuing prosperity and the savage repression of labour organisations. In the 1920s, large numbers of the immigrants were pouring into the city from the poorest regions of Spain, many of them uneducated or without particular skills. There was work for them, if all else failed, in the construction industry[68]. Every year, from 1920–30 on average, 14 000 homes were built as well as many new industrial premises. This was done largely through private enterprise and the bottom third of the population were very poorly housed[69]. Barcelona acquired its first "shanty" town in 1914. City planning and civic culture patently excluded the poor.

More effort began to be put into modernising the city's infrastructure, though, even if much had had to be done by private enterprise. Plans were put in hand for the first of two metropolitan railways to service Greater Barcelona. The Metro Transversal line was located running parallel with the shore. It was the cheapest and most direct option for bringing people to the docks and industrial areas and out again. In 1925, the underground Gran Metro was built, running beneath the Passeig de Gràcia. The development of a mass transit system was part of the preparation for the new World Exhibition. There had been fresh talk in the early 1920s of using this nineteenth-century method of self-promotion and display of industrial prowess, as problems of world trade continued after the war. Plans were drawn up and money raised to pay for such an event in 1929 even though there were few funds for public housing or other social programmes. Since Puig i Cadafalch had failed in 1905 to get support for a new Exhibition which might have led to the adoption of Jaussely's new extension plan, this idea had nevertheless continued to seem attractive as a way of promoting the fortunes of Catalan industries. In 1913 a new attempt was made, promoted by the business men in the electrical industries which, since 1912, had included the Canadian-owned "Barcelona Traction Light and Power Co". The idea was to demonstrate how far advanced Barcelona was in this rapidly growing industry. The Exhibition, scheduled for 1914, was cancelled because of the First World War. It was to have been sited in the new park, Parc Laribal, purchased by the city in 1908, a by-product perhaps, of Jaussely's comments on the lack of public open spaces in the city.

The park was on Montjuïc and it was on this great hillside to the west of the city that much of Barcelona's special city planning efforts were to be expended in the years of the Primo de Rivera dictatorship. A cable railway to take visitors up to the proposed exhibition site on the hilltop was begun in 1926, though it was not completed until 1931 when the Exhibition was over. The Parisian official gardener, Jean C.N. Forestier, was employed to lay out the slopes of the hill which he did with monumental flights of steps, fountains and terraces. Puig i Cadafalch was to obtain his dream of the monumental with the redevelopment of the ancient castle site as the Museum of Catalan Art, reached by a grand avenue from the Plaça d'Espanya which he redesigned. For the first time, the Plaça d'Catalunya was also both reorganised and tidied up for the occasion. The Exhibition itself was organised in conjunction with the Ibero-American Exposition in Seville. The two together were called the General Exposition of Spain. Barcelona had been brought to heel and the King and Queen came to the opening of this soon-to-be fiercely Republican city. There were two elements of the Exposition which had particular cultural resonances: the Spanish village and the German pavilion of Mies van der Rohe[70]. The first was an extraordinary collection of rural buildings from all over Spain. It exuded a nostalgia for a lost rural past, a *Heimat* which was disappearing fast. The second was an astonishing vision of the future. Neither had much to do with the city's past or its citizens' future. The city was left to dream about its future, contemplating the fantasy of the "Future Barcelona" produced by N.M. Rubió i Tudurí and shown at the 1929 Exhibition[71]. In the 1930s, the process of modernisation was reborn again as the city began to assume a metropolitan scale, though the civil war meant a break in achieving a new civic identity for the city.

CITY PLANNING AND "MODERNITY" IN MUNICH

If Barcelona's launch pad towards a modern identity had been the 1888 Exhibition, in Munich it was also a cultural event: the Secession in 1892. It was soon followed by the Secessions in Vienna and Berlin but Munich was first as befitted Central Europe's undisputed capital of the visual arts. This break with the past was engineered by a group of artists who wished to go beyond the rules of the established Art Academies and develop their work, unhindered by classical conventions. These avant-garde artists were to exhibit their work in their own specially built gallery, one of the first outstanding examples of the new architectural style, Jugendstil. For at least a decade, the Munich Secessionists' Exhibitions were a landmark in progressive artistic achievements[72]. The term "avant-garde", however, has to be treated in this context with caution. It conjures up the image of impoverished artists, working in garrets, sacrificing their well-being and livelihood in a commitment to the ideal of "art for art's sake". In fact, period of the 1860s to the 1880s was something of a "golden age" for Munich artists. For the most successful of them, it was possible to become very rich indeed and they were also accorded high social status. Leopard von Kalckreuth and Franz von Stuck, for example, made fortunes from their work. Stuck actually became one of the richest men in Munich. In 1892, Stuck was 29 years old. What he and his fellow Secessionists were doing were initiating a highly controlled and commercially successful revolt of youth. Their success lay in their ability to "express visually their pent-up frustrations with the repressions of a 'civilised' society"[73]. Munich was set on the path to "modernity".

If science and technology created the modern city, then artistic endeavour was the route to emancipating society to enjoy these new conditions. This was an entirely different view of art from that held by the Wittelbachs earlier in the century. They had endowed Munich with Art Galleries and patronage of the arts as a measure of the city's cultural standing. Ludwig I's famous comment: "I want to turn Munich into such a city, that no one shall know Germany who does not know Munich[74]." needs to be read in this light. What the Secessionists began, however, the following generation took to extreme lengths. Stuck was to tutor Kandinsky and Klee, two immigrant artists, drawn to the city by its promise of support for the arts. If the Secessionists broke with convention, the next generation pitted themselves with passionate commitment to the question: what is art? and what should it be? In the context of the Munich art world (which provided a livelihood for more indigenous painters than Stuck in the form of commissions for book illustrations, advertisements and design work), Kandinsky and others were to embark on a fertile period of experimentation. By the First World War, Kandinsky had reached the point when colour and expression had become the essence of his work and he made the breakthrough to an abstract art. An important part of his inspiration had come from artistic commissions outside pure painting, of which the experimental modern theatre developing in the city was a prime example.

The theatre as an art form occupied a central place in the burst of cultural creativity to be found in Munich in the two decades before the war. Experimental theatre involved many different art forms: prose, poetry, acting, music, dance and painting and support for such an innovative art form bound together the intelligentsia of the city. In 1890, the city only had four theatres, three of them dominated by the court and the fourth, which was privately owned, survived on a diet of programmes offering popular entertainment and Bavarian folk culture. Serious modern drama which addressed not only the question of "what is art?" but also "what is society?" and "how might it be reformed?" could only be seen in the city in private theatre societies. These circumnavigated the heavy hand of censorship and at least gave plays an airing. New ideas were tried out in cabarets attached to particular cafés and nightclubs. The problem of censorship arose since the dramatists attacked religion and politics in their examinations of modern society and the plays of the most talented of them all, Frank Wedekind, had a sexual explicitness which the politically conservative found pornographic. The cultural creativity in the theatre thus existed in a state of constant expectation of repression and Wedekind's major work, *The Spring Awakening*, did not get a public performance until 1908 and only then, in a heavily expurgated version[75].

This climate of repression was to be found all over Germany as the State had moved to ban what were termed obscene publications, especially those attacking the Church and State. For accidental local reasons, censorship in Munich was considered to be less strictly enforced than in Berlin, its closest competitor in the evolution of modern drama[76]. Munich writers and artists were able to sustain periodicals such as the famous *Simplicissimus* which allowed them the all important means of communication to a wider public and a method of sustaining the impetus of their innovations[77]. The liveliness and quality of the new plays also encouraged the building of a new theatre for the Schauspielhaus theatre group in 1901, and the avant-garde architect, Max Littmann, was commissioned to build two new theatres, the Prinzregententheater in 1901 and the most experimental of all, the Künstlertheater in 1908. The style and location of the 1901 Schauspielhaus theatre gave an indication of the cultural climate in the city. It was located, not on a conspicuous site on a main thoroughfare but in the interior courtyard of a housing block on Maximilianstrasse. The Jugendstil style of its architecture emphasised its womb-like site. It could only be entered by covered passageways. Hidden away from public view, its delicate, Jugendstil interior offered a glimpse of a revitalising, youthful, exciting, "modern" context within which dramatists could reveal the wickedness of capitalism and modern society[78]. It was an irony therefore, that it was paid for by donations from a multi-millionaire Munich brewer.

A sympathetic multi-millionaire brewer was not enough, however, to sustain Munich's place as the cultural capital of Germany. Another of the great ironies of this period of cultural achievement in the city has to be seen against a background of rapidly declining sources of patronage for the arts. Much of this had to do with political changes. The overarching framework of change was the decline of the artistic community's greatest patrons, the Wittelbach family. With Ludwig II's premature death in 1886 and the ascension to the throne of his schizophrenic brother, necessitating a regency, the decline became marked so that its final extinction during the Weimar Republic seemed inevitable. The Prince Regent Liutpold was an ardent collector of art but he was not able, for legal reasons, to expend state funds on it. He had to fund his own collecting habit himself. Exhibitions at the Glaspalast had helped to bring the art collectors of the world to Munich but in the mid-1880s, the most important foreign buyers, the Americans, ceased to come in such large numbers as the US government imposed a heavy import tax on art works brought to America. Just as the Munich Secessionists hoped they were setting up Munich as the art centre of Germany in competition to Berlin, it became ever more evident that the Munich market was shrinking. Berlin, in contrast, had a growing number of very affluent entrepreneurs interested in buying art. The prospect of declining patronage for the arts in Munich was already apparent by 1900.

What to do about this was a political issue which the city of Munich was ill equipped to solve. How important was the image of City of Art to Munich's future?

Figure 1.12 *Poster by Paul Bruno for the Elf Scharfrichter cabaret 1902, a version of the "modern woman" with disapproving old women looking on* [By permission of Houghton Library, Harvard University]

Since the end of Ludwig II's reign, a Bavarian Centre Party (of Catholic orientation) had been struggling for power with the liberals. As the power of the Wittelbachs declined, so the power of the Bavarian State parliament grew and so did the power of the Bavarian Central Party. It also grew in influence in Munich City Council. It was not the nature of the party to be sympathetic to the avant-garde art scene. The cultural life of the city was left in the hands of the liberals with declining powers, the intellectuals and university professors resident in the city's most famous "artistic" suburb of Schwabing and those of the industrial bourgeoisie with an interest in art. There was little contact with the working classes. In 1890, when the anti-socialist legislation was lifted, Munich returned two members of the Social Democratic Party as representatives of the State in the Reichstag. On a local level, however, the SPD was both uninterested in trying to dominate city government and concerned to develop a separate cultural context for the leisure hours of their members which would tie them ever more firmly to an SPD mentality. Such a response had grown out of the years of repression of the

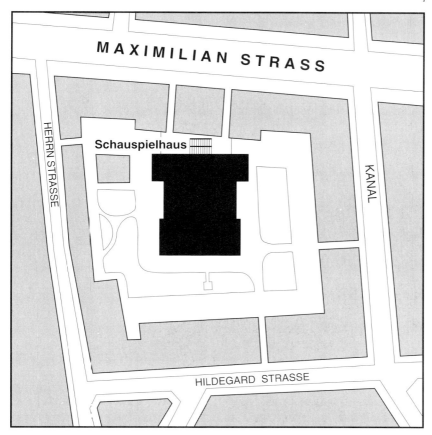

Figure 1.13 *Plan showing enclosed site of the Schauspielhaus* [Map drawn by Chris Lewis]

party from 1875–90[79]. For a brief moment in the political revolution of 1919 in its SPD phase, some of the Schwabing intellectuals offered leadership and support for the workers. But the artistic and literary scene of Munich was heavily focused on the lives of the bourgeoisie.

Yet despite these increasingly tenuous links with the changing political life of city and state, the Munich art world was to continue to have an enormous influence on the city's image. Through the dedication of individuals and professionals, this influence, in turn, was to be a strong force in the city's physical development. In Munich, town planning came to be practised as an art. The Wittelbach's legacy of creating the fairest city was self-consciously translated into a judicious balance of

Figure 1.14 *Fischer's early work in Munich: surrounding the old and the new art galleries with more space, 1912* [By permission of Professor Dr Winfried Nerdinger]

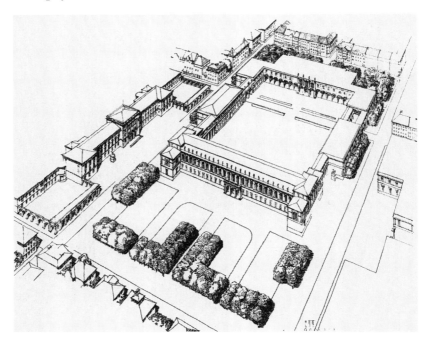

preservation and innovation as the city was modernised as it was extended. The key figure in this was the architect Theodor Fischer, who not only became the City Extension Officer from 1893, but also, in 1908, Professor of Architecture in the Technische Hochschulen of both Munich and Stuttgart. Throughout his career, he had a busy private practice. Fischer had three passions: for new architecture; for developing the ideas of Camillo Sitte; and for Munich as a city of art. He was a seminal figure well beyond the local scene with his work in Stuttgart and his role in developing the German Werkbund. He was either teacher or mentor of what Collins describes as a "heterogeneous group of architects, including JJP Oud, Walter Gropius and Bruno Taut". Collins suggests that Fischer served "as a bridge between Sitte and the progressive architects of the 20th century"[80]. In Munich, he struggled to modernise the city while also enhancing the quality of the urban environment. He did not believe there needed to be conflict between such objectives.

The competition for the plan for Munich's extension had raised the profile of modern town planning in the city. Establishing his office on a professional basis, Fischer set about getting maps drawn and collecting data on the city's layout and

Figure 1.15 *Fischer's early work in Munich: redesigning Maximilianplatz 1912* [By permission of Professor Dr Winfried Nerdinger]

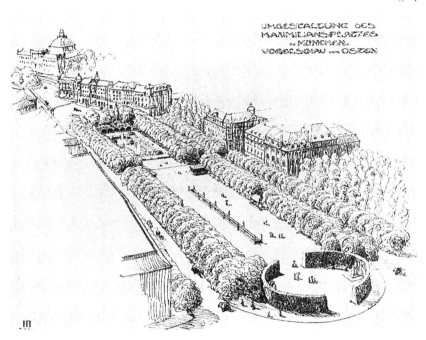

structure[81]. He was deeply conscious of his responsibility for preserving the existing heritage. There was much debate about the layout of new roads. The one element of Munich's historical legacy which was much criticised was the Ludwigstrasse, King Ludwig I's impressive but very straight and very boring great thoroughfare. The followers of Sitte argued for the beauty of curved streets and irregular squares which offered the eye a whole range of aesthetic pleasures. The Arnulfstrasse was duly laid out with a curving line and Fischer expended much effort on the design of squares and plazas that offered a variety of shapes. But he was no mere disciple of Sitte. His experience as City Extension Officer taught him pragmatism and the need to work out a method of city development which would suit the city administration and private enterprise, since most development was in the private sector. Gradually he worked out a set of principles which were embedded in regulations which were so successful that they remained unaltered until 1979.

The secret of this long-term success was in the flexibility offered by Fischer's ideas. He started from the premise that the people of Munich liked their city and that city extensions should be just that: "city" extensions. New areas were to become "epicentres" of Munich itself, a not unreasonable idea in a *Residenz-stadt*[82]. Fischer controlled the buildings along the main streets to maximise density of housing for the poorer classes and to sustain the market economy of the street. Behind the main streets was lower density development of higher quality homes for the richer people. This suited the property developers who wanted a higher return on their outlays. Industries could also be located behind the main streets. It was possible to develop the land according to demand: as high-class residential suburbs with low densities and large gardens, or industrial sites. There was no effort to "zone" the extension areas exclusively for one use or another. In fact, market forces dictated that most of the development of industry took place to the west[83] and middle-class residential development to the north. Some of Fischer's earliest extension plans were for Schwabing, the famous suburb which had become the artists' colony as well as home for many of the university faculty. Here his idea of "epicentres" of urbanity was completely successful.

Schwabing was not a suburb but an important urban centre within the framework of the city as a whole. The texture of the place was totally urban with wide streets, apartment blocks, cafés and markets. It was to play a dominant role in the development of Munich's image and self-identity as a place where creative artists could live freely; where social and sexual experimentation was tolerated; where people, especially women, could be free of the stifling social norms of Wilhelmine Germany. It has been suggested that in Schwabing "was generated the most powerful of all imaginative resistances to the patriarchal Germany of Bismarck"[84]. It was Schwabing, not Munich as a whole, which produced this image. Schwabing was established before Fischer became the City Extension Officer, but he nurtured the image. He and other Jugendstil architects also built the apartments which made the area attractive to its inhabitants. Long after its heyday in the 1890s, the fame of Schwabing was to live on and it was here that the young Hitler came to live when he was intent on becoming an artist[85].

By 1904, Fischer had developed what was described as a *Staffelbauplan* for the city. In all old and new suburbs, the "feel" of a large city was reinforced by building regulations on width of streets and heights of buildings. All building heights everywhere were regulated but there were nine different levels which could be chosen according to location and use. To avoid monotony, Fischer encouraged the retention of former boundaries marking ownership and field patterns. Development should follow these, providing echoes of the past, thus giving individuality to each new city area. For all the practical nature of the *Staffelbauplan*, though, the dominant idea was still to make the city beautiful. Public utilities such as the gasworks were built in "Heimat" style or a new municipal savings bank as a renaissance palace[86]. School buildings (the responsibility of the city since 1870) and public baths were designed to be beautiful. Almshouses, cemeteries, new community centres were carefully monitored to make sure they contributed something to the city's built form. But such ardent concern could lead to difficulties. Sometimes modern needs such as transport could have the opposite effect.

Figure 1.16 *View of interior of a photo and reproduction studio probably that of Franka in Kanalstrasse in first decade of twentieth century* [By permission of the Stadtarchiv München]

Figure 1.17 *Fischer's design for a new departmental store for Paul Schwabe in Kaufingerstrasse 1912* [By permission of Professor Dr Winfried Nerdinger]

Fischer had produced plans for a new rail network in the city, especially a branch line to Schwabing in 1895[87]. An Artists Association, led by Frank Lenbach, the rich and famous portrait painter, demonstrated against both the railway and the idea of wires in the streets for electric trams. Munich did not get its U-bahn but modern technology could not be held at bay. The first German Electricity Exhibition had been held in the Glaspalast in 1882. By 1883, the introduction of electricity in the theatres had transformed productions. Over the next decade, electric street lighting was introduced. Munich's trams were electrified in 1895 and two years later, the system was taken over by the municipality. The crucial change was the lowering of fares, the first sign that the municipality was becoming conscious of the needs of its poorer citizens. Fischer's brief had not included the idea of giving priority to the poor. He did not think in terms of cheap mass transit, nor did he put in hand municipal housing projects for the poor before the First World War. The greatest fear had been that Munich would be swamped by suburbs of low-class housing in great building blocks as had happened in Berlin. Fischer's energies were concentrated on combating that.

Yet in the first decade of the twentieth century, the city acquired 60 000 new inhabitants but between 1903–9, only 6000 new housing units were produced. The

Figure 1.19 *Fruitseller in Zweibrückenstrasse in 1905* [By permission of the Stadtarchiv München]

Figure 1.20 Munich in the inter-war period showing Fischer's plan for Schwabing [Map drawn by Chris Lewis]

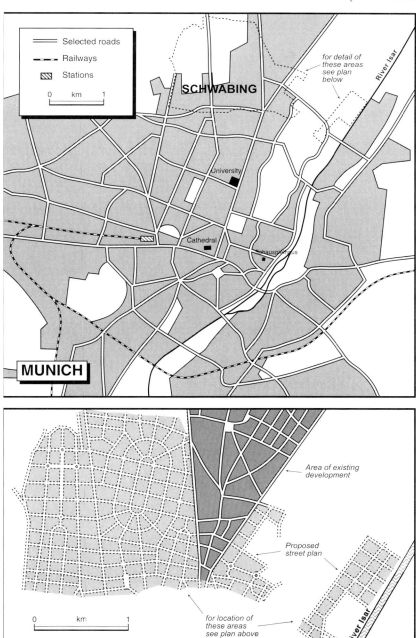

issue of housing and city extension would have to be faced. Munich was a relatively healthy city but it already had a long-term problem of overcrowding. A survey of 1910 gave the average number of residents per house in Munich as 36.6. This put it roughly on a par with Hamburg at 38.7, but much worse than Hannover with 20 and Frankfurt am Main, with 17.1[88]. Of course the figure for Berlin was very much worse at 75.9 but Berlin's speed of growth and housing problems outstripped every other city. In Munich, as in all German cities, the First World War was a turning point. Defeat accompanied by hyperinflation of the currency brought great suffering for the poor and the context for revolution and political instability[89]. The socialist revolution of the early months of 1919, led by the mild-mannered Eisner, collapsed in the political turmoil following his assassination and the weight of dealing with the daily problems of food and work for the people.

It was followed for two short but glorious weeks at the end of April 1919 by a Communist coup whose leaders declared Germany a new Communist state[90]. As the poor came from the crowded quarters of the city to hear the leaders such as Levine give passionate speeches, he promised them immediate access to new houses. At the outbreak of war, 5% of new housing in the city was actually empty, since property developers had overestimated the demand of the middle-class market. The communist promises of better homes had to be empty. Two weeks was not long enough to institute change. But serious changes had already occurred which were to transform the housing conditions of the city. All rent rises (following inflation) were forbidden and it became impossible to evict tenants. A Munich Housing Authority was set up in 1919 which was given the right to look into all future housing developments. Rents continued to be frozen[91]. In 1920, they were only 14% of their pre-war value. In 1923, as the mark finally collapsed, and Hitler organised his abortive Munich putsch, they were only 3.4% of the 1914 value. Even as the national currency was stabilised under the American Dawes Plan of 1924, there could be no going back to pre-war conditions.

In 1925, Munich acquired an energetic new Mayor, Karl Scharnagl, of the Bavarian Centre Party. He went cap in hand to the USA and to Britain to negotiate for loans for housing programmes for the city. Between 1924 and 1932, 80% of new dwellings were publicly financed and 26 944 were built[92]. It was a massive effort which unluckily, with the world economic depression in 1929, was to cost the city dear. Fischer had been called in to start a public housing project in the early 1920s and he had adopted a garden city ideal with gardens and vegetable plots for the residents. This proved too expensive but it established the principle that new developments should fit in with what already existed and the city's architects did not go in for the latest functionalist styles. They chose, in the words of a recent historian of the city, "Munich's middle way between traditionalism and the avant-garde"[93]. But during the Weimar Republic, Munich had definitively lost its cultural pre-eminence to Berlin.

In 1925, at the grand opening of a new German museum for technology and industry, the new Mayor Scharnagl, protested unconvincingly that: "to the realm of the arts, which we cultivate so lovingly, and to the domain of the sciences, which we hold in such high esteem, we now add technology, which for some time has provided a solid base for our cultural and intellectual life"[94]. Not even the acquisition in the same year of Franz Lenbach's mansion and art collection as a new city art museum could give substance to his words. The leading painters, artists and avant-garde dramatists had gone. One of the most famous of Munich's writers still remained. Thomas Mann did his best to sustain a creative environment. In 1926, he organised a *Münchener Gesellschaft* to help the city recover its cultural and intellectual strength which he believed had been poisoned by anti-Semitism and extreme nationalism[95]. His efforts merely underlined that the city was no longer the centre of cultural creativity that it had been. The moment had passed but the city still bore the physical legacy, in its streets, suburbs and centres, of former aspirations for the City of Art when great care had been lavished on the process of its modernisation. Like Barcelona, in the 1930s, its cultural life was to be subsumed in the political struggles of the state.

Figure 1.21 *A handsome hostel for unmarried men designed by Fischer* [By permission of Professor Dr Winfried Nerdinger]

WHOSE CITY? CIVIC IDENTITIES AND SOCIAL SPACE

In both Barcelona and Munich, the modernisation of the cities had taken place at a time of great cultural creativity. Artistic endeavour had, in both cases, created civic identities at a time when expansion was obliterating the past. The introduction of modern town planning had been culturally and politically determined. It was not just a matter of coping with the elements of modernisation: the increased scale, public health measures, transport, workers' housing, gas, water, electricity and the internal combustion engine. Each city had adopted all these elements but, more important, were the ideals and ambitions that inspired people to contemplate change. Collectively, these produced civic identities which were recognisable by citizens and visitors. The comparison of Barcelona with

Figure 1.22 Small housing complex designed by Fischer in the 1920s [By permission of Professor Dr Winfried Nerdinger]

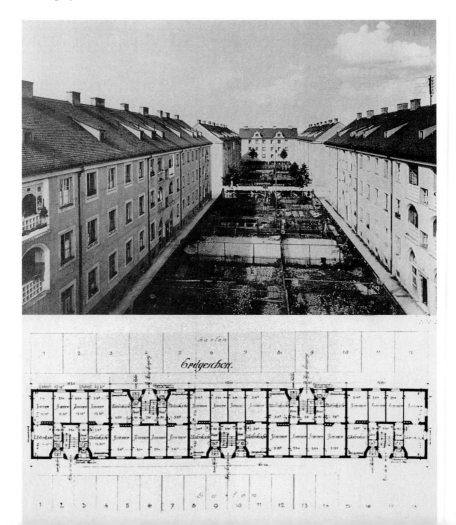

Munich has highlighted just how different these images could be in two cities of similar size and regional status. In both instances, totally different histories, traditions and cultures were reinterpreted anew. As the cities grew in scale beyond the purview of any single personal or political influence, they had still managed to achieve a sense of a specific civic identity. It was an identity based on the history, traditions and culture of city and region. It had been reinterpreted in the present in the lay-out of the expanding city, in its architecture and use of space.

The physical form of the enlarged city and the evolution of cultural institutions were reference points. These had been created in both Munich and Barcelona in the early twentieth century with the resources of a bourgeois elite. Yet they were not exclusive. Cultural institutions, parks and open spaces, swimming baths and sports facilities were open to the public. In fact, one of the most important social and cultural changes in both cities was the growing influence of the working classes. In both Barcelona and Munich, highly sophisticated subcultures of the working classes had developed in parallel with those nurtured by the bourgeoisie. The work of Temma Kaplan, RJ Evans and others[96], has shown how these cultures adapted to the new circumstances of mass urbanisation. As they adapted, so new civic identities were born which were to be as powerful as any of the others in sustaining the independence, affection and commitment of citizens to their city which was to be such a significant force in facilitating successful adaptations in the future[97]. To conclude this comparison of Barcelona and Munich and the recreation of their sense of civic identities at moments of great change will be a brief review of how the enthusiasms of the working classes contributed to changing the use of space in the city and new civic identities.

In the course of the period 1890–1930, one of the most significant impacts on the use of space in the city was the growth of modern sport. Even as the period of high artistic endeavour in Barcelona and Munich was fading, a new revolution in organised sport was taking shape. In the 1920s, Barcelona had not only tried to mount another International Exhibition, it had also tried to get itself selected as the location for an Olympic Games[98]. This new civic movement, invented in 1896, was to offer fresh grounds for competition between cities. It might have been dedicated to modern sport, but the civic hosts gained prestige and even economic spin-offs. Barcelona was never successful in this period in its bids but its efforts meant the transformation of the Montjuic area to one dedicated to sporting facilities. The huge Olympic stadium on Montjuic was first built in 1929, to increase Barcelona's chances of bidding for the 1936 Olympics. It lost famously to Berlin, supported by the ambitions of the Third Reich. Barcelona's Olympic bid was, however, an indication of how enthusiastic the bourgeoisie was in the pursuit of sport. From the 1890s, the city had sported smart clubs devoted to most modern sporting activities such as yachting, cycling, polo, golf, tennis, shooting, boxing and by the turn of the twentieth century, automobile clubs, followed soon by flying clubs. Yet the great growth sport of the first quarter of the twentieth century in both Barcelona and Munich was to be football[99].

Barcelona Football Club was founded in 1899, just one month before the Catala Football Club[100]. Yet the bourgeois did not have a monopoly on enthusiasm for the game. In Cerdà's Eixample, the existence of empty lots in many squares gave opportunities for local football clubs to proliferate. The game also began to develop as a spectator sport, which was to transform the fortunes of the Barcelona Football Club. In 1922, the first large stadium, which could hold 20 000 spectators, was built. Three years later, the new dictatorship of Primo der Rivera banned Barcelona Football Club because of fears of what the massed spectators might do. In the second half of the 1920s, many small sports clubs did become "fronts" for sustaining a sense of Catalan identity, along with recreational clubs of all kinds, in a manner reminiscent of the Socialist recreational clubs in Munich in the nineteenth century, which were also products of repression.

Organised sport for the workers in Munich, however, had expanded well beyond the confines of the socialists. Gymnastics and athletics became extremely popular. Munich was also at the forefront in promoting leisure activities which took the workers out of the city. The first German group of the Natur Freunde, set up in Vienna in 1895, was established in Munich in 1905 and reached a peak in 1923. Its members went walking and rambling in groups[101]. One way of assessing the impact of sport on the physical fabric of the city is to explore the provision for organised sports of all kinds. In Munich, it was impressive. By the early 1930s, the city was equipped with 13 sports pitches of more than 3 hectares in size and 217 smaller ones. There were facilities for a huge range of other sports including facilities for gymnastics and athletics, tennis, swimming, boating, cycling, shooting, riding, camping and ice sports[102]. Such a range was indicative of the great variety of choice to be found in a large modern city in forms of recreation and leisure. The German Workers Cyclist Movement had 250 000 members, making it the largest cycling movement in the world and its magazine had a circulation of 45 000.

Variety, choice and scale were similar in both Munich and Barcelona, though the Munich working classes had far better provision. Both were regional centres and citizens could expect to find a wealth of social and cultural facilities. Yet it is a mistake to believe that, gradually, large modern cities were becoming very similar. The perceived identities of Barcelona and Munich were not the same. The bland terminology: "regional centre" obscures how city and citizens had fought for decades to construct their own and their cities' social identities. What they achieved was individualistic, multi-faceted and subject to change. What is a city's social identity? It remains a very hard concept to pin down in an historical context. This chapter has tried to demonstrate the interaction between the creation of the built environment and the social and cultural history of particular places, in this case Barcelona and Munich. Two very different cities have been compared in the hope that comparison will underline the effort that was expended to achieve a sense of civic identity in an ever more self-conscious way as cities grew, new technology was introduced and modern town planning methods were first articulated.

NOTES

1. J Richardson (1992) *A Life of Picasso Vol I 1886–1906* London, Pimlico, 57–257.
2. P Weiss (1970) *Kandinsky in Munich: the formative Jugendstil years* Princeton, NJ, Princeton University Press.
3. F Roca (1994) "Ildefons Cerdà: 'el hombre algebraico'" in A Sànchez (ed) *Barcelona 1888–1929: modernidad, ambición y conflictos de una ciudad soñada* Madrid, Alianza Editorial, 155–66; GR Collins and CC Collins (1986) *Camillo Sitte: the birth of modern city planning* New York, Rizzoli.
4. A Sutcliffe (1981) *Towards the Planned City: Germany, Britain, the United States and France 1780–1914*, 2. The cities were: London, New York, Paris, Berlin, Chicago, Vienna, St Petersburg, Philadelphia, Manchester, Birmingham, Moscow, Boston and Glasgow.
5. J-L Marfany (1996) *La Cultura del Catalanisme: el nationalisme catala en els sens inicis* Barcelona, Editorial Empuries.
6. D Blackbourn (1997) *The Fontana History of Germany 1780–1918* London, HarperCollins, 264–5.
7. CM Cipolla (ed) (1973) *Fontana Economic History of Europe*, Vol 3 London, Collins.
8. R Carr (1966) *Spain 1808–1939* Oxford, Clarendon Press.
9. DC Large (1997) *Where Ghosts Walked: Munich's road to the Third Reich* New York and London, WW Norton and Co. This book claims Munich had a special set of circumstances which made it the ideal centre for the National Socialist Party. This is perhaps to overstate the case and sets up an analysis of those factors conducive to the outcome, which gives a distorted picture of the city's history.
10. AF Weber (1899 repr. 1965) *The Growth of Cities in the Nineteenth Century: a study in statistics* Ithaca, New York, Cornell University, 80–93.
11. A Lees (1985) *Cities Perceived: urban society in European and American thought 1820–1940* Manchester, Manchester University Press, 205.
12. VK-M Heartle (1988) "Münchens 'verdrdägte' Industrie" in F Prinz and M Kraus (eds) *München: Musenstadt mit Hinterhöfen: Die Prinzregentenzeit 1886–1912* Verlag CH Beck, Munich, 164–74.
13. M Makela (1990) *The Munich Secession: arts and artists in turn of the century Munich* Princeton, NJ, Princeton University Press, 7.
14. Makela (1990) *The Munich Secession*, 14–15.
15. R Hughes (1996 2nd edn) *Barcelona* London, Harvill Press, 257.
16. T Kaplan (1992) *Red City, Blue Period: social movements in Picasso's Barcelona* Berkeley, CA, University of California Press, 13–36.
17. Richardson (1992) *A Life of Picasso*, 237–44.
18. Weiss (1970) *Kandinsky in Munich*, 119.
19. B Ladd (1990) *Urban Planning and Civic Order in Germany 1860–1914* Cambridge, Mass., Harvard University Press, 91–2. Ladd offers a short discussion on the question of the destruction of city walls.
20. M Green (1974) *The Von Richthoven Sisters: the triumphant and tragic modes of love* London, Weidenfeld & Nicolson, 86.
21. Collins and Collins (1986) *Camillo Sitte*, 410.
22. MZ Brooke (1970) *Le Play: engineer and social scientist: the life and work of Frédéric Le Play* London, Longmans.
23. F Estapé (1996) "Ildefons Cerdà I Sunyer" in *Contemporary Barcelona, 1856–1999* Catalogue of Exhibition, Centre de Cultura Contemporània de Barcelona, 55.
24. VM Lampugnagi (1996) "Cerdà's Plan or progressive urbanism" in *Contemporary Barcelona*, 57–8; I Cerdà (1867) *Teoría general de la urbanización y aplicación de sus*

principios y doctrinas a la reforma y ensanche de Barcelona Madrid, Imprenta Española, Archivo General de la Administración.

25. Lampugnagi (1996) *Contemporary Barcelona*, 63.
26. Cerdà is credited with inventing the term.
27. Lampugnagi (1996) *Contemporary Barcelona*, 59.
28. The blocks were all to have the same width in the 1855 plan. The sides of their square forms, not counting the chamfered corners, measured 113 metres and covered 12 370 square metres, of which at least 800 sq.metres were intended to be garden. Lampugnagi (1996) *Contemporary Barcelona*, 57.
29. Sutcliffe (1981) *Towards the Planned City*, 7–46; G Fehl and J Rodriguez-Lores (eds) (1983) *Stadterweiterungen 1800–1875: Von den Anfängen des modernen Städtebaues in Deutschland* Hamburg, Christians.
30. Ladd (1990) *Urban Planning*, 36–77.
31. DJ Olsen (1986) *The City as a Work of Art: London, Paris and Vienna* New Haven and London, Yale University Press, 58–82.
32. Ladd (1990) *Urban Planning*, 38–43.
33. The sub-title of the work was *Der Städtebau* but it is referred to as the *Handbuch* by GR and CC Collins and others to differentiate it from the work by Sitte with the same title. Collins and Collins (1986) *Camillo Sitte*, 429 and 45. See also comments on Stübben by Ladd (1990) *Urban Planning*, 104.
34. J Stübben (1907) *Der Städtebau nach seinen Künstlerischen Grundsätzen* Stuttgart, Alfred Kroner Verlag. It has been translated by GR Collins and CC Collins (1965) *City Planning According to Artistic Principles* London, Phaidon Press.
35. Collins and Collins (1986) *Camillo Sitte*, 64–70.
36. Collins and Collins (1965) *City Planning*, 190.
37. Collins and Collins (1986) *Camillo Sitte*, 97–9 and 44–5; Ladd (1990) *Urban Planning*, 133–6.
38. *Deutsche Bauzeitung* XXVII 1893, 193–4. There is an account of the whole Munich competition in this volume.
39. G Fehl (1994) "Carl Henrici (1842–1927): pour un urbanisme allemand" in J Dethier and A Guiheux (eds) *La Ville, Art et Architecture en Europe 1870–1993* Paris, Editions du Centre Pompidou, 136–7.
40. Collins and Collins (1986) *Camillo Sitte*, 71–91.
41. S Fisch (1988) *Stadtplanung in 19. Jahrhundert. Das Beispiel München bis zu Ära Theodor Fischer* Munich, R Oldenbourg Verlag, 211–17.
42. Another classic example was the growth of Budapest in a wave of Hungarian nationalism. See J Lukacs (1993 pbk ed.) *Budapest 1900: a historical portrait of a city and its culture* London, Weidenfeld & Nicolson, 69–72.
43. D Mackay (1985) *Modern Architecture in Barcelona 1854–1939* No 3, Anglo-Catalan Society Occasional Papers, University of Sheffield, 13–41.
44. See the discussion on the celebration of May Day in Barcelona from 1889 in T Kaplan "Civic Rituals and patterns of resistance in Barcelona 1890–1930" in P Thane, G Crossick and R Floud (eds) (1984) *The Power of the Past: essays for EJ Hobsbawm* Cambridge and Paris, Cambridge University Press and Édition de la Maison des Sciences de l'Homme, 173–93.
45. M Guardia y Albert García Espuche (1994) "1888 y 1929. Dos exposiciones, una sola ambición" in Sánchez (1994) *Barcelona 1888–1929*, 25–43.
46. Mackay (1985) *Modern Architecture in Barcelona*, 6.
47. The ancient universities of both Barcelona and Munich had been allowed to move back into the cities in the course of the nineteenth century, having previously been banished to rural outposts as a method of controlling seditious behaviour. In both cities, the

universities and their faculty and students were to play an enormously important role in cultural activities, in providing training and expertise (especially for architects and lawyers) and in nurturing the cultural images of each city.

48. This evolved from the Escola de Mestres d'Obres (School of Master Builders) set up in 1859 by the Madrid government in imitation of the French École Polytechnique in Paris. J Rosell (1996) "'Catalan construction' for modern architecture" in *Contemporary Barcelona*, 71.

49. J Casassas (1994) "Batallas y ambigüedades del catalanismo" in Sánchez (1994) *Barcelona 1888–1929*, 127–40.

50. For Nice Exhibition see chapter on Nice and Blackpool.

51. JM Montaner (1997) *Barcelona: a city and its architecture* Cologne, Taschen, 38.

52. R Aurin (1996) "Pere Garcia Fària" in *Contemporary Barcelona*, 75–7.

53. Mackay (1985) *Modern Architecture in Barcelona*, 15–17; Montaner (1997) *Barcelona*, 38–42.

54. C y E Mendoza (1989) *Barcelona Modernista* Barcelona, Editorial Planeta, 83; Mackay (1985) *Modern Architecture in Barcelona*, 20.

55. Mackay (1985) *Modern Architecture in Barcelona*, 35.

56. Montaner (1997) *Barcelona*, 134–41.

57. There is a huge literature on Gaudí and his achievements. Still useful in the study, GR Collins (1960) *Antonio Gaudí* London, Mayflower.

58. JJ Lahuerta (1994) "Antonio Gaudí: poeta visionario, arquitecto demiurgo" in Sánchez (1994) *Barcelona 1888–1929*, 166–81.

59. Carr (1966) *Spain 1808–1939*, 548–52.

60. J Castells (1994) "Guía urbana de la diversión" Sánchez (1994) *Barcelona 1888–1929*, 233–4.

61. "Els Quatre Gats" became a popular meeting place for artists. It was fitted up by the painter, Pere Romeu in imitation of "Le Chat Noir" in Paris.

62. H Geretsegger and M Peintner (1970) *Otto Wagner 1841–1918: the expanding city, the beginning of modern architecture* London, Pall Mall.

63. Mackay (1985) *Modern Architecture in Barcelona*, 46–7.

64. N Toutcheff (1994) "Léon Jaussely 1875–1932. Les débuts de l'urbanisme scientifique en France" in Dethier and Guiheux (eds) (1994) *La Ville*, 169.

65. His book was not published until 1913: A Soria y Mata (1913) *La Ciudad lineal como arquitectura nueva de ciudades* Madrid; C Sambricio (1994) "Arturo Soria y Mata (1844–1920), La Cité linéaire" in Dethier and Guiheux (eds) *La Ville*, 162–3.

66. Carr (1966) *Spain*, 497–9.

67. Mackay (1985) *Modern Architecture in Barcelona*, 48–9.

68. In 1902, 6800 were employed in the construction industry. *Annuaire Estadistico de la Ciudad Barcelona*, 1903, 1482.

69. The first annual statistical report of Barcelona city, published in 1903, did a survey on housing which demonstrated the huge differences in densities between the old city and the Eixample. Dividing the city into ten districts, the best had 6 inhabitants to a house, the worst 31. The worst four districts with 31, 30, 26, and 25 inhabitants per house were all in the old city. *Annuaire Estadistico de la Ciudad Barcelona*, año 1, 1902, 92.

70. Montaner (1997) *Barcelona*, 190–7.

71. PJ Ravetllat (1996) "Future Barcelona" *Contemporary Barcelona*, 87–9.

72. Makela (1990) *The Munich Secession*, 6–18.

73. Makela (1990) *The Munich Secession*, 108.

74. Jelavich (1985) *Munich and Theatrical Modernism: politics playwriting and performance* Cambridge, Mass., Harvard University Press, 20.

75. E Boa (1987) *The Sexual Circus: Wedekind's Theatre of Subversion* Oxford, Basil Blackwell, 26–53.
76. R Lenman (1980) "Politics and Culture: the State and the avant-garde in Munich 1886–1914" in RJ Evans (ed) *Society and Politics in Wilhelmine Germany* London, Croom Helm, 90–109.
77. Boa (1987) *The Sexual Circus*, 8–12.
78. Jelavich (1985) *Munich and Theatrical Modernism*, 156–7.
79. R Geary (1987) "Working Class Culture in Imperial Germany" in R Fletcher (ed) *From Bernstein to Brandt* London, Edward Arnold, 11–16.
80. Collins and Collins *Sitte*, 92.
81. Fisch (1988) *Stadtplanung*, 201–53.
82. W Nerdinger (1994) "Theodor Fischer: le plan d'occupation des sols, Munich" in Dethier and Guiheux (eds) *La Ville*, 138–9.
83. S Bleek (1991) *Quarterbildung in der Urbaniserung. Das Münchner Westend, 1890–1933* München, R Oldenbourg, 9–18.
84. Green (1974) *The Von Richthoven Sisters*, 85.
85. Large (1997) *Where Ghosts Walked*, 3–5.
86. W Zwischau (1988) "Heimatstil und Funktionalismus. Fabrikbau in München" in Prinz and Kraus *München*, 114–18.
87. Fisch (1988) *Stadtplanung*, 246–53.
88. Ladd (1990) *Urban Planning*, 153.
89. MH Geyer (1993) "Munich in Turmoil: social protest and the revolutionary movement, 1918–19" in CJ Wrigley (ed) *Challenges of Labour: Central and Western Europe 1917–1920* London, Routledge, 51–71.
90. A Mitchell (1965) *Revolution in Bavaria 1918–19: the Eisner régime and the Soviet Republic* New Jersey, Princeton University Press; R Leviné-Meyer (1973) *Leviné: the life of a revolutionary* Farnborough, Saxon House, 106.
91. W Rudloff (1992) "Notjahre. Stadtpolitik in Krieg, Inflation und Weltwirtschaftskrise 1914 bis 1933" in R Bauer (ed) *Geschichte der Stadt München* München, CH Beck, 336–68.
92. J Lindauersche (1938) *Statistisches Handbuch der Hauptstadt der Bewegung für 1927–37* München, Universitäts-Buchhandlung, 79.
93. Rudloff (1992) "Notjahre", 360.
94. Large (1997) *Where Ghosts Walked*, 210.
95. Large (1997) *Where Ghosts Walked*, 212–13.
96. Kaplan (1992) *Red City, Blue Period*; RJ Evans (ed) (1980) *Society and Politics*; L Abrams (1992) *Workers' Culture in Imperial Germany: leisure and recreation in the Rhineland and Westphalia* London, Routledge.
97. F Bianchini and M Parkinson (1993) *Cultural Policy and Urban Regeneration: the West European experience* Manchester, Manchester University Press.
98. X Pujadas and C Santacana (1990) *L'Altra Olimpíada. Barcelona '36. Esport, societat i política a Catalunya (1900–36)* Barcelona, Llibres de l'Index.
99. C Eisenberg (1991) "Football in Germany: beginnings, 1890–1914" *International Journal of the History of Sport* 8, 2, 205–20.
100. J Artells (1972) *Barca, Barca, Barca* Barcelona, Laia; E Pérez de Rozas (1994) "¡Barça, Bar-ça, Bar-ça!: el catalanismo sentimental" in Sánchez, *Barcelona 1888–1929*, 213–25.
101. HJ Teichler and G Hauk (1987) *Illustrierte Geschichte des Arbeitersports* JHW Dietz Nachf. 249.
102. *Statistisches Handbuch*, 188.

CHAPTER 2

PLANNING, SOCIETY AND THE URBAN ENVIRONMENT: VIENNA, BUDAPEST AND PRAGUE IN THE 1920s[1]

Patrick Geddes, the pioneer international prophet of modern town planning, believed one thing implicitly: that there was a link between the health and well-being of a society and the physical environment in which people lived and worked[2]. Furthermore, as an evolutionist, Geddes believed that the factors which sustained a continuous process of change and development of any built environment were ultimately cultural. Economic and technological change determined the resources available but how they were used depended on decisions made in specific cultural contexts. Geddes illustrated his ideas through his famous Cities and Town Planning Exhibition which he had created for the first International Town Planning Conference in London in 1910. He went on to win the Gold Medal at the International Exhibition at Ghent organised by the Belgian peace campaigner and urbanist, Paul Otlet, in 1913[3]. This "Congrès International de l'art de construire les villes et l'organisation de la vie municipale" specifically made connections between the will and enterprise of municipal governments and citizens and the changes they brought to the physical environment of cities. This congress was the last attempt to understand cities and social change before Europe was engulfed in the First World War. The aftermath of the war was to provide the ultimate testing ground for these pre-war ideas. The extreme case had to be the experience of Vienna, Budapest and Prague in the 1920s.

Vienna, Budapest and Prague were not just large cities but capital cities. Vienna, the glittering capital of the Austro-Hungarian Empire before the First World War, and its rivals, Budapest and Prague, had become thoroughly modern metropolitan cities (though Prague was still modest in scale and dominated by its medieval core). Pre-war Vienna has been described as the cultural cradle of modernity. It contained many outstanding individuals in the worlds of science and art, music and literature, who struggled to reveal the complexities of the human condition in the twentieth century. The work of Carl Schorske, Donald Olsen and many others has produced insights into the physical and social environment of the city at this time[4]. Budapest, on the other hand, was the epitome of modern commercial and industrial endeavour. Budapest enjoyed such a period of entrepreneurial vigour and industrial growth in the half century before the war that its transformation has been likened to that of New York at the end of the nineteenth century[5]. Its flamboyant history has received a considerable share of scholarly attention, John Lukacs' study being the most accessible assessment of the city and its cultural achievements at the end of the nineteenth century[6].

Prague, meanwhile, was not only an industrial centre, it also began one of its modern careers as a tourist attraction. The astonishingly beautiful medieval core of the city was a revelation to visitors. The railways of the mid and late nineteenth century had opened up Central Europe to eager travellers from America as well as the Europeans from west and east. The "cultural context" of Vienna, Budapest and Prague has thus, in one sense, been charted. This, however, was not the only kind of cultural context which Geddes was using to explain the relationship between the physical environment and social change. He was also more in tune with the process of urbanisation, economic and social change and local history[7]. He was as interested in local assumptions, aspirations and achievements as the manipulation of power and influence. What he sought was a synthesis of the factors which produced a specific local environment: local, urban and regional. A perspective influenced by his ideas on these three cities stimulates a different range of questions about social and cultural change and the physical environment.

Currently, there has been a new wave of urban history in Central Europe which has taken a path more akin to the Geddesian perspective though it has happened entirely independently of Geddes' work. To offer just one example, in a recent edited volume on Vienna, Prague and Budapest in the period from 1867–1918, the editors, Gerhard Melinz and Susan Zimmermann, have been addressing some new questions[8]. They are interested in asking, not "how did Prague and Budapest catch up with the Imperial capital Vienna?" but "how did cities in very different circumstances in relation to scale, population and economic structure, relate to the challenges common to them all?" They argue for a balance in explaining change between an appreciation of the particular and the common factors. They warn against the problems of comparative histories of even these three central European capitals which too easily degenerate into a simplified over-arching discussion of the relative "progress" made by each towards solving their common problems. There is need for more research into many more issues such as the relationship between family structures and size and the housing of the people, the nature of industrialisation and its location, and in the twentieth century, the crucial issue for old established cities, the physical and cultural connections between their inner core and the ever-growing outer suburbs. The culture and politics within which solutions to these issues were found were local and municipal as much as national. The differences in what happened in Vienna, Budapest and Prague in the inter-war years were thus as important as the similarities. Much of their response to the catastrophe of the First World War was individually determined before it ever began.

But first it is necessary to outline the catastrophe. The First World War was the greatest catastrophe for Central Europe since the Thirty Years War centuries before. At a stroke, in the Peace Treaty of Versailles which followed the First World

War, the Austro-Hungarian Empire was dismantled. The map of central Europe was redrawn. Because the First World War had reduced Europe and the international trade of the world to ruins; because Russia was in turmoil with its own civil war; and because the new superpower, America, was only flexing its political muscles, the Peace Settlement was dominated by Britain and France[9]. The Central Europeans were at the mercy of the negotiators. New boundaries were deliberately drawn which paid no attention to present or more ancient boundaries: Austria became a tiny rump of its former self, limited to the Austrian provinces alone. Hungary was also very heavily reduced to less than one-third of its former size, leaving it without its industrialised perimeter; and Czechoslovakia was created out of parts of the ancient kingdoms of Bohemia and Moravia as well as the northern Highlands of the former Hungarian kingdom. The three historic capital cities, Vienna, Budapest and Prague, thus faced adjustment to totally different social and physical hinterlands in the inter-war period. The driving force behind the Versailles Treaty was twofold: to make the Germans "pay" for the suffering that the allies over-self-righteously claimed they had caused and to make sure that subject nationalities within the former Austro-Hungarian empire would have a chance of self-determination in their future. For the drafters of the Treaty, the new countries thus had a nationalistic agenda as "buffer zones" against any future German imperialist aspirations and as repositories of the hopes of the many different national groups whose fortunes had been mingled together over the thousand years of the Holy Roman Empire (the Habsburg Empire having inherited its polyglot nature).

What happened to Vienna, Budapest and Prague in these greatly changed circumstances? What needs to be said at the outset is that nationalism was not actually an issue for any of them, although there were great movements of population in and out of the three capitals as ethnic minorities became fearful for their futures. In the course of the inter-war period, some new national institutions were also built, mainly administrative ones. Being capitals of small nations, though, had little to do with nationalism. Major concerns were political stability, economic development and providing the infrastructure for growth[10]. How to meet the challenges of industrialisation and modern social life were the main priorities. Of key importance to the position they found themselves in at the end of the First World War was the economic legacy of the past on the macro-scale of the Austro-Hungarian Empire. As industrialisation had swept in fits and starts over Europe in the second half of the nineteenth century, the lands of the Austro-Hungarian Empire had achieved a degree of regional specialisation in economic development which had never before been experienced. Protected by tariffs within the empire, the process of industrialisation could continue unimpeded by national boundaries and, with improvements in transport, each region (including the capital cities and their hinterlands) was able to concentrate on those areas of industrial and commercial activity in which it had an advantage[11]. By 1914, 43% of the total industrial labour force of Austria-Hungary was located on the territory which became Czechoslovakia[12] although the old city of Prague itself had been left behind by the growth of industrial suburbs outside its jurisdiction. Budapest, the amalgam of three cities, Óbuda, Buda and Pest, joined in 1873 to become the new capital city of Hungary, had been a thriving commercial, financial and industrial centre. Finally Vienna, at the centre of Dual Monarchy and Empire, was both the seat of government and administration and the centre of the Imperial banking system. Each city and its region were complementary to the other, though where there were economic conflicts, Vienna had asserted her political power to keep the advantage.

The First World War had already destroyed this system before the peace settlement. War had led to a dramatic decline in both agricultural and industrial production, with industry heavily geared to war. The result was that economic and social conditions for ordinary citizens in all three cities, but especially the larger cities of Vienna and Budapest, became life-threatening. Famine and disease were accompanied by the breakdown of basic services. The consequences could be seen in high mortality figures. In Vienna, people were kept alive on a ration of 10–15 decagrams of bread and flour a day and by 1919, milk consumption was 7% of its pre-war figure[13]. The influenza epidemic of 1919 killed thousands while infant mortality in 1920 in Vienna was 24% and in Budapest, 23%. All this was compounded by the migration and immigration of ethnic minorities. They were driven by fear and compulsion. A large number of Germans were expelled from Czechoslovakia. The Austrian Germans from Moravia and Bohemia fled to Vienna. Yet Vienna still lost population. Those that left Vienna were Slavs, Czechs, Slovaks and Poles though some ethnic groups who had become dominant in a particular industry actually stayed. Viennese builders and bricklayers were mostly Czech and they stayed in their own quarter, Favoriten, close to the brick factory. Hungarians in both Vienna and Prague were forced to return to Budapest. Many who had worked in the vast Imperial civil service now found themselves totally destitute or lucky if they could find employment as menial labourers. The most unfortunate of all the refugees were those who, made stateless by the end of the Austro-Hungarian Empire, yet had no country they could call their own. Anti-Semitism had been rife in pre-war nationalistic parties such as the Czech National Party and in Vienna, against the Polish Jews. In Budapest there had been considerable assimilation of Germans, Jews and Slovaks[14], though the position of the Jewish communities in Vienna, Budapest and Prague was to become ever more perilous in the inter-war period with the onset of Nazi dominance. Ever present latent forces of anti-Semitism were released by the economic and political crisis.

By 1923, Vienna's population had shrunk from more than 2 million to 1.85 million. This still made the city almost twice as large as Budapest which just topped a million if the industrial suburbs (outside the city limits) were counted. Prague was the smallest with a mere 700 000. Their efforts to overcome the economic and social catastrophe that had befallen them was determined by three factors: 1. The relationship of the city to its newly formed nation; 2. The elements for economic recovery to be found within the city itself; and 3. The strength and efficiency of its municipal government. The balance between these factors was very different in the three capital cities. It should be remembered that no national government in Eastern, Central or Western Europe had, before the First World War, been engaged in detailed economic and social planning. The relationship between city and state and the role of government in the implementation of new social policy, especially public health and education, had been developing before the First World War but only slowly. As for economic policy, governments were extremely keen on such activities as taxation, the safeguarding of the national currency and the regulation of trade, especially import and export tariffs, due to the fact that government income depended on it. Active policies to control the trade cycle or invest in industry were tolerated, though not applied in a systematic fashion as they had been since the 1880s by the German Government under the autocratic rule of Bismarck. In the post-war world, the governments of the new nations found themselves engaged in a balancing act between a political need to appear independent and an economic imperative to continue co-operation[15], a context which was to help Central Europe spawn some of the world's leading economists by the middle of the twentieth century.

The war had profoundly changed the understanding of the government's role in economic and social life. Governments had had to take on the role of equipping the armies and feeding the people. The inability of the government to do that had facilitated the Russian Revolution. The chaos in Europe after the war raised the hopes of communists and left-wing activists in all three capital cities that revolution might be possible in these newly formed countries. The political power and institutions of the Austro-Hungarian Empire had depended on a vast civil service dominated by the nobility. In Czechoslovakia, the political parties of the bourgeois and the proletariat could not wait to get rid of the monarchy. There were violent political scenes in all three capitals as activists sought to seize power in the vacuum left by defeat. Left-wing governments came to power but a fear of communism and its consequences split the left-wing parties, just as it concentrated the minds of the opposition on the right. In Austria and Hungary, the first national democratic left-wing governments proved to be short-lived, and reactive, even repressive regimes were to gain power. What happened in the capital cities, however, did not necessarily follow what happened to the state, with one exception: in Czechoslovakia, the Social Democratic framework for national politics established by Tomăs Masaryk, the nationalist leader, was mirrored in the municipal government of Prague. State and city were politically allied. In Budapest the relationship was far less amicable. Forces of reaction in the form of Admiral Miklós Horthy, hostile to left-wing governments and the city which he believed (with some justification) was their power base, dedicated himself to giving the city "well deserved" punishment for its errors and "sinful ways"[16].

The state and city which were most at odds, however, was Vienna. A potential political divide between city and the rural regions of Austria had begun to emerge

Figure 2.1 *Poster by Bíró Mihály "Let's have a republic!" Hungary 1918, where the revolutionaries were least successful* [By permission of the Budapest Archives]

9. Bíró Mihály: „Köztársaságot !" c. plakátja

during the First World War. Survival for citizens, cut off from normal supplies of food and fuel, had led to systematic plundering of Vienna's rural hinterland. The immediate problems were simply to feed the population and to stem the massive rise in inflation which undermined the possibilities of any economic recovery. During the war, an organisation was formed, the Wirtschafts-Zentralen, run by bureaucrats in co-operation with business men, which obtained food by force and at prices determined by the organisation. At the end of the war, this organisation continued to try to meet the needs of the people of Vienna but the only agricultural areas with a very modest surplus were the Alpine provinces of Upper Austria. Forcibly removing these surpluses set the Austrian peasants against the city and encouraged the implacable rift between city and country which was developing. When the new Austria was being created, there had been a majority of Social Democrats which had facilitated the passing of a Liberal state constitution. But left-wing sympathies even for the non-revolutionary Social Democrats were quickly extinguished in the rural regions which became solidly and fiercely conservative. In the federal structure of the country, however, the city was so large that it was made into a province (or *Land*) alongside the other regions. Vienna was thus able to sustain a Social Democratic political regime which was at odds with what happened in the rest of the country as, under the new state constitution, it was able to get state funding directly. In 1920, a democratic city constitution was put in place under which a Social Democrat Mayor was elected. In 1922, the Mayor of Vienna then also became the President of the Viennese *Land* when Vienna gained her new status as a *Land*. The Social Democratic Party remained in power in Vienna until 1933, in contrast to conservative domination elsewhere. Between 1918 and 1933, Vienna was often out of step and out of sympathy with the national government. It was at the very extreme in the relationship between capital city and state in terms of lack of state control.

What did all this mean for the three capital cities, intent on modernising, and their citizens, intent on recovering from the disaster of the First World War? What follows in this chapter cannot be in anyway comprehensive. It will be concerned only to highlight some of the most significant physical changes to the urban environment of each city and how these emanated from a specific historical context. A comparison of the three cities of the former Austro-Hungarian Empire will help to reveal how, in adjusting to their futures, one of the most important resources was what had been achieved in the past.

THE DEVELOPMENT OF PRAGUE

It was Prague, the smallest of the three and the least rent by political extremism, which was able to set about the task of reconstruction first[17]. Right from the earliest post-war years, legislation, such as the Construction Act of 1919 which was directed towards building housing blocks containing small, low-rent housing for workers, was put into place. Political circumstances were favourable as Tomăs Masaryk was a charismatic figure, a democrat as well as a nationalist, able to stamp his authority on the new nation–state. There was also the advantage that becoming a nation–state for the first time generated a great deal of enthusiasm among the Czech people[18]. Furthermore, in Prague and Czech society as a whole, the scale of social divisions: class and nationality, were less extreme than elsewhere though it might not have felt like that for the Jewish communities in Prague[19]. The other group who would have felt similarly at odds with the present were the leading business men and merchants in the many Czech towns still dominated by upper-class Sudetan Germans. There was also the problem which was to become chronic and insoluble between the more industrialised Czech provinces and the more agrarian and backward Slovakia. Masaryk was intent on creating the image of a hard-working, egalitarian but capitalist society, willing to make sacrifices for the benefit of the future. To some extent he succeeded. When Jaroslav Císař and F. Pokorný wrote their propaganda tract in 1922 on the Czechoslovak Republic, they painted a picture of an advanced "continental nation" with a sophisticated, political, cultural and economic infrastructure[20]. At least, it conveyed the determination of the Czechs to succeed and a keen awareness of the two factors which would determine the outcome: economic development and planning. In central Europe, unlike anywhere else, the stark contrast between the Russian way forward and the capitalist systems of the West was very evident. Between 1917 and 1923, the outcome in Russia was uncertain. The Czechs meanwhile worked to stabilise their currency and develop their economic links with the West.

Czech fortunes, in this and all other respects, were inextricably bound up with Germany[21]. Many of the industrial towns of the new Czechoslovakia were dominated by German minorities. Brno, the historical capital of the ancient kingdom of Moravia, was the largest town outside Prague. It had been one of the first industrialised towns in Central Europe in the eighteenth century[22] and became known as the Czech "Manchester", but the town itself actually had a German-speaking majority[23]. So did some of the smaller towns such as Ústí n./L., Opava, Liberec and Jablonec. These were centres of the textile industries, machine tools industries, sugar refining, chemical works, trade centres for lignite and corn and luxury goods such as glass and fancy goods. The collapse of the Austro-Hungarian Empire had two effects. Many firms engaged in these industries in Vienna relocated to Prague because its financial structure was more robust; but at the same time, markets for their products were hard to find. The Czechs only had a couple of options. To find new markets for their current goods or to invest heavily in new technology in order to compete with America, Britain and France. Initially, their financial circumstances, though better than elsewhere in Central Europe, ruled out the latter, so great efforts were put into selling Czech goods world-wide. The dilemmas of the Czech economy, however, reinforced a commitment to two objectives: modernisation and planning. Unlike Britain, where the new National Government elected by the "Khaki election" of 1918 wanted to dismantle wartime controls as quickly as possible and allow the free rein of market forces to operate as they had done until 1914, the Czech government was committed to planning. This was an unusual commitment for a capitalist society and it was nationalistic endeavour that helped to sustain it.

Saving the value of their currency in the face of the hyper-inflation which took place in Germany between 1921 and 1923 made such a commitment a necessity. The massive hyperinflation suffered by Germany, which reached its peak in 1923, pulled Austria and Hungary down in its wake. Yet the Czechs were able to stave off runaway hyperinflation through the harshly deflationary measures put in place by a fierce Chancellor of the Exchequer, Alois Rašn (whose fate was to be assassinated by a mad communist revolutionary in 1923, though not before he had put the Czech economy on the road to recovery before everyone else)[24]. With this degree of financial stability, the Czechs were able to begin reconstruction and modernisation almost immediately after the war. Top of the list was the planned development of their capital city, Prague. Here again, the consequences of the past were favourable to this objective. Prague had not enjoyed the massive growth of Vienna and Budapest in the half century before 1914. It was thus still a "manageable" scale and the extent of suffering and poverty of its poorer citizens was not so overwhelming as in, for example, Budapest. The Municipal Government and the State could agree on the need for a State Planning Commission to oversee the future of the city and Greater Prague. In the extreme circumstances of the immediate post-war period, the Commissioners were able to utilise the best traditions of urban planning that had emanated from Vienna and ultimately from Germany, and weld them to a policy of modernisation for their capital city. The nine-member State Commission, appointed in February 1920, contained architects and town planners, transport and civil engineers, one public health expert and representatives of the municipality and business associations. Drawing on professional expertise, it did not, of course, include any women.

The Commissioners were saved from the prospect of producing a macho Master Plan for Prague, such as had existed before the war for Chicago and New York. What saved them was context and pragmatism. Viennese models of modern urban planning dated back at least to the plans for the Ringstrasse, announced by the Emperor in his Christmas speech of 1857. Further, in the Viennese tradition of planning, there was greater awareness of the need to be flexible and meet many different kinds of aspiration. The Prague Commissioners, in any case, had to gather together the necessary technical expertise to deal with a wide variety of issues. Their aims and objectives were not shaped by an ideal so much as the need to meet immediate demands for a transport system and civil engineering activities controlling (or failing to control) the river. The Commissioners were given a brief, however, which extended well beyond the problems of the physical environment. They were enjoined to work out a detailed plan for the development of the Greater Prague "within the widest possible context of economy, social and educational aspects, public health, technology and the arts"[25]. Given the breadth of their brief and the lack of technical back-up, they proceeded in an *ad hoc* manner, finally dividing up the area into four parts and working alongside the developments as they took place. It was the best possible combination in the circumstances, of a state authority which could make things happen, giving relatively free play to the local forces for change. Resources were always far too limited to carry out many cherished schemes but the enthusiasm engendered by the prospect of modernising the city created a context which had many extraordinary outcomes. One of these was that Prague became a formative centre for modernist architecture. The

Figure 2.2 *Prague in the inter-war years showing historic core* [Map drawn by Chris Lewis]

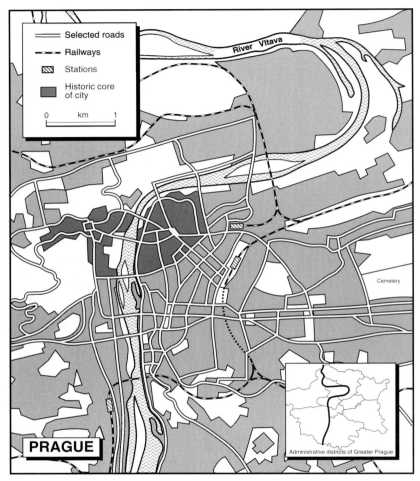

development of Prague nurtured a flowering of an avant-garde modernism which was actually to lead the industrialised world. For modern architects, Prague in the 1920s was an exciting place to be.

The Prague Municipal Government set out in a workmanlike manner to put new building and planning in hand as soon as possible. The three key areas were: new national buildings; the integration of the Greater Prague with the old city, sustaining the infrastructure of both old and new areas; and planning for social

Figure 2.3 *Competition project for the Czech Press Agency building, 1927* [By permission of Professor Rostislav Švácha]

development of the people, in terms of schools, hospitals and housing for the workers. An Act of 1921 created the administrative units of the Greater Prague adding ten new districts to the existing seven. The Czechs were modest at first about what could be achieved but cautiously ambitious and competitions were held for ministerial buildings and for the planning of Greater Prague. The Professor of Architecture at the Academy of Fine Arts in Prague at the end of the war, and until his untimely death in 1923, was Jan Kotěra. He is credited with being the founder of modern Czech architecture[26], though he was personally disappointed in not being given large commissions for new public buildings. The development of the modernist style at this time was very fluid, moving from simplified but still traditional buildings covered with historicist murals, to rondo-cubism, to a rational and pragmatic functionalism, which became the basis of modern architecture before the Second World War. Czech versions of the latter, however, did not carry the didacticism of Le Corbusier and the Congrès International d'Architecture Moderne (the CIAM, founded in 1928). There were few high rise buildings. New stylistically innovative buildings such as Josef Gočár's Czechoslovak Legiobank

1921–23 (Gočár became the Professor of Architecture in 1923) were built alongside the older buildings and fitted into the cityscape. The Bat'a shoe store in Václavské Náměstí, built between 1927 and 1929 by Ludvik Kysela was pristinely modern and functional, bearing no ornament but the slogan, Bat'a, on its façade[27]. Yet it was situated alongside much earlier buildings whose ornamentation merely complemented the new functionalist style.

The building of airports, schools, hospitals, the giant building to house the Prague Trade Fair, all encouraged new ideas, but architectural ambitions were constrained by the practicalities of cost and the demands of those who commissioned the work. Some architects felt frustrated at the inherent

Figure 2.4 *Bat'a store in Prague, architect, L. Kysela* [By permission of Professor Rostislav Švácha]

conservatism that this engendered. One of the fierce critics of compromise was
Karel Teige, an architectural journalist and theorist (a comparable figure to
Sigfried Giedion who had publicised the work of the Bauhaus), who co-founded a
journal, *Levá fronta*, recognised as leading among the avant-garde. Teige helped to
develop the identity of Czech modernism and to put forward many futuristic ideas.
He was keen on solving the shortage of housing by inventing new ways of living,
which eliminated the single family house dwellings. He envisaged an urban lifestyle
serviced by the building of great blocks where the only private space were
"sleeping cabins" and all other functions, such as eating, studying and leisure,
were to be undertaken in public rooms. Such experiments had already been made

Figure 2.5 *Prague Trade Fair building,
interior 1924–8, architects O. Tyl and J.
Fuchs* [By permission of Professor Rostislav
Švácha]

Figure 2.6 *Müller house, 1928–30, architects A. Loos and K. Lhota* [By permission of Professor Rostislav Švácha]

in Russia. Teige himself lived in such a cabin, though it was in a building which only had two sleeping cabins and public rooms shared by the occupants of these. Such ideas, however, were not generally taken up. The middle classes in the course of the mid to late 1920s when the Czech economy was thriving, began to build themselves family villas in the Greater Prague, albeit in the modern style. Prague still has one of the greatest collections of modern villas built in the inter-war period.

Ideas of modernity among the bourgeois did not extend to undermining ideas about home and family. Middle-class Czech women barely moved outside the nineteenth-century social conventions of separate spheres of action for men and women. Some had taken part in developing voluntary associations, especially

Figure 2.7 *Interior (living hall), Müller house, 1928–30, architects A. Loos and K. Lhota* [By permission of Professor Rostislav Švácha]

Figure 2.8 *J. Krejcar and J. Špalek,
Competition project for the Greater Prague
transport plan 1930–31* [By permission of
Professor Rostislav Švácha]

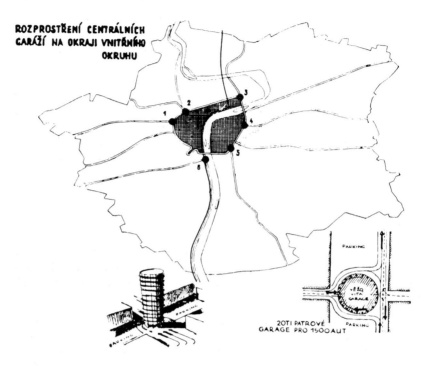

philanthropic ones and some had gained higher education[28]. But one of the few
women architects, Elly Oehlerová, was only able to practise alongside her husband, Oskar. The new Prague was to create more jobs for women in the future but
in the 1920s, decisions about the future urban environment were firmly in the
hands of men. For them, however, there were great opportunities in a number of
fields. Civil engineering projects caught the imagination of youthful practitioners.
One such was a competition in 1930–1 for the handling of the prospect of
increased traffic between the Greater Prague and the old city. Jaromir Krejcar and
Josef Špalek put forward a proposal to ban all motor traffic in Old Prague,
"expropriating" the area for public transport. The city centre was to be made
accessible by surface express rail, complemented by street car and trolley bus
services[29]. It was never implemented and the motor car was allowed access.

Yet there was no wholesale destruction of the city as there had been in Paris in
the mid-nineteenth century to facilitate traffic circulation. The old city was
cherished by politicians, the people and the technical experts. The new was

carefully grafted on, the new areas of Greater Prague retaining the sense of their separate identity as, most importantly, they had not been part of the city until the post-war period. The reminiscences of a former inhabitant of Prague in the 1930s, Eric Dluhosch, Professor Emeritus of Architecture at the Massachusetts Institute of Technology, highlights this juxtaposition of the ancient medieval city and the most modern outer suburbs. He paints a somewhat romantic picture of a largely unspoilt old city where the main form of transport was the red and white, noisy but efficient electric trams. For part of the 1930s, he also lived in a well-planned modern suburb outside the city which he also loved. In retrospect he feels he now understands how he came to love the old city and yet be dedicated to "the spirit of all things modern". In Prague, because of accidents of timing and scale, the old and the new were brought together. Municipality and State Commission acted sensitively as the midwives of the modernisation of the city. Problems of working-class housing especially, still remained, but by and large, the period 1918–38 was a minor "golden age" for civic development in Prague.

THE DEVELOPMENT OF VIENNA

Prague was perhaps more fortunate than Vienna in a number of ways, not least because it escaped the limelight focused on Vienna as the former Imperial capital. A great deal has been written about Vienna at the end of the war and in the decade afterwards. Eric Hobsbawm has suggested that:

> it produced an extraordinary outburst of literature . . . No set of political events in the twentieth century has had a comparably profound impact on the creative imagination . . . an empire destined to collapse as a metaphor for a Western elite culture itself undermined and collapsing: these images had long haunted the dark corners of the Central European imagination[30].

What has to be separated out, however, is the history of the end of the Empire and the history of the city. That is not so easy since the political history of the city was shaped by its relationship with the small Austrian state. The Social Democrats who had drafted the liberal national constitution were ousted from national power but were able to use their power base in the city to institute a social experiment there, which was designed to be the flagship of Social Democracy. The historiography of the city in this period is much exercised by this attempt and there are passionate eulogies and hostile criticisms, according to political persuasion, of "Red Vienna" and its achievements. Fighting their way through this conflict over the last couple of decades, a number of urban historians of Vienna have struggled to establish a new understanding of how the city responded to the challenges of the post-war world.

Perhaps the best place to start is with some of the parameters that dictated the city's fortunes. Vienna had been one of the rapidly growing centres of industry in the Habsburg Empire in the late nineteenth century and it also retained many small primarily artisanal shops and medium-sized factories. There were thus many layers of working class and petit-bourgeoisie although, at the bottom there was a vast pool of underemployed or unemployed people such as was found in every major capital at that time. Labour was attracted to the city, both because of its size and its industries, just as the poor and the rural had flocked to London in the early nineteenth century. Vienna was, in fact, the same size at the outbreak of the First World War as London had been in 1851. The technology of the mid-Victorian industrialism had thrived on a large pool of casual labour, unskilled, untrained and constantly replenished by immigration from the countryside. In some respects, Vienna had still been like that at the turn of the century. Most of the migrants came from Bohemia and Moravia and most were of peasant origin. One of the telling statistics in relation to the housing of these people is that in Vienna, 17% of the population did not even have separate rooms or part of rooms as they might have done in London. Instead, they rented beds on a rotation basis to fit the working shifts demanded by the factories. Those who had factory jobs were considered lucky as unemployment was always a problem. After the war, the immigrants were mostly Austrian Germans ousted from Czechoslovakia and else-where, many of urban origin. But this did not help their employment prospects. They were to get worse immediately after the war and became catastrophic by the end of the 1920s when the Great Depression finally brought about the collapse of much large- and small-scale manufacturing in the city. Vienna's achievements in the period 1918 to 1934 (when the civil war conclusively ended the reign of the Social Democrats) has to be seen against this constant struggle to sustain the city's economy.

Work, housing and welfare had to be top of the agenda of any civic government in the 1920s, aiming to keep the allegiance of the people. The new constitutions of state and city had enfranchised all adults including women. The idea of an active municipality was not, in itself, new. The Christian-Social Party, in power in the city since 1895, had, under their charismatic Mayor, Karl Lueger (1844–1910), pioneered a form of "municipal socialism". The city's water supply and sewerage disposal systems were overhauled, there was heavy investment in public transport, suburban trains and trams, and the provision of essential services such as town gas was municipalised. There were new schools, hospitals, a municipal savings bank and insurance company. The result had been to create one of the largest and most efficient municipal service bureaucracies in Central Europe that could rival any to be found in Germany. The need to plan for the future expansion of the city had been forcibly brought to the fore with the destruction of Vienna's military fortifications in the 1850s. The famous Ringstrasse, built on the land of the old city walls, with its exceptional public buildings, had been acclaimed all over the world. An attempt was made to celebrate the achievements of the city in the accepted "modern" style by holding a great International Exhibition there in 1873 which was supposed to launch the city as a tourist attraction but, in this respect, it

Figure 2.9 *Vienna in the inter-war period*
[Map drawn by Chris Lewis]

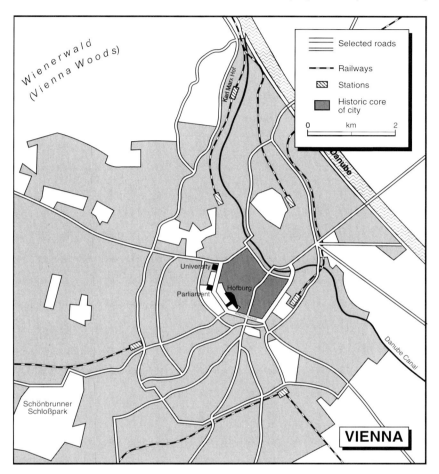

proved impossible to compete successfully with Paris. However, as a result of the planning activities, the municipality had developed a far-sighted policy of acquiring land in order to control future growth. Mayor Lueger was not only concerned with the economic and social development of the city, he also dreamed of preserving the Vienna woods and the Danube meadows as permanent pleasure grounds for the Viennese people.

Before the war, though, the municipality was little concerned with the relief of poverty and the social condition of the people. That was left to private or religious philanthropy, supported especially by upper-class women. The unenfranchised Christian Socialist women had their own organisation, the Katholische Frauenorganisation (KFO), whose Presidents were drawn from the aristocratic Metternich family. Within the framework of a Catholic culture, they cared for working women, women's education and the problems of the poor: hunger, orphaned children, clothing and household relief. Even here, there had been a perceived need for change. Gradually the aristocratic women were losing their influence and new recruits, such as Alma Seitz, a middle-class but highly educated woman, were taking over and bringing a new degree of professionalism and efficiency to their work. Alma was made the secretary of the KFO before the war and President of the Viennese KFO in 1924 when it was reorganised. She, and many other women philanthropists, had been forced to realise the desperate limitations of their work in the context of the sufferings of the poor during the First World War. When women were enfranchised under the new constitution, Catholic women were an important electoral force, agitating for welfare reforms and putting municipal government under pressure. Alma Seitz became their vociferous spokesperson on the Municipal Council when she won an election for a seat against the odds (since she was a member of the CSP) in 1919.

The party which emerged with a new political programme to alleviate distress was that of the organised workers, die Sozial-demokratische Arbeiterpartei (SDAP). The SDAP had its power base amongst those in work and the skilled and semi-skilled workers. It was thus on the social reformist wing of the labour movement always, in electoral terms, fighting off challenges from the usually Catholic Right and Communist Left. And 1919 brought the SDAP its first major chance. The prize of electoral power would come if it could address Vienna's economic and social problems and come up with coherent policies. What they had in their favour was threefold: first, financial resources of a kind brought by the new ability of the Viennese municipality to levy taxes as a *Land* and to have a share of state resources; second, a municipal civil service which, although it was old-fashioned, was of such scale and expertise that it could be relied upon to put in hand municipal enterprises and sustain them; and finally, a link with the trade union movement which gave the party a power base among the workers in trade unions (who tended to be the better-off "respectable" working class). This link was sometimes tenuous as SDAP objectives and trade union objectives did not always coincide. There was also an extremely influential group of SDAP supporters amongst Viennese intellectuals who were often attached to the university, such as Julius Tandler, a Professor of Anatomy in the Medical School. These were the people who were to be the powerhouse behind the development of the social theories that guided SDAP policies. Tandler was elected to the Municipal Council and in 1920 was put in charge of the public welfare department. At the heart of the problem of needing to create a new social policy with few resources, Tandler used his scientific background, allied with a form of social evolutionism, to develop a theory based on demographic changes[31].

The birth rate in Vienna had been falling since the 1870s (as in all other advanced Western European nations) though only among the upper classes. After the war, the other social orders were following suit. Tandler based his ideas on what he thought was demographically positive and demographically negative: policies which enhanced the quality of the population as opposed to policies which offered relief for those with some form of physical disability, from old age to the infirm. With limited resources, the aim was to fund the former at the expense of the latter since the ultimate objective had to be to transform the economic and social opportunities of the now smaller poor families to help themselves. In the extreme circumstances at the end of the war, it was a policy of helping the survival of the fittest to achieve more than they might on their own. The famous motto over the children's asylum read: "he who builds palaces for children tears down prison walls"[32]. It was in this context that the SDAP set out on the most spectacular element of its social policy in the 1920s: the building of working-class homes. It was a policy which fitted theory, possibility (since taxes could be levied directly to pay for it), and practice (as the municipal bureaucracy could handle it). It was also an electoral winner as housing for the workers after the war became a widely supported issue, not only in Vienna but in all European capitals. The SDAP also had the further incentive that the municipality owned land all around the city and thus new housing could be located in many different electoral wards and tenancies allocated to SDAP supporters. Above all, it was a policy that could be marketed and advertised: the SDAP were building a "new city" for the new people, the proletariat.

For the first time in its history, the municipality was going to serve the people, meaning all the people. In 1927, the city published a multi-volume work, *Das Neue Wien*, which trumpeted their proposals. Mostly, of course, the "brave new world" of the Social Democratic Workers, was not so modern. The Social Democratic Workers' Party and its allies, the trade unions and labour movement nurtured ideas and values which had been articulated for at least half a century before the First World War. The section of the working class on which the SDAP built its power base was the "respectable" workers, factory workers, organised labour. The aspirations of these people could be supported by the petit-bourgeoisie and some of the middle classes. But the extent to which the "cultural aims" of the SDAP and working-class culture generally coincided is only one of the many contentious subjects among historians. For our purposes here, all we need to accept is that the SDAP in Vienna set about a clear programme for the physical transformation of parts of the city. How it was achieved in the difficult circumstances of the time, and what was achieved, provide the basis for our comparative study.

The new SDAP Mayor, Jakob Reumann, made municipal housing his top priority. Since rents had been frozen in all major cities during the war to minimise the hardship of those whose labour was vital to the war effort, the building of new housing had become uneconomic for the private landlord. This was not a Viennese problem alone. It was found in Western European capital cities such as London and Glasgow as well. What the Viennese were able to do, however, was to be very much more efficient than their western counterparts in tackling this problem. The end of the First World War marked a turning point in housing reform in all of Europe and America. The debate was no longer a problem about poverty and the housing of the poor: it was about modern conditions and workers' housing. Beyond that, in the absence of more directed economic planning and with a regard for the political context, housing became a means of achieving a modern future. The war had forged new links between professionals, municipal bureaucrats, employers, working-class political parties and trade unions in which improved housing was the

Figure 2.10 *Mural on wall of municipal housing illustrating the dignity of the workers* [Author's photo]

key to co-operation and mutual endeavour. The housing programme in Vienna, however, was the most publicised and famous. From the start, political propaganda was made out of it. The Viennese were particularly conscious of image. The Ringstrasse had symbolised the cultural life of the city before the war: aristocratic, glittering, fostering the avant-garde of the world with bourgeois wealth. The Social Democrats set out to use the outer ring of municipal owned land to create another Ringstrasse: die Ringstrasse des Proletariats.

The model for the "modern" form of urban dwelling for the proletariat, however, had very little to do with architectural modernism and new styles. The work of Renate Banik-Schweitzer has shown how the form of Vienna's public housing in the 1920s followed an evolutionary pattern of working-class housing stretching back to the last quarter of the nineteenth century, from corridor-type barrack blocks with few private facilities to small units in similar sized blocks with some degree of privacy in the supply of essential services such as water supply and toilets[33]. Her careful analysis of the form of working-class housing from the mid-nineteenth century onwards has demonstrated how these changes were dictated by the special circumstances of Vienna, though they were paralleled elsewhere (for example, in Berlin). The relative cheapness of land and the control of much land by the municipality, and a unique tax system based on rents, formed the strongest parameters determining what was built. The dominant form was the multi-storied tenement house. Since the end of the nineteenth century, social reformers such as those who formed the Emperor Franz-Josef Jubilee Foundation for People's Housing and Welfare, had worked on ways of "modernising" the lives of those who lived in them. An example of what they achieved was to be found at the tenement block, Lobmeyerhof, which contained 480 flats organised around 16 staircases surrounding a central courtyard with a playground and lawns. The tiny flats had their own essential services and each complex had, in addition, communal facilities such as shower rooms, laundry rooms, libraries, lecture halls and rooms available for medical staff to undertake personal consultations[34]. In essence, this was the pattern which was to be adopted by the Social Democrats but there was a real difference. In a word, it was scale.

In 1923, the Viennese passed a resolution to build 25 000 flats during 1924–8 at an average of 5000 flats a year. Such was the efficiency in the administration of the projects, the target was reached in four years. But 1927 was a testing time. The power of the right-wing establishment began to be articulated against the workers. A general strike in the city was quashed by federal troops and the Palace of Justice was burned down by a mob, deeply angered by the power of the Right to manipulate the judiciary. The Social Democrats felt under threat, as a general election was imminent. The promise of more flats was held out as an election pledge. It was in this context that the famous Karl Marx-Hof was completed. It contained 1325 flats and was more than 1 kilometre long. Each complex contained communal facilities including laundry and drying rooms and recreation areas. By 1934 the municipal government had built 63 070 dwelling units, of which 54 000 were multi-storey buildings and about 6000 were row houses and two-storey family houses on the urban periphery. In the early days after the war, the Viennese Social Democrats had harboured ambitions to build more "modern" municipal housing which was seen at that time in terms of low density, family homes in the outer suburbs, on a garden city model. They even managed to find the finance to build prototypes such as Siedlung Flötzersteig in 1921 which had 154 dwellings. It was a drop in the ocean for Vienna's housing needs. Obviously a much more economical form was necessary and the city became committed to the larger and ever larger apartment blocks.

Figure 2.11   *Karl Marx-Hof façade close-up*
[Author's photo]

Figure 2.12 *Karl Marx-Hof rear view*
[Author's photo]

Much of the new accommodation was very cramped. Some 75% of apartments built before 1927 were only 38 square metres. But they represented a huge political and social achievement. They also transformed the periphery of the city. There was no totally separate Greater Vienna. All the outer suburbs were linked by an excellent public transport system so that the city remained a more or less cohesive whole. The blocks of flats were sited close to congested areas and near already provided infrastructure services: transport, schools, hospitals. The SDAP made sure of the political capital they could draw on through their efforts in choosing new tenants for the blocks who were expected to vote Social Democrat and were drawn mostly from the respectable working class and the petit-bourgeoisie. The introduction of the superblocks in different districts of the city created new kinds of "social mix" against the trends of social segregation which had begun to develop as the old central tenement blocks, which had included all classes together, each living on different floors of the same blocks, became an increasingly insignificant proportion of Vienna's housing stock. Yet the architectural style of the buildings, for all the "brave new world" propaganda were not avant-garde functionalist. Their scale was softened by detailing and sometimes even gable ends and pitched roofs and most of them carried lengthy inscriptions on their façades, giving the dates and details of their construction, and are named after members of the City Council or Socialist heroes. The first block was named Jakob-Reumann-Hof after the Mayor. Another early example was the Giacomo-Matteotti-Hof, named after the Italian Socialist Labour leader murdered in 1924 by the Fascists. The special political, economic and cultural circumstances of Vienna in the 1920s had produced a unique result. Given the condition of city and citizens during the First World War, what was achieved was quite remarkable.

BUDAPEST

Budapest, in the early 1920s, had neither the economic strength of Prague nor the democratic municipal government of Vienna. Of the three major capital cities of central Europe, it was the most vulnerable. It had achieved the largest size after Vienna before the war, reaching a million inhabitants, but the legacy of that expansion and the economic and social factors which had underpinned it, did not help in the aftermath of war, followed by revolution and counter-revolution. The vulnerability of the city was based on an amalgam of factors mostly outside its control. The savage dismantling of the territory which had been Hungarian before the war, reducing the country to a third of its former size, was to leave Budapest as a hydrocephalus, at least 15 times larger than the next largest Hungarian town. Yet even before the war, there were some very severe problems. Although it was so large, the social consequences of scale and rapid industrialisation had not always been vigorously addressed. Partly that was the result of the speed of growth. Budapest had grown in size very dramatically in the decades before the turn of the century, increasing by 45% in the decade 1890–1900 alone. Partly it was the difficulty of setting up the appropriate political institutions and raising adequate revenue to undertake public works.

Increasing in intensity from the moment of the signing of the Dual Monarchy agreement in 1867 (which gave Hungary a degree of autonomy), there had been a great desire to make Budapest a capital city which could rival Vienna and of course, the ultimate model, Paris. Such longings reached a peak at the time of the Millennium Celebration of 1896, celebrating roughly the thousand years since the conquest of the Carpathian basin and the start of the reign of Hungary's first king, King Stephen (later canonised as a saint). Between 1884 and 1904, a new Parliament building was constructed, which, despite its extraordinary mixtures of style (mostly neo-Gothic), was based in spirit on the model of the Houses of Parliament in London, the model of western-style democracy. Its fate, however, for virtually the next century was that it never became a fully democratic institution. Enyedi and Szirmai, in their study of Budapest, argue that the evolution of the capital can only be understood in the context of this desire for change on Western European lines which was always at odds with the realities of political, economic and social power[35]. Social democracy was not able to dominate the Municipal Assembly because neither the power base of the social democratic parties nor the city's trade union movement was strong enough to overcome the political forces against them. The remnants of the feudal past, still strong in surrounding neighbouring countries, could not be quickly overcome.

Budapest's aristocratic ruling class was often involved as capitalists fuelling the spectacular economic growth. The *haute bourgeoisie* were small in number and never powerful enough to marginalise the influence of the nobility. Budapest's period of rapid industrial and commercial growth coincided with the stage of economic development which required considerable capital. The Hungarians were competing with the giant cartels and trusts of Germany and America, and large-scale industries in Britain, France and elsewhere, for a share of world markets[36]. It was hard to become a Hungarian capitalist unless you were very rich already. There was little upward mobility. This left a tiny social strata of elite who provided the political leadership who were themselves divided and conditioned by memories of the feudal society of the past and the capitalist aspirations of the present. To complicate matters further, there was the anomalous position of ethnic minorities within the nation–state and the process of "Magyarisation". At the time of the inception of the Dual Monarchy in 1867, Magyars were in a minority in Hungary. Of key importance here was the role played by the Jews. In Hungary, they were not treated as an ethnic minority but rather as a religious group and they were to contribute, out of all proportion to their numbers to "Magyarisation", to the development of Hungarian capitalism, and through their dominance in key professions, to the modernisation of the country.

In 1910, 5% of Hungary's population were Jews, numbering about one million. Many were to be found in Budapest, where they dominated in financial institutions

Figure 2.13 *View of Hungarian Parliament building across the River Danube* [Author's photo]

and the professions: 12.5% of the country's industrialists, 54% merchants, 43% employees of credit institutions were Jewish; as were 42% newspaper men, 45% of lawyers, 49% of doctors. At the census counts in the early twentieth century, they were allowed to return themselves as Hungarians by nationality and their assimilation tilted the ethnic balance in favour of the Magyar[37]. Because of their professional and business status, many Jews were able to have seats in the Municipal Assembly. By an Act of 1920, the franchise to the Municipal Assembly was extended. The old system of *virilism* was abolished and it was possible for women, craftsmen, shopkeepers and junior clerks and other representatives of the people to get elected. This reform, however, had the effect of radically reducing the proportion of Jews among the aldermen. During the inter-war years, Jews wishing to get elected could only do so if they were on the list of the liberal-democratic bourgeois parties or in the SDAP. Those that went for this option tended to be more left-wing and they played an important role in sustaining elements of democratic government for the city. They were to be expelled in 1941 by an act of state (Act 19: 1941) against the Jews: 108 elected aldermen were expelled[38].

In these complicated political and economic circumstances, Budapest's Municipal Assembly did not become a breeding ground of democratic politics. Most massively under-represented were the workers who, by their immigration to the city, so dramatically swelled the population figures. In fact, although there were periods especially from the 1890s when liberal mayors nurtured a greater degree of social responsibility towards all of Budapest's citizens, the Municipal Assembly itself largely operated through a bureaucracy with professional officials who undertook the necessary management of public works. This had a well-established history. In 1870, the state had set up a Board of Public Works on the model of the London Metropolitan Board of Works.[39] Half the Budapest Board was nominated by the state and half from the Municipal Assembly. It was this body which decided on the locations for the infrastructure of roads and transport and the regulation of building developments by codes. From the start, financial capital was raised by borrowing and this was a model that the Municipal Assembly continued on its own account, the raising of taxation being a continual problem. In the early days of the Dual Monarchy, the Prime Minister, Andrassy, had commissioned an engineer, Ferenc Reitter, to write a report on the future physical shape of the city. It was to be an outstanding early example of capital city planning[40]. It was followed by a competition to plan the city rather in the way that the Viennese had held a competition for the planning of the Ringstrasse. Subsequently, the Board of Public Works was directed to carry out an amalgam of the plans which were submitted. Most energy was expended on such projects as the construction of grand avenues leading to the city centre and three rings of boulevards leading to bridges over the Danube (which, in rather typical fashion, were not actually built until later when the resources could be found)[41]. Budapest was to gain the first underground railway in Europe, built in 1896 to run, again typically, to the Millennial Monument in Heroes Square.

Figure 2.14 *Budapest in the inter-war period showing Városliget Park* [Map drawn by Chris Lewis]

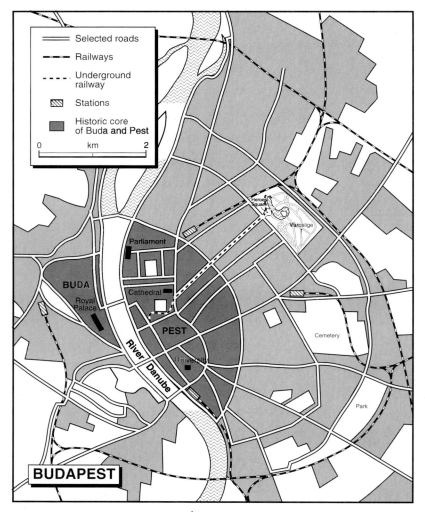

The social consequences of growth were a long way down the agenda and only surfaced in the 1890s with the increasing crisis in working-class housing and the dire social consequences of little investment in social capital. Acts were passed to outlaw the use of basement dwellings which were often the most overcrowded and unhealthy. Eventually, as Gabor Gyáni has shown, the state, under the influence of Wekerle, in 1908 Minister of Finance, began a vigorous policy of state housing[42]. At that time, Budapest had a reforming Mayor, István Bárcy, who also took up the cause. He borrowed vast sums of money on 50-year loans from the French and invested it in homes, schools, hospitals and other social institutions. By 1914, 10% of the working classes was housed in the public sector. Some of the very worst conditions were being eliminated, yet there were still large numbers of people in conditions either of dense overcrowding or living in shanties and sheds to get a roof over their heads. In the period 1867 to 1914, the city population had grown from 280 000 to about 1 000 000. The war which brought the subsequent revolutions and the economic collapse of city and country was to magnify the suffering. The initial post-war political turmoil did not result in the establishment of greater social democracy[43]. There was some extension of the limited franchise for the Municipal Assembly, especially the extension of the franchise to women for the first time, but the first elections in 1920 brought the conservative Right Christian Municipal Party to power. There was an equally important change in 1925 when the Social Democratic Party, as the political representatives of the workers, was allowed in the Municipal Assembly but the liberal, more left-wing block was always the minority. Political stability in Hungary after the revolutions had been restored by Admiral Horthy, who also led the Hungarian armed forces and, as President, put social control above democratic politics. Any hint of trouble and the Municipal Assembly was overruled by the state. A government commissioner was appointed to run the city directly in 1920 and 1924 though, generally, the government was able to bring the municipality more and more under its control by constitutional means. Parliament, also dominated by the right-wing party, was happy to sanction Acts concerning the control of Budapest[44].

Yet it was not only politics which tied the hands of the Municipal Assembly. The lack of resources was overwhelming. Even the basic needs of Budapest and the country as a whole could not be met by industry and agriculture (neither achieved their 1914 level of production for the entire inter-war period). On top of this, Hungary was supposed to pay war reparations to the allies in addition to finding the capital to rebuild itself. In desperation, one finance minister in the early 1920s actually increased the rate of inflation of the currency in an attempt to wipe out such imposed burdens on the country. With the collapse of the German currency in 1923, the Hungarians found themselves in a completely impossible position. In the moment of dire need, they were baled out by the League of Nations (in fact led by the Americans) who offered a loan of $20m in a bankers trust for a loan period of 35 years. A further 250 000 000 gold crowns was lent by the merchant bankers, Rothschild and Sons, for the country's reconstruction and health policies. In 1923, Budapest still had an infant mortality rate of 23% and few medical facilities available to the poor. With this help, it was possible at least to achieve some financial stability. A new currency was set up, the pengő, in 1927 which retained its value. Lack of capital, however, was to restrict severely what could be achieved in the modernising of the city in the 1920s. The city had to rely heavily on what had been achieved before the war.

Figure 2.15 *The poor constructing shelters for themselves* [By permission of the Budapest Archives]

Figure 2.16 *Cave-dwellers in Budafok in the early 1930s* [By permission of the Budapest Archives]

Reconstruction in the inter-war period was, in any case, a daunting task. It is estimated that about 220 000 people did not have separate accommodation on a family basis of even the most basic kind. One of the major works on Hungary in the inter-war period, *Budapest Története* Vol. 5, has photographs of the poor putting up rough wooden shelters themselves or living in the caves in the rocks in the Budapest hills[45]. Formerly middle-class Hungarians, government officials (including high court judges, mayors, army officers and even a land-steward) from the lost territories in the north and south of Hungary and Transylvania, were to be found living in railway freight cars at the railway stations[46]. Some of the latter were to conceive the idea of building themselves, through co-operative organis- ation, a model garden city colony. It was almost ten years before financial and legal obstacles were overcome and the actual building of St Imre garden city in Pestlőrinc, a suburb of Budapest, took place between 1930 and 1936. By dint of supreme persistence, an area of 170 acres was developed to accommodate between 300 and 400 buildings in the garden suburb style. The result was that Budapest finally acquired almost 20 years later, a garden city suburb which had been considered the most modern urban form immediately after the First World War elsewhere in Europe. Unlike the bourgeois villas built in Greater Prague in the 1930s, the style of the houses was far from functionalist modern. The historian of this development, Istvan Teplán, has emphasised the rural and bourgeois models of a former lifestyle which influenced the design[47].

For the rest of Budapest's poorer inhabitants, there were public housing pro- grammes which, especially after the stabilisation of the currency and the ability of the country and the city to borrow resources by the late 1920s, were undertaken with vigour. Between 1920 and 1944, 96 000 new flats were built which increased the whole building substance of the city by one-third.

However, unlike Vienna, there was no programme to build a new Budapest or at least there was no propaganda campaign of that kind. Yet, once the currency had been stabilised, the municipality set out to do what it could. Its budget, with the help of loans, was almost doubled in the period 1925–29. The increased resources were used for the reconstruction of the road network, two new bridges over the Danube, urban planning of the extension of the city to the south and the reconstruction of the health service facilities as well as the housing programme. As several industries in the city, especially engineering and food processing, became adversely affected by the difficulties of world trade, culminating in the Great Depression, the municipality turned to tourism as a possible new source of income. A programme was put in hand to modernise and develop the potential of the city's hot springs which for centuries had been providing pleasure and recreation for Budapest's citizens. There was a special programme to create a City of Spas. This was, of course, building on what had been established before the war and a couple of centuries before that, when the Turks had occupied the city. One of the most elaborate spa swimming baths, the neo-baroque Széchenyi Baths, were completed in 1913. These were located opposite the Zoological Gardens, also

Figure 2.17 *Budapest International Fair in 1937. In the middle is a rail-bus made by the Ganz Work* [By permission of the Budapest Archives]

completed before the First World War, part of the great complex of the people's park, the Városliget.

This park had, for more than a century, played a key role in the cultural life of the city. From its inception, it had been planned as a park for the people. The city's Embellishment Committee had organised a competition for a public park in 1813. Gabor Gyáni suggests that this was probably the first competition in the history of landscape architecture ever held. The winner was the Bavarian German landscape designer, Christian Heinrich Nebbien. He sought in his design to create a public space that was "the purest expression of the great virtues of a people and the product of the spirit, the taste, the patriotism and the culture of a noble nation". He amply succeeded as it became a favourite haunt for all classes of citizens who flocked there regularly every Sunday, summer and winter[48]. The designer had deliberately set out to make a public park which was not, as was customary in the eighteenth century, created out of magnanimity towards the public by those in power, but which was "to be the immediate possession and

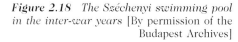

Figure 2.18 *The Széchenyi swimming pool in the inter-war years* [By permission of the Budapest Archives]

creation of the people"[49]. There were a large number of monuments dedicated to the great personalities of the past (Heroes Square was placed at the park entrance), and an architectural folly consisting of a small-scale version of a great castle of the Hunyadi clan to which has been attached, somewhat incongruously, small parts of buildings representing the different styles of Hungarian architecture up to the nineteenth century. Most of the monuments had been erected in the decade immediately preceding the Millennial Exhibition of 1896. The park itself was 600 000 square metres and, in the nineteenth century, the various social classes had specific areas where they congregated. It was not just a park, it was a national and civic monument and the weekly pilgrimage was more than recreational, it created a sense of identity and belonging. In the inter-war period, when the political ethos of city and nation was sternly repressive, the cultural aspects of the park took on greater significance. In this sense it played a more significant role than the Prater did in Vienna, which was otherwise very similar in many ways. May Day parades started and finished there; processions, mass meetings and demonstrations were held there; and giving hope for a better future, mass displays of schoolchildren, performing gymnastics. The park had a vital role in providing the context for the aspirations and interactions of the citizens of Budapest.

Patrick Geddes would have fully understood the significance of Városliget. His own first commission to undertake practical planning work had been from the

112

Figure 2.19 *Monument in Heroes Square to Hungarian leaders* [Author's photo]

Carnegie Dunfermline Trust who had asked him to lay out the Pittencrief Park in Dunfermline in Scotland. He had produced a plan which had made the park the central feature of this ancient little capital city of Fife[50]. The message was that social evolution, the whole purpose of modern change, needed as much investment and attention as economic activities. In the Dunfermline plan, there was a moulding of the natural features of the park with a range of social institutes, which were designed by Geddes for the "social development of the people". He would have recognised the Városliget, for all its nineteenth-century origins, as the crucial component of the modernisation of twentieth-century Budapest, bringing natural elements into the urban environment and creating a social context for all citizens in which the future was developed in direct contact with the historical memory of the past. Indeed, the analysis he gave in his exhibition at the Ghent "Congrès International de l'art de construire les villes et l'organisation de la vie municipale" of 1913, would have fitted very well the subsequent history of Prague, Vienna and Budapest in the inter-war years[51].

These three capital cities, of territories somewhat arbitrarily carved out of the former Austro-Hungarian Empire, adjusted to the dramatically different conditions they found themselves in after the First World War by drawing on their past and reinterpreting it for the future. The relationship between political and cultural

Figure 2.20 *Gymnastic exhibition on the sports grounds of the school in People's Park 1937* [By permission of the Budapest Archives]

change and the physical environment was marked in all three cities. The combination of crucial factors: the relationship between city and state, the economic circumstances and the vision of municipal government, had been quite different in each case. Yet all three cities faced similar problems in the need to develop the physical infrastructure, handle growth and provide better social conditions for all their citizens. How they responded had little to do with the role they were assigned by the negotiators of the Treaty of Versailles after the First World War. In each, the interaction of local, regional and national factors produced unique results, even in the face of ever increasing technological links in communications and transport, and their vulnerability to the economic fluctuations of the world economy, that brought them into closer contact with the rest of the world. Their fate, by 1939, was to be in the hands of the same Western European powers who had given them such impossible conditions to meet after the First World War.

NOTES

1. I should like to acknowledge, with warm thanks, the help of Dr Ilona Sármány-Parsons, Visiting Fellow of the Institute of Russian and Central European Studies, University of

114

Nottingham, who read material in several languages for me, especially Hungarian and gave me the benefit of her advice.

2. H Meller (1990) *Patrick Geddes: social evolutionist and city planner* London, Routledge, 18–55, 156–200.

3. W Boyd Rayward (1975) *The Universe of Information: the work of Paul Otlet for Documentation and International Organisation* published for the International Federation for Documentation by the All-Union Institute for Scientific and Technical Information, Moscow, 190–6.

4. CE Schorske (1980) *Fin-de-Siècle Vienna: politics and culture* London, Weidenfeld and Nicolson; R Wagner-Rieger (1969) *Das Kunstwerk im Bild – Vol I* of *Die Wiener Ringstrasse: Bild einer Epoche*, Vienna, Hermann Böhlaus Nachf; see also E Timms "Images of the City: Vienna, Prague and the Intellectual avante-garde" in RB Pynsent (ed) (1989) *Decadence and Innovation: Austro-Hungarian life and art at the turn of the century* London, Weidenfeld & Nicolson.

5. T Bender and CE Schorske (eds) (1994) *Budapest and New York: studies in metropolitan transformation 1870–1930* New York, Russell Sage Foundation.

6. J Lukacs (1993) *Budapest 1900: a historical portrait of a city and its culture* London, Weidenfeld & Nicolson.

7. P Geddes (1915) *Cities in Evolution: an introduction to the town planning movement and to the study of civics* London, Williams and Norgate.

8. G Melinz and S Zimmermann (eds) (1993) *Wien, Prag, Budapest: Blütezeit der Habsburgmetropolen: Urbanisierung, Kommunalpolitik gesellschaftliche Konflikte (1867–1918)* Vienna: Promedia. Introduction.

9. J Rothschild (1974) *East Central Europe between the two World Wars* Seattle and London, University of Washington Press, Intro. 3–25.

10. IT Berend and G Ránki (1974) *Economic Development in East-Central Europe in the 19th and 20th Centuries* New York and London, Columbia University Press, 171–241.

11. A recent work suggests that this interdependence was to remain after the War and the redrawing of national boundaries, see A Teichova and H Matis (eds) (1996) *Österreich und die Tschechoslowakei: 1918–1938. Die Wirtschaftliche Neuordnung in Zentraleuropa in der Zwischenkriegszeit* Vienna, Böhlau Verlag.

12. VS Mamatey and R Luža (eds) (1973) *A History of the Czechoslovak Republic 1918–1948* Princeton, NJ, Princeton University Press, 190.

13. IT Berend and G Ránki (eds) (1974) *Economic Development*, 174.

14. G Gyáni (1995) "Ethnicity and Acculturation in Budapest at the turn of the century" in S Zimmerman (ed) *Urban Space and Identity in the European City 1890–1930s* Budapest, Central European University 107–13.

15. A Teichova and H Matis (eds) (1996) *Österreich und die Tschechoslowakei: 1918–1938.*

16. T Bender and CE Schorske "Introduction" in T Bender and CE Schorske (eds) (1994) *Budapest and New York*, 9.

17. A Teichova and H Matis (eds) (1996) *Österreich und die Tschechoslowakei.*

18. See Chapter 3.

19. NM Wingfield (1992) "Czech, German or Jew: the Jewish Community of Prague during the inter-war period" in J Morison (ed) *The Czech and Slovak Experience* London, Macmillan.

20. J Císař and F Pokorný (1922) *The Czechoslovak Republic: a survey of its history and geography, its political and cultural organisation and its economic resources* London, T. Fisher Unwin.

21. J Kren (1996) *Konfliktgemeinschaft: Tschechen und Deutsche 1780–1918* Munich, R Oldenbourg Verlag. See also E Wiskemann (1938) *Czechs and Germans: a study of the*

struggle in the historic provinces of Bohemia and Moravia London, Oxford University Press.

22. H Freudenberger (1977) *The Industrialisation of a Central European City: Brno in the eighteenth century* London, Edington.

23. Actually almost 95% of its population was German before the First World War.

24. AH Herman (1975) *A History of the Czechs* London, Allen Lane, 172.

25. R Švácha (1995) *The Architecture of the New Prague 1895–1945* Cambridge, Mass., MIT Press, 148.

26. Švácha (1995) *The Architecture of the New Prague*, 192.

27. See Chapter 3 on Zlín.

28. H Volet-Seanneret (1988) *La Femme Bourgeoise à Prague 1860–1985: de la philanthropie à l'émancipation* Paris, Slatkine.

29. Švácha (1995) *Architecture of the New Prague*, 322.

30. E Hobsbawm (1994) *Age of Extremes: the short twentieth century 1914–1991* London, Michael Joseph, 188–9.

31. G Melinz (1995) "'Red' and 'Catholic' Social Integration and Exclusion: municipal welfare policy and social reality in Vienna (1918–1938)" in S Zimmermann (ed) *Urban Space and Identity in the European City 1890–1930s* Budapest, Central European University, 59.

32. Melinz (1995) "'Red' and 'Catholic'", 60.

33. R Banik-Schweitzer (1990) "Vienna" in M Daunton (ed) *Housing the Workers: a comparative history, 1850–1914* Leicester, Leicester University Press, 107–48.

34. E Lichtenburger (1993) *Vienna: bridge between cultures* London, Belhaven Press, 97–9.

35. G Enyedi and V Szirmai (1992) *Budapest: a Central European capital* (English trans.) London, Belhaven Press, 71.

36. S Pollard (1973) "Industrialisation and the European Economy" *Economic History Review* Vol XXVI 4, 636–48; for the social structure of Hungary see I Romsics (1999) *Hungary in the Twentieth Century* Budapest, Corvina, 36–53.

37. G Jeszenszky (1990) "Hungary through World War I and the end of the Dual Monarchy" in P Sugar, P Hanák and T Frank (eds) (1994) *A History of Hungary* Bloomington, Indiana University Press, 274–5.

38. ZL Nagy (1994) "Transformations in the City Politics of Budapest" in T Bender and C Schorske (eds) *Budapest and New York*, 47.

39. G Gyáni (1990) "Budapest" in MJ Daunton (ed) *Housing the Workers*, 149–50.

40. T Hall (1997) *Planning Europe's Capital Cities: aspects of nineteenth century urban developments* London, E & FN Spon, 245–54.

41. Gyáni (1990) "Budapest", 151.

42. Gyáni (1990) "Budapest", 163–78.

43. ZL Nagy (1985) "State Power, Autonomy, and Liberal opposition in Budapest 1919–1945" in *Études historiques Hongroises* Vol II, Budapest, 73–89.

44. ZL Nagy (1994) "Transformations in the City Politics of Budapest: 1873–1941" in Bender and Schorske (eds) *Budapest and New York*, 46–8.

45. H Miklós (ed) (1980) *Budapest Története: a Forradalmak Korától a Felszabadulásig* Vol V Akadémiai Kiadó, Budapest, 241 and 295.

46. I Teplán (1994) "St Imre Garden City: an urban community" in Bender and Schorske (eds) *Budapest and New York*, 164.

47. Teplán (1994) "St Imre Garden City", 174–9.

48. G Gyáni (1994) "Uses and Misuses of Public Space in Budapest, 1873–1914" in Bender and Schorske (eds) *Budapest and New York*, 90–2.

49. D Nehring (1985) "The Landscape Architect, Christian Heinrich Nebbian, and his design

116

for the Municipal Park in Budapest" *Journal of Garden History* 5, 3, 269–72 quoted in G Gyáni (1990) "Budapest", 90.

50. P Geddes (1904) *City Development: a study of parks, gardens and culture institutes. A report to the Carnegie Dunfermline Trust* Bournville, the Saint George Press and in Edinburgh, Geddes and Company.

51. P Geddes (1913–14) "Two Steps in Civics: cities and town planning exhibition" *The Town Planning Review* IV, 78–94; P Abercrombie (1913–14) "The International Congress of Cities: the Ghent International Exhibition, 1913" both in *The Town Planning Review* IV, 205–18.

CHAPTER 3

EUROPEAN RESPONSES TO THE GARDEN CITY IDEAL: THE EXTRAORDINARY EXAMPLE OF ZLÍN

The keynote of European responses to the garden city ideal is variety. In the first quarter of the twentieth century, the garden city ideal became a recognised model of modern urban development. In the second quarter, as the model was taken up more widely and tested, the outcomes varied according to context. Tracking down the uses made of Ebenezer Howard's ideas provides an exciting example of cultural transmission in which local, national and international factors combine to produce concrete results: modern settlements designed according to garden city principles[1]. It is the different combinations of these factors which produced different results. The period of influence of garden city designs in Europe stretched from the earliest days following the "Garden Cities and Town Planning Conference" held in Bournville in 1902, to the Second World War[2]. Yet the heyday, without doubt, was immediately after the First World War. The growing internationalism of planning ideas and architecture was massively accelerated by the First World War. The seismic changes brought by global war in politics and social change, including the Russian Revolution and the collapse of the Austro-Hungarian and Ottoman Empires, fed new social aspirations at all social levels. A key aspiration was to improve living conditions, especially the homes of the workers[3]. The garden city offered an ideal, yet realisable, model of what a new modern city could offer to all its citizens.

The concept of a garden city in the European context, however, needs defining. Basically, the only elements which readily made the transition to Europe were those relating to the achievement of high-quality housing for the workers, the creation of a "healthy" environment measured in terms of maximising light and air (incidentally the key factors in the fight against the major killer disease, tuberculosis) and the decongestion of old-established cities by building new settlements to absorb the excess population. Howard's carefully worked-out scheme for his Garden City, which included a new social deal for citizens, a balance between town and country and, above all, the financial structure which encompassed both capitalist and communal elements, generally did not make the transition[4]. Finance was by far the most important constraint. The reason why the period 1918–1925 was the heyday of the garden city ideal in Europe had everything to do with the aftermath of the First World War which loosened financial constraints on workers'

Figure 3.1 *Poster for selling site plots organised by the Federation of Co-operatives for the war wounded, c. 1921* [By permission of the Archives d'Architecture Moderne, Bruxelles]

housing projects for a variety of reasons. For a brief period, leaders of city authorities, co-operative housing associations, and government social housing schemes were prepared to experiment. The political urgency of placating the people, the recognition of the rights of the industrial working classes who had endured the worst hardships on both the war and the home fronts and contributed most to the war effort, briefly overcame the barrier of cost. There was a period of trial and error. There was a willingness to discover precisely how much the new kind of housing settlement would cost.

German hyperinflation and the collapse of payment of German reparations in 1923 virtually brought an end to this period in most of western Europe. The currencies of central Europe were also in dire crisis. There was simply no resources available for building working-class housing in garden cities which were perceived as being an unprecedented luxury. Even in the USSR, with a state dedicated to the proletariat and an economy outside the fluctuations affecting the rest of the world, the ideal of the garden city appeared to be a luxury out of reach. A post-revolutionary garden city, Sokol, built near Moscow from 1918, had been designed on such a scale of lavishness that there was no likelihood that a programme of garden cities in a similar style could follow[5]. The key word here is "style". Projects for housing the workers continued. Established cities were still overcrowded and growing. The pressure to build and the cost-effectiveness of building healthy homes for the workers kept many of the garden city principles alive. Yet the problem of funding high-quality housing projects set in acres of land, a very unproductive way of using capital, began to test both political commitment and led to questions on the apparent lavishness of the styles adopted by garden city architects. In the context of the inter-war period, these considerations touched the nerve ends of societies trying to come to terms with revolution and political change and the creation of new nations in the wake of the First World War.

GARDEN CITIES AFTER THE FIRST WORLD WAR IN BELGIUM, FRANCE, GERMANY AND THE USSR

The impetus to build garden cities after the war was political. The garden city was a symbol of a political shift in favour of the lower classes. It was also a rallying point for left-wing politicians who eschewed revolution. The garden city offered a pragmatic, practical form of immediate social change, without revolutionary upheaval. It could be celebrated as an end result without disruption. There were also, of course, other elements which contributed to experiments in garden city building. The most significant of these was the search by urban designers for a modern idiom. The whole prospect of urban design and planning which had been given momentum in the nineteenth century by the large city competitions such as Vienna and Cologne, and the German extension schemes, was changed by the war. In country after country, legislation was passed admonishing local town councils to adopt comprehensive planning measures. The only profession in a position to offer urban design skills was architecture. Young architects threw themselves into this kind of work, on the one hand, because rich private patrons were harder to find, on the other, because they were inspired by the prospect of giving form to ideas of modernity. The garden city was the most up-to-date version of what that was.

This combination of politics and architecture was very evident in Belgium, scene of some of the worst physical devastation of cities during the First World War. At first, much effort was put into reconstructing the ancient medieval cities which had been destroyed, as a means of reaffirming national identity for the future. This reconstruction work gave little scope to the group of young Belgian architects who had been dispersed during the war to Holland, England and France and were longing to design something new and modern[6]. Their chance came when the Minister of Reconstruction and other housing bodies such as co-operatives decided that better quality housing for the workers should be built as a memorial to the war dead and war veterans. The model for such schemes was often the garden city. Some of the earliest examples were named specifically as war memorials such as La Cité des Veterans ou Combattants at Dour (Hainault), the work of Louis Herman de Koninck[7]. The Belgian Minister of Reconstruction funded

Figure 3.2 *The Cité-jardin of Le Logis-Floréal at Watermael-Boitsfort (Bruxelles), 1922–1930. A teacher with her pupils* [By permission of the Archives d'Architecture Moderne, Bruxelles]

the earliest post-war *cité-jardin* for 100 inhabitants at Roulers in 1919, just to find out exactly how much it cost.

Roulers happened to be the birthplace of Raphaël Verwilghen, a key figure in the transformation of urban planning in Belgium. He had been made an inspector in the National Public Works Department in 1913 and was to spend the war in England, where he met Howard and Unwin and studied garden city development. After the war, he used his position as director of the building department of l'Office des Régions Dévastées, to put in hand a number of garden city schemes. The Roulers venture, however, proved too expensive. A way around the cost was found by two housing co-operatives that joined forces to build the largest and most successful Belgian garden city at Watermael-Boitsfort. This was the Cité Le Logis-Floréal. The overall planner and architect was Louis van der Swaelmen and he employed a group of talented young architects: Raymond Moenaert, Lucien François and Jean-Jules Eggericx (the latter was to work closely with Verwilghen on other projects). Planner and architects drew on the knowledge they had personally gained during the war years: of modern design for workers' housing from the Amsterdam school in Holland; the planning models of Parker and Unwin in England; and the new ideas on architectural style emerging in Paris[8]. With co-operative funding, careful planning, economical architecture (using new techniques of reinforced concrete, etc.), this major project was able to continue until completion in 1940[9]. One thing, however, about the garden city in French-speaking countries which has to be made clear (they themselves do not always make the distinction) is the meaning of the term *cité-jardin*. There is no question that in terms of scale, planning and social intent, Cité Le Logis-Floréal was the nearest thing to a garden city to be found in the inter-war period in Western Europe. But *cité-jardin* as a term was used to describe any suburb or new settlement with some greenery in it. The elements which made up the special nature of the garden city or even the garden suburb (as in Hampstead Garden Suburb which originally had a social purpose[10]) were not always present.

For financial and administrative reasons, the full-scale implementation of Howard's ideas was rarely practical. The French exponent of Howard's ideas, Henri Sellier, became the Mayor of Suresnes in 1919. In this position he encouraged the Office de Public Habitation de la Seine (OPHDS) to work to facilitate the building of high-quality working-class housing[11]. He was under no illusion, however, that the model of the garden city could be used in all its aspects. In 1919, he wrote that the OPHDS had a more limited objective:

> qui consiste à édifier les agglomérations propres à assurer le décongestionnement de la ville de Paris et de ses faubourgs, à servir d'example aux lotisseurs qui depuis 30 ans ont littéralement saboté la banlieue et à montrer comment, tout en tenant compte des conditions économiques et morales normales de la vie urbaine, il est possible d'assurer à la population laborieuse, manuelle et intellectualle, un logement présentant le maximum de confort matériel, des conditions hygiéniques de nature à éliminer les inconvénients des grandes villes, et des modes d'aménagement esthétique contrastant singulièrement avec la hideur des formules antérieurement pratiquées[12].
> [which consists in building urban areas which are designed to alleviate congestion in the city of Paris and its suburbs, to serve as an example to the developers who, for thirty years, have literally sabotaged the suburbs, and to show how, whilst recognising the economic and social conditions endemic in urban life, it is possible to guarantee for the working population (manual and intellectual) a form of housing which offers the maximum of material comfort, hygienic conditions which are designed to eliminate the disadvantages of cities, and modes of aesthetic planning which contrast remarkably with the hideousness of former designs.]

Such pragmatism from the man who had been heavily involved in the pre-war years in the study and debate about the future of cities as a follower of Albert Thomas and collaborator with Marcel Poëte, was an indication of political reality[13].

Sellier's career provides an excellent example of the transformation of European responses to the garden city idea from the pre-war to the post-war period. His career also spans another crucial element which facilitated experiments in improving the quality of working-class housing: the growing professionalism of city authorities in managing growth and improving sanitary conditions. Sellier's interest in Howard's Garden City was as a model of what a healthy, well-administered social environment should be. As he climbed up the political ladder as a civil servant in the Ministries of Commerce and Labour, his interest in cities and social change had been stimulated and informed by his meeting in his youth (he was 19 in 1902) with Albert Thomas, syndicalist leader working for social and political change[14]. Sellier became a syndicalist and served as the President of the Confédération du Travail (the French equivalent of the British Trades Union Council) at its Congress in Amiens, in 1906. He brought to his work both a passionate commitment for improving the quality of urban life for the working classes, and a belief in the need for a more scientific approach to urban problems. Just before the war, he was made the Vice President of the International Union of Towns, a body which was set up at an international congress on cities and their problems, held in Ghent, in 1913[15].

The President was Paul Otlet, the Belgian peace campaigner. The congress encouraged the further development of international professional associations who could share their expertise in dealing with urban growth, but the congress itself was still dependent for funding on philanthropy[16]. In contrast, at the end of the war, Sellier joined Marcel Poëte to set up L'École des Hautes Études Urbaines to train young students to study urban conditions and to improve professional responses to them[17]. After the war, the concept of the garden city, born in an era when social reform was a philanthropic concern, had to survive in a world which was highly politicised and increasingly professional. In this changing context, a key question was the political complexion of the very concept of a garden city. Howard had suggested that the Garden City was the path to real reform. Was such reform a conservative or radical proposal? Did it pacify the workers and keep them quiet or did it bring them the dues to which they were entitled?

The answer to these questions had a special significance in Germany. Since the rapid industrialisation of the united German state from 1870 and the rise of the heavy industries, especially coal, iron and steel, employers had taken a keen interest in the subject of workers' housing. The pioneering workers' estates built by the Krupp Company at Essen from the 1860s, were to be transformed stylistically from the 1890s onwards by the development of more single-family homes set in their own small gardens[18]. The physical image of *rus in urbe* promoted by the industrial village of Bournville and Howard's Garden City at Letchworth had been keenly studied by Germans interested in these ideas and a society for promoting garden cities, the Deutsche Gartenstadt Gesellschaft, had existed as early as 1902[19]. Yet although the image was transplanted to Germany, the Krupp housing projects and those of other German industrialists, such as Siemens in Berlin, were, in concept, less a model of a future urban civilisation and much more a management technique in the handling of labour[20]. Was the garden city, then, a capitalist ploy? This had seemed to be the case in pre-war Germany.

In the aftermath of the First World War, the idea of the garden city simply seemed irrelevant. Germany, as the defeated nation, had also experienced an abortive political revolution. The leaders of the new Weimar Republic faced enormous difficulties balancing the demands of the people with the obligations to pay war reparations, in money and kind, forced on them by the Treaty of Versailles, drawn up without their consultation. The "right to a sound dwelling", however, had been incorporated into the new Constitution of the Weimar Republic, so the provision of workers' housing was on the political agenda[21]. Basically, there were three possible routes for achieving this objective: through co-operative building societies or municipal administrations (both funded by the State) or by big business. The first two were largely unable to function between 1918 and 1924 because of lack of funds and, in the turbulent, post-war period, big business had been less than interested in anything approaching garden city planning ideals. Post-war business magnates, like Hugo Stinnes, may have been forced to accommodate the demands of labour to a greater extent than before, but they did not have their sights set on developing stable, balanced communities. Stinnes' rapacious business empire stretched across a whole range of industries from coal and iron and steel works, machine building, electro-technical and automobile factories, shipbuilding and shipping lines, paper printing and publishing, textiles, sugar production, petroleum companies to banks, farms, hotels and much more. His was a business technique of asset stripping and accumulation on a truly vast scale. He made a famous agreement on a national basis with the leader of the socialist Free Trade unions about wages and hours of work, not housing and community building[22].

However, by 1924, the situation had changed, at least for the co-operative housing associations and municipalities concerned with housing. In the wake of the American Dawes Plan, which stabilised the value of the mark after the hyperinflation of 1923, the German government was able to introduce new policies of taxation. One of the first was a new tax on the rents of existing properties to raise funds for building. It was to provide the financial basis for an extensive programme of building workers' housing in the second half of the 1920s. With its efficient administrative structures, especially in the municipalities, which could handle large-scale projects, Germany experienced a building boom with municipalities putting in hand commissions for hospitals, schools, market halls, public baths, stadiums and above all, workers' housing[23]. The question has to be asked, however, to what extent were the new suburbs of workers' housing, found in city after city, a legacy of garden city ideals?

One of the most studied examples of what was achieved in the 1920s has been the city of Frankfurt, mostly because of the talent of the city architect, Ernst May, and his ability to promote his ideas on workers' housing. His work impressed the American Catherine Bauer, a member of the radical Regional Planning Association of America and friend of Lewis Mumford, who disseminated European ideas on modern housing and town planning to America at the crucial time of "New Deal" politics in 1934[24]. Nicholas Bullock has argued that there were important links between garden city ideals and what happened in Frankfurt[25]. May had studied housing and town planning in England and had been a close friend of Unwin. There are, no doubt, a number of cultural assumptions that May brought to his work which could be traced to Howard's ideas, such as the importance of satellite communities, the desirability of low-rise building, and the importance of personal identity. Yet the context within which May worked had three major differences from anything found in England.

The first was the administrative structure. Frankfurt had gained a new, vigorous and professional *Oberbürgermeister*, Ludwig Landmann, in 1924. He was determined to undertake giant schemes of urban expansion and housing development. He chose May as the man to carry it out and he facilitated the means for enabling him to do it by creating the special office of *Dezernent für Bauwesen* for him. May was given huge powers. A second difference was that when May came to design his new workers' housing, he was deeply influenced by the ideas of the architects of the Modern Movement in terms of style. A distinction, however, has to be made here. The functionalist architecture of the Modern Movement has been seen as aggressively different from the ideals of community building inherent in the garden city ideal. In the former, a rational approach to use takes precedence over other considerations such as old-fashioned assumptions about family life, social harmony and Howard's view on the balance needed between town and country. What Bullock rightly suggests in his study of May, however, is that the dichotomy can be exaggerated and that in the case of May in Frankfurt, ideas from his understanding of the garden city model were reinterpreted in modern idiom in "Das Neue Frankfurt"[26]. Bullock argues that May and his colleagues, although they all joined the Congrès Internationaux d'Architecture Moderne (CIAM) at its foundation in 1928, already had enough experience of building in Frankfurt to give them grounds for disagreeing with Walter Gropius and others on such issues as high rise versus low rise, densities, and the building of communities[27].

Yet there is no doubt that the excitement which had come from the prospect of a totally new architecture in tune with modern culture, which had put architects such as Bruno Taut and Walter Gropius at the forefront of the avant-garde, facilitated May's experiments in Frankfurt and helped him to achieve the support of city council and citizens. "Das Neue Frankfurt" itself became a hopeful symbol of the future for the whole of Frankfurt and its region, in a way which went far beyond the garden city ideal. The third and final factor in the major building projects in Germany in the late 1920s, in contrast to the English garden city propaganda, was the emphasis on housing and satellite towns rather than new towns on greenfield sites. What May built in Frankfurt were essentially major housing estates for workers and the emphasis was on finding the cheapest way of building housing. From 1926, May had begun experiments with prefabricated building in an effort to cut costs. Even with this effort, however, the new housing was always beyond the means of the poorer workers. "Das Neue Frankfurt" was for well-paid artisans and above, echoing the results of attempts to build workers' housing stretching back over the previous half century. What happened in Germany was thus very much a continuation of what had happened before the war only on a greater scale and with ever greater levels of professional expertise[28].

In one sense, the ideal of the garden city as the path to real reform had been less a matter of specific plans and more a commitment to planning, to achieving a balance between society and environment, which was sustainable and life-enhancing. In Germany, this was fully appreciated. In the Ruhr, this even led to the beginnings of more co-ordinated regional planning. In 1920, an overarching planning organisation, the Kommunalverband Ruhrgebeit, was set up in the *Land* of Westphalia, which was not concerned with town extensions, but with co-ordinating the environmental initiatives emanating from different municipalities within the area[29]. The challenge of this huge industrialised area, however, was overwhelming and trying to reverse environmental destruction on this scale was to nurture a wider professionalism and a handling of the environment quite outside Howard's vision. Parks and open spaces were purchased and the very long-term effort begun to turn the whole area from an industrial, heavily polluted wasteland to a cultivated landscape. In the German context in the inter-war years, the garden city ideal was absorbed as one source among many others of how to shape the urban and rural environment of the future. Issues of scale, resources, and conflicting ideals from the exponents of functionalism, ruled out any closer attempt to modernise Howard's ideas.

POLITICAL AND PROFESSIONAL INTERPRETATIONS OF THE GARDEN CITY IDEAL

Was the garden city thus left as a utopian, possibly left-wing ideal? In the post-war period, the left-wing credentials of the concept of the garden city seemed to be increasingly uncertain. Howard had drawn on radical and alternative traditions when developing his ideas, using especially the American land reform campaigner, Henry George's work, *Progress and Poverty*, and the ideas of the Russian anarchist émigré, Peter Kropotkin[30]. He was also aware of communitarian experiments in Britain and America and the attempts in France to build high-quality housing for the workers[31]. One of the most successful of the latter was the pioneer workers' city in the industrial area of Mulhouse begun in 1853 and completed in 1897. Yet the ultimate test of the political dimension of Howard's ideas was to be in the only Socialist state after the First World War, the USSR. Here, however, context rather than politics, determined the reception of Howard's ideas. The garden city had been seen in Russia as a suitable model of modernisation in a country which had only begun the process of rapid industrialisation in the decade that Howard wrote his book. Between 1905 and 1917, there were a number of garden city style developments on the outskirts of cities from Riga in Latvia[32], to Petrograd, Kiev, Kharkov, Odessa, Ekaterinburg, Tula, and even Barnaul in Siberia[33]. A leading

Russian architect, Vladimir Semionov, had spent the years 1908–12 in England and had been deeply influenced by Howard. He went back to publish a book on modern town planning, *The Welfare and Planning of Towns*, in 1911 and to design and build Prozorovka, the first Russian garden city for the railway workers on the Moscow/Kazan railway, 40 km from Moscow. A Russian Garden City Association was formed in 1913, and a book published in the same year by V. Dadonov entitled, *Socialism without Politics: garden city of the future and present*[34]. By 1917, the garden city was seen as the model for the modern city of the future.

The test came after 1917. Was the garden city both radical and modern? In some ways, it fitted the Russian context very well[35]. Land was cheap and the garden city was dependent on innovations in transport and communications technology which made it appear modern. Further, a key element in cost, the type of housing used for workers could be kept low by using the traditional, low-cost, wooden cottages which had housed the poor for generations in Russia. In the mid-1920s, there was an academic debate between two organisations, one architectural and one devoted to housing, about the merits and drawbacks of low-rise housing as against high rise. The architects, members of the Union of Contemporary Architects, favoured high rise; the housing reformers, of the national Housing Co-operative Movement, founded in 1924, favoured the low rise. Marnikov, leader of the latter, denigrated high-rise buildings as "generated and maybe justified only by super urbanistic aspirations . . . built on the planning theories of Le Corbusier"[36]. This was a truly socialist sneer against the bourgeois cult of the great individual architect. The debate, however, had ceased to be academic by the end of the 1920s[37]. By then, the costs of the infrastructure of low-rise building, especially roads with wide verges as demonstrated by the Sokol experiment in Moscow, gave victory to the architects. Style won against social considerations and Howard's ideas were castigated as hopelessly bourgeois. By 1929, he was seen as "the father and main influence behind contemporary bourgeois town planning"[38].

Thus the political complexion of the garden city ideal was subject to an idiosyncratic fate. In the USSR, even after he had been castigated as bourgeois, they went on building new cities. By the end of the twentieth century, there are more than 800 of these. The key matter for a communist state was not only massive industrialisation but also building settlements for the workers as the majority of the nation became urbanised. In appearance they may not look like Howard's Garden City but such a programme of building had its roots in Howard's vision of the future. He had said as early as 1904 that:

I venture to suggest that while the age in which we live is the age of the great, closely-compacted, overcrowded city, there are already signs, for those who can read them, of a coming change so great and so momentous that the twentieth century will be known as the period of the great exodus . . . when by a great and conscious effort a new fabric of civilisation shall be reared[39].

The great and conscious effort was to produce an overall national programme of urban planning of which the new towns were one component. There is thus a thread connecting Letchworth and Welwyn Garden city with the new cities of the USSR. Their appearance could not, however, be more different. By the end of the 1920s, Howard's Garden City had ceased to be the model for the future.

In the immediate aftermath of the First World War, Howard's ideas had seemed like the ideal for the future development of European cities. But, in fact, the scale of the problems of urban growth and the cost of workers' housing, the desperate need for investment in industry and the problems of the resulting pollution it caused, made garden cities seem an unrealisable Utopia. It needed state involvement to co-ordinate and underwrite schemes and this was only possible in small countries with low levels of industrialisation. Ebenezer Howard published a small book with Halfdan Bryn, a Norwegian housing reformer, with the title: *Garden Cities and Farming Cities of Norway*. Norway developed a state system of planning from the war years and among the many new suburbs around the capital, Kristiana (Oslo), some, such as Ullvål Garden City[40], were built on garden city lines[41]. Similar attempts were made in Greece but usually lack of public resources meant that the little that was achieved were settlements for the bourgeois classes. Yet scale, cost and politics were not the only challenges to the garden city ideal. The First World War had also given a huge boost to those who were committed to the Modern Movement. For Walter Gropius and the architects of the Dessau Bauhaus, the garden city ideal was no model for the future but rather a coda to nineteenth-century ideas on urban design. The use of concrete for building, the desire to use new technology in everyday life, the advent of mass markets, the new power of advertising and the media, created a context which architects everywhere, but especially Germany, Holland and France, wished to exploit.

The clash between those who adopted the ideas of the Modern Movement and those who did not follow the leadership of Le Corbusier and the Congrès Internationaux d'Architecture Moderne has often been oversimplified. In its early years, what united the architects within the CIAM was hostility to the Beaux-Arts tradition[42]. What was understood as modern "functionalist" architecture varied considerably, much influenced by the context within which architects received commissions and what they had to build. At the centre were key issues about professionalism and it was these which, at a stroke, made Howard appear to be part of the past instead of the future[43]. Howard was the gifted amateur and social reformer. The leaders of the Modern Movement wanted to be the professionals of the new era but professionals still with a moral purpose: to restore a new cultural equilibrium to a world transformed by technology and scientific progress. Howard's vision of the garden city was that of an amateur shaped by cultural assumptions about civilisation and citizenship and the ideal environment for raising a family.

The men of the Modern Movement were much more self-conscious. They wanted to develop a new lifestyle as much as developing a new style of dwellings, both of which were to be expressions of a modern culture which people could be taught to enjoy. Architecture, of all the activities which were becoming professionalised in new ways in the inter-war period, was still particularly elitist. Members of the profession, especially in Germany and France, had, through their rejection of the past, their skills in a variety of the plastic arts, and their expertise in propaganda, placed themselves at the forefront of the avant-garde. They believed they were the arbiters of the direction which modern art and culture should take. Sigfried Giedion, the art historian and organiser of the CIAM, gave a series of lectures in America in 1938–39, which were subsequently published during the Second World War[44]. He spoke of the new ways in which art and science had been brought together, juxtaposing the discoveries of mathematics and physics with the "optical revolution" of modern art from the turn of the century. Art, science, philosophy, architecture were, he stated, the basis of modern culture, away from the historicism of the past or old-fashioned approaches to social welfare. The future was to be one without precedent, with buildings defined now in terms of space, light, air and, above all, a new functionalist approach to everyday living.

Yet in fact, the architects did not get it all their own way. The inter-war period was marked by a dramatic increase in the process of professionalisation of a number of activities linked with modern management and social welfare: social workers, factory superintendents, factory and workshop inspectors, personnel workers, public health officials, city planners, housing managers[45]. There were marked differences between national cultures as to the implications of this trend: in America and Britain, it led to independent professional bodies; in Germany, the professions developed within an existing civil service structure[46]. As for the exchange of international expertise on social welfare issues, the first international conference on social service was organised in Paris in 1928, the year of the Athens Charter of the CIAM. What professionalisation meant in all these different occupations was not always clear but their activities were increasingly underpinned by "scientific" study based on research undertaken in urban communities[47]. Here was another path towards Howard's "real reform". There was a chance for Howard's ideas to undergo "modernisation" rather than to be discarded if the context was right. It was beginning to be understood that the "modern" urban environment was more than a matter of fashionable urban design. However, to bring the *professionals of place* (architects and urban designers) together with *professionals of people* (social and educational workers), required the right political context, largely absent in most of Western Europe.

In fact, it required a combination of private resources with democratic public institutions, strong leadership countered by the interests of the many, and no historical baggage from the past. There was one intriguing example where the context was right and it actually happened. This was in the new country of Central Europe, Czechoslovakia. Here, a 100 kilometres from Brno, around the nucleus of a little market town, serving its agricultural hinterland, a modern city was built. The town was Zlín and from its inception, it was meant to create not just a new

Figure 3.3 *An early photo of Zlín before development* [By permission of the Muzeum Jihovýchodní Moravy ve Zlíne]

environment but a new civilisation. The entrepreneur who invested in it was Tomáš Bat'a, the shoe manufacturer, and the only model of a modern city he had ever heard of, was the garden city. What was built in Zlín, was a garden city in a modern idiom. By adopting a modern, functionalist approach to the problems of the built environment and using modern materials and techniques of construction, Zlín was to take the concept of the garden city and give it a form which could not have been further from that of Letchworth Garden City in England. There were no echoes of Arts and Crafts of the 1890s. Instead, Zlín was uncompromisingly modern. It was the garden city for a new era. As such, it provides a fascinating example of how the garden city concept might have developed, a "might-have-been" which was definitively put out of reach of the rest of Europe by the Second World War.

ZLÍN: GARDEN CITY BUILDING IN A MODERN IDIOM

In the new country of Czechoslovakia, the process of "modernisation" was studied with total commitment by business men, politicians and members of the professions who recognised that the only hope for the future prosperity of their little country was to be at the cutting edge of technology and its exploitation[48]. The latter required a modern approach to every aspect of life, from working

Figure 3.4 *Tomáš Baťa (1876–1932)* [By permission of Mr Pavel Novák]

conditions for the workers in industry, to their homes and social life, to the quality of the urban environment. One man particularly was dedicated to achieving this. He was Tomáš Baťa (1876–1932), a leading Czech business man and entrepreneur, who made his fortune turning the craft industry of cobbling shoes for the workers into a mass production industry which would supply new, lightweight, even fashionable shoes to the entire world. Baťa was passionate about modernisation and he consciously chose an American model of industrial production and personally adopted an American lifestyle. He set out to create, not only the most advanced modern methods of manufacturing but also a modern city which could grow up around it and pioneer the "modern" spirit of the new nation–state of Czechoslovakia.

The result was Zlín. The model he used, however, was the English one of Howard's Garden City. Baťa was no architect and urban planner but he had heard of the English garden city and in the early 1920s, it did seem to be the model of the future. What Baťa decided, however, was that in this instance, in his new town of Zlín, it was to be a garden city with all the social and cultural elements, put forward by Howard, "modernised" by teams of professionals[49]. Architects worked alongside factory managers, social workers, landscape gardeners and town planners, municipal officials and many other professionals to achieve a modern city. The result was a garden city translated into the idioms of the twentieth century.

Zlín became, in many respects, the model of the garden city of the future. It had a unique cultural quality from the beginning. As its chief architect said in 1934: "We have made efforts from the outset of building this town that it might grow organically in style from the industrial architecture, as a new form of expressing the architects' view of the work and life of an industrial town"[50]. Instead, the Second World War made this model a cul-de-sac in the Modern Movement. After the war, the development of new towns became the prerogative of state governments with different control mechanisms determining what was built on the ground and how it functioned in economic and social terms.

For Zlín, the most important factor controlling its success was the vision of Tomáš Bat'a, and the context within which he carried out his experiment[51]. He personally decided that the model should be Howard's Garden City and he was powerful enough to stamp his authority on everyone who worked for him including the architects. He was a moderniser with a mission: he wanted all who worked for him to use the latest materials and techniques and yet to make sure that the result did not alienate the people. He had a business man's concern that his efforts would produce a healthy and stable, creative and contented labour force[52]. Zlín thus offers an example of a modern urban environment for the age of mass society which did not lose its humanistic scale and values. In confirmation of this, the Bat'a company had a head-on collision with Le Corbusier himself. He had been invited to Zlín to judge an international model housing competition in 1935 and was deeply intrigued by the extent of the town building. In 1934, plans had been commissioned to increase the town's population from 30 000 inhabitants to 100 000. Le Corbusier put forward a plan which was rejected: he wanted a linear development for the town with workers' apartments in high-rise blocks placed on the hill slopes[53].

The Bat'a company was dedicated to developing districts with workers' housing in the form of single-family homes with gardens along garden city lines. Only after the Second World War were Corbusier's blocks built, but that was in another political era. In the formative period from the First World War to his untimely death in an air crash in December 1932, Tomáš Bat'a was able to control the development in every respect. He was able to attract young Czech architects from Prague, such as Frantisek L. Gatura, and to bring back young Czech architects working abroad, such as Vladimir Karfik, who had been working in America but who had become alarmed at the prospect of the loss of work because of the Great Depression. What attracted them was the challenge of such a large-scale enterprise with so much work. Bat'a's intention, however, in employing Czech architects was not overtly nationalistic. It was much more pragmatic. Always at the forefront of his thinking were the economic imperatives of keeping his enterprises successful and he had no wish to be encumbered by a world-class architect offering him a masterpiece of urban design. He made clear from the outset that the modern functionalist design that he favoured must meet his economic and social plans for the future and be dedicated to development of his workforce.

Figure 3.5 *View of some workers' housing in Zlín in 1930* [By permission of Mr Pavel Novák]

MODERN MANAGEMENT AND THE PHYSICAL ENVIRONMENT OF ZLÍN

In the early 1920s, Bat'a had developed a particular brand of management which became known as the Bat'a system. It was based on individual motivation with separate workshops in the production process being given autonomy. Each kept their own accounts and dealt with the other Bat'a units as supplier to customer. Such autonomy led to a wage policy which reflected profit or loss. People were thus motivated to work for themselves and Bat'a placed great emphasis on the importance of the individual and the development of personal talents. He did this alongside the introduction of mass production methods, which he had pioneered in his industry during the First World War as he had secured the contract to make boots for the Austro-Hungarian troops. The 1920s were an extremely successful time for Bat'a when ever more employees made, exponentially, ever more pairs of shoes: in 1922, 1800 workers made 8000 pairs daily; in 1928, 12 000 employees made 75 000 pairs daily; in 1932, 18 700 employees made 144 000 pairs daily.

To sell these, Bat'a used to the full the modern techniques of advertising, the very emphasis of which was to underline the "modernity" of his products, his methods and the resulting low prices. A key feature of his advertising campaign was a network of retail outlets in all Czech cities and abroad. A Bat'a shop was itself an advertisement and a hallmark of Bat'a's methods. In terms of retailing it was a complete modern experience. Pavel Halik, at a conference on Zlín in 1991, recounted the pleasure he had experienced as a young boy in the inter-war years, buying his shoes at a Bat'a store: "even here the presence of Zlín radiated through Bat'a's salesroom, all glazed, with lightweight armchairs from metal tubes, full of light and airy, pleasantly smelling of rubber." The Bat'a stores, some built by Vladimir Karfik, were a revelation in their locations in Prague and Brno, Bratislava, Ostrava, Karlovy Vary and soon outside Czechoslovakia, in Amsterdam and elsewhere. Their spare and elegant modernism (their only ornament the slogan "Bata") was in the greatest possible contrast to the classical and historicist buildings with which they were surrounded.

Zlín itself was just as exciting and novel to those who visited it (including many foreign architects such as the French architect, Auguste Perrot). The town was recognised as the most complete example of modern functionalist architecture. Yet it was a functionalism bereft of the ideological baggage of the CIAM. The key physical feature of the buildings which created the indelible and recognisable stamp of the place, was not even the work of particular architects. It was actually the fact that Zlín was built, to a large extent, in prefabricated blocks which limited the freedom of architectural design. The town, the factory building, and all the ancillary buildings were constructed by teams of architects, engineers and construction workers, working together. The standard block with which they invariably started was a reinforced concrete rectangle measuring 6.15 metres in length × 3 metres in width. From 1924 onwards, when the factory management was comprehensively overhauled and a new building programme put in hand, this standard unit was used universally. Its benefits were that it was cheap, flexible and could greatly expedite the building process. The new five-storey factory building of 1924 was built in just five months, from the day the foundations were dug to starting shoe production.

This was in great contrast to the shoe-last factory built by Walter Gropius in Germany for a German entrepreneur, Karl Benscheidt, in 1911. Gropius had produced a revolutionary design. This was the first true use of a glass-based curtain wall for the exterior of the building, made possible by the use of cantilevered steel frame construction. But it took three years to get from foundations to the finish and it needed extensive loans to pay for the factory building from the United Shoe Machinery Corporation of the United States[54]. Bat'a was not interested in this kind of "cutting edge" architecture. Vladimir Karfík, one of two most important of Zlín's architects (the other being F. Gahura) has quoted what he heard the Chief (as they used to call Tomáš Bat'a) say on the subject:

> I get the impression that the majority of architects are mostly interested in building monuments to themselves. We aren't interested in that: a building should serve us and our people. There are other factors as well: time, science and technology, and of these the most valuable to us is time[55].

So what made Zlín a true garden city as opposed to an industrial settlement built along garden city lines? It had certainly started as the latter. Bat'a had built his new settlement as part of the management structure for his special management methods. Yet also from the start, Bat'a had given a great deal of thought to the kind of social and physical environment he was creating. He was enough of a modernist to recognise that the two were connected. It was both in his business interests (which were anti-union) and his personal belief that Zlín should have an independent, multi-layered urban civilisation which would engage the interests of all citizens. Ever the propagandist, Bat'a had coined the slogan: "Work as a collective, live as an individual". There was a strong emphasis on family values. All the housing in Zlín was to be in small family homes with gardens. There were, of course, hostels for young men and women who flocked to the town in search of work. Zlín was situated in an agricultural area with high unemployment. Many of Bat'a's workers came from the land. In Bat'a's view, they needed to be turned into citizens.

Like Howard, Bat'a was prepared to develop schemes for his town which would create a new social ideal for all citizens. He was prepared to try and achieve a balance between town and country. From plan, to housing, to social and cultural activities, Bat'a sought to transform this place which he had come to in 1894, when it had been a modest agricultural market town, into an industrial city and centre of modern urban life without destroying its rural context[56]. He is quoted as saying: "Buildings: these are just piles of bricks and concrete. Machines: these are only a

Figure 3.6 *View of Bat'a Memorial building flanked by the Technological Study Institute, built in the standard blocks* [By permission of Mr Pavel Novák]

lot of iron and steel. It is only people who breathe life in them[57]." Bat'a was given to pronouncing maxims of this sort and they were used extensively as propaganda for creating the cultural environment. Fortunately for workers and citizens, Bat'a had a broad view of what was good for business and what was good for the people. It was Bat'a's idea of a peaceful path to real reform.

His construction engineer and architect, M. Drofa, had solved, at the price of a certain degree of monotony, the vital problem of building workers' housing cheaply enough. There were just two types: one with a slightly pitched roof and the other with a flat roof (though Drofa designed four types, the latter costing more). Each unit of housing was totally standardised with the result that it could be built at the cost of between 25 000 and 30 000 Kcs in the mid-1920s when workers' housing, for example, in the cheapest development in Novy Dum in Brno (Czechoslovakia's largest industrial city) cost five times that amount[58]. This was the single most crucial issue. By cutting the costs of the houses in this way in Zlín, it was possible to go for a low density layout with each house located in its own garden. This created the double advantage of mass production with, at the same time, the greatest possible freedom for each inhabitant to have their own private family home and to determine the quality of their own environment. The initial success of the firm in building the factory and workers' housing so cheaply was to be repeated as the firm began to expand overseas just before the Second World War.

Bat'a began to colonise the world, building factories and workers, housing on the Zlín model in Ottmuth, Germany; in Mohlin, Switzerland; in Borovo, Croatia; in Chelmek, Poland; at Tilbury, England; Best, Holland; Hellcourt and Vernon, France; Martfu, Hungary; Batanagar, India; Belcamp in the USA, so that by the end of the century, developments were to be found in 90 countries[59]. In Zlín itself, however, by 1935, the perennial need for cheap housing was becoming supplemented by an increasing demand for privately owned, higher-quality homes. The success of Zlín led to the development of a private housing market, an indication of a growing independent economic base. One of Bat'a's most talented architects, Miroslav Lorenc, who had been in Zlín since 1930, wanted to escape from the strait-jacket imposed by the company on his work. He was able to set up in the town as a private architect, building private houses and shops for patrons who gave him freedom. His career is an indication of the extent to which the town had become a self-confident, self-propelled community, dominated by the Bat'a company, but no longer entirely dependent on it[60].

ZLÍN AND THE CREATION OF A MODERN URBAN CIVILISATION

Zlín's claim to be a garden city rests on more than the fact of its low-density, family housing with gardens. Howard had believed that his garden city idea would be at the forefront of modern civilisation because of its exploitation of modern technology

Figure 3.7   *The market place in Zlín in 1927*
[By permission of Mr Pavel Novák]

and its pursuit of culture. Bat'a had a passion for these things. He, and his successor as head of the firm, his half-brother, Jan Bat'a, exploited new technology: the phone, the car, the cinema, radio and aeroplane, to the utmost, to create a satisfying form of modern life. Both of them loved planes and modern travel; both were intensely interested in healthy living and sport; both were deeply committed to modern advertising and films and all forms of modern communication. The Bat'a company made Zlín a centre for all these things in competition with established urban centres which, historically, had tended to monopolise the social and cultural life of the nation. Zlín was a pioneering place to live in the inter-war period, just as Letchworth had been in the decade before the First World War.

Its position as a centre for the Czech film industry happened almost by accident, though it was no accident that Zlín provided a receptive context[61]. Bat'a's had used Prague film studios to make advertising material in the 1920s. By 1928, this had become prohibitively expensive. The firm set up its own film unit. By 1935, the unit had collected a number of young professionals from Prague and other places. They were sent to Moscow and to America (where they bought the latest equipment) and by 1936, they were given new studios, built in the Zlín style. Their exuberance spilled over from their advertising work (they used a clip of Greta Garbo as Queen Kristiana, in the film of that title, being so vigorously greeted by the English king that he lifts her off the ground, the Zlín technicians adding footage of her shoes falling off, naturally Bat'a shoes!) into educational work and documentaries. It was the Zlín team who made a documentary of Tomáš Masaryk's life: he actually died while they were filming it so that it became a national memorial. It was also a Zlín team who made documentary films of Nazi provocations in Bohemia in a vain attempt to rouse the sympathy of Western countries. The Zlín film studio, that had begun as a unit to produce advertising for the firm, was able to progress into a modern independent unit responsible for its own financial future.

The route from a perceived need for the firm, to a cultural outcome for the community, was one which was followed quite often in inter-war Zlín. In a small country, grappling with high unemployment and poverty, especially in the 1920s and during the world economic depression of the early 1930s, all initiatives were dependent on what could be achieved with limited resources. As the firm progressed in the 1920s, so ever more funds were made available for social and cultural purposes[62]. An original top priority was education. Starting modestly with a nursery school for children of employees within the factory grounds, the company went on to fund schools for boys and girls, the Tomáš Masaryk schools, in the mid-1920s. The Bat'a company obviously needed an educated labour force but the intention of architects and planners was to make this provision in a modern and culturally significant way. They conceived of a "school quarter" which would concentrate all the schools for children of various ages and, by these densities, create a learning environment as well as pay attention to a very practical consideration – the sharing of facilities such as large assembly halls and sports facilities. Gahura had been the architect and he conceived the idea of a school district for the new town. He was also responsible for the various Zlín extension schemes of 1921, 1927, 1931 and 1934 and he planned such a cultural and educational area for each new major suburb. From the 1927 plan onwards, Gahura was able to achieve his original ideal. In 1931, Lorenc had built Zlín its first business school to complete the original school district of the town[63].

With school districts concentrating on primary and secondary education, a need was felt for an advanced educational institution to serve the whole town. The crowning achievement of the firm and the town council working together was to found a Technological Study Institute which would bring Zlín in touch with world developments in science, industry, technology and art[64]. The occasion which brought it into being was the death of Tomáš Bat'a in 1933 (in an air crash) and the decision to build a suitable memorial to him. Even in the death of Bat'a, Zlín was fortunate. His drive had created the town but equally, his death had freed it to develop a new relationship with the Bat'a industry. Gratitude was expressed in the building of a very fine memorial to Tomáš Bat'a, located in the centre of the proposed new Study Institute. It was designed by Gahura and is considered to be one of the finest examples of classical functionalist architecture[65]. Placed high on the hill on the north–south axis of the town, the glass building, supported by the Zlín standard concrete modules, reflects the evening light. It was a fitting memorial to the pioneer modernist. Its spacious and airy interior supported a model aircraft suspended from the ceiling. Even in the commemoration of his death, there was a desire to look to the future.

This spirit was nurtured in the new Technological Study Institute which flanked the memorial. Originally it was intended to have four large rectangular buildings in the Zlín style, dedicated to science and technology, social science and art. Financial constraints meant that only two buildings were completed in 1935, those for science and technology. Yet, from the outset, the Institute was intended to be a new kind of centre of advanced study, open to all who wished to learn, closely related to economic and cultural concerns, using the most advanced technological means of communicating and learning[66]. To encompass the first objective of encouraging all to learn, exhibitions of science and technology were laid out, since the starting point of all education had to be observation, curiosity and information. Initially the exhibitions of science and technology did not fill the space designated for them in the new buildings. Since the newly-appointed Director and his committee did not want to open the new Study Institute with empty rooms, the space was given to a sub-committee charged with mounting an exhibition of Fine Art. There was always the intention of finding a place for the arts, both pure and applied, at the Institute even if there was no money at first for a separate building. Thus, at its opening, the Institute had a wide range of exhibitions covering science and technology, art and industry.

Ebenezer Howard had argued that his Garden City could be a centre of modern civilisation because industry, art and culture no longer needed the historical links

Figure 3.8 *View of the play facilities in a school area, architect F. Gahura* [By permission of Mr Pavel Novák]

Figure 3.9 *The Bat'a Memorial* [By permission of Mr Pavel Novák]

Figure 3.10 *Interior of the Bat'a Memorial – note the plane in the top right corner* [By permission of Mr Pavel Novák]

with established cities in order to grow and develop. The ease of travel and the speed of communication meant that location in the provinces was no disadvantage. The Director and the management committee of the Technological Institute in Zlín tried to bring this vision into effect. The aim from the outset was to provide a university-style education but one that was more broadly based than purely academic study. This was easier to achieve in the more applied subjects such as textiles and the study of appropriate uses of new materials such as rubber. In chemistry, there was both pure and applied activities as students received lectures from university academics and also experimented with the design of specialised machines in the process of chemicals. Some studies had direct links with business interests. In 1938, one of the last departments opened was for Oriental Studies. The aim was to train workers for jobs abroad and prepare them for working the markets of the Far East. One of the innovations of the Institute was the intro- duction of a technical news service, offering up-to-date information in a wide range of subjects and issuing regular bulletins. Bulletins were broadcast, using the new means of information technology.

What this combination of academic study, from the practical to the academic, meant for the prospective students can be illustrated by the history of the evolu- tion of the arts-based subjects. From the opening exhibition in 1936, the Zlín Art Salons went from strength to strength[67]. At the first Salon, 90 000 people turned up to an exhibition of the work of young Czech artists. The Salon was held annually and was soon to become an important institution in Czech national culture, offering space for the exhibition of the work of sculptors, painters and all kinds of artists. National ministers and leading politicians attended the openings of the Salon and its proceedings were widely reported in the local and national press. Not least of its attractions was that work exhibited in Zlín tended to get sold. It was typical of the determinedly modern atmosphere of the Institute, however, that, also from the beginning, there was an equal emphasis on commercial art. At the original opening in 1936, on the next floor above the Salon devoted to Fine Art, was another exhibition devoted to commercial art. It contained advertising posters from all over the world and displayed the latest polygraphic techniques and commercial graphic work.

These initiatives were boosted after the 1937 World Trade Fair in Paris where the Bat'a company had its own pavilion (designed by Karfík when Le Corbusier's design was rejected). International competition sharpened the efforts made to train the best local talent so that they could compete in world markets. In typical Bat'a fashion, students were self-financing, aided by a sympathetic framework provided by the company (which also gave many of them their first commissions for work of all kinds). Students were able to work in the firm during the mornings to earn a wage and then attended the Art School in the afternoons until 7.00 p.m. On Saturdays, they attended the Art School all day. The subjects they studied were deeply influenced by the Bauhaus view of an appropriate education for the modern world[68]. It was an esoteric syllabus which included: drawing, graphics and applied graphics, advertising, book-binding, modelling, carving and sculpture, stucco work and mould casting, ceramics, toy-making, anatomy, geometry, chemistry, architecture, interior decoration, exhibition design, joinery, how to make mosaics, fashion design, decorative and figure painting, art history, literature, aesthetics, photography, window-dressing, landscaping, restoration work, folk-art and, finally, book-keeping. The Director of the Technological Institute had similarly practical and academic courses for the scientists and engineers. The Institute was designed so that every working person from any sector of modern industry would find courses appropriate to their needs.

Provision of other social and cultural facilities for the citizens of Zlín developed along similar lines. The initiative often came from the firm; the institution or activity was then developed and supported by the town council. Always the emphasis was on offering the most modern and up-to-date facilities. One of the most outstanding was the Corporate House in Zlín. It was an 11-storey building, described as the main "collective" town centre. It was built in 1931 by M. Lorenc and contained restaurants, a café, clubs, gambling rooms and public rooms. There was also, within it, a hotel with 300 bedrooms, each equipped in the latest modern style with its own en suite facilities. On the eleventh floor was a terrace from which the entire town could be viewed. It was used for dances in the summer months. Immediately in front of this building was added, two years later, the Zlín cinema. This could seat 2270 and was built as a huge rectangular building, a construction made possible with a steel framework. Earlier in the 1920s, the emphasis had been on health and welfare. In 1924 there was a building devoted to health and social welfare built at the factory gates; to be followed by the House of Social Care in 1925. Zlín's first hospital was begun in 1926. A covered swimming pool was too expensive and one was not built until 1950. But in the 1930s, as houses were built for the film workers near the new studio, a pool was constructed to serve as a water reservoir and an open-air pool. Zlín naturally had its own airfield and Bat'a representatives flew regularly.

CONCLUSION

The success of Zlín meant that it was emulated in at least three new settlements in Czechoslovakia: at Bat'ovany (now Partizanske), Zruc nad Sazavou and Sezimovo Usti-Velky Dvur. The Second World War, however, brought an abrupt end to the development of both Zlín and its imitators according to the Howard-inspired Garden City lines. What happened to Zlín had parallels with what happened to new settlements in Britain and continental Europe after the war, especially in the 1950s. State planning and development costs helped to dictate the need for high-rise buildings for residential areas, linear patterns of development (with increasing use of the internal combustion engine for transport) and a completely different approach to basic beliefs as to how an urban civilisation could be created on a

Figure 3.11 *The cinema in Zlín* [By permission of Mr Pavel Novák]

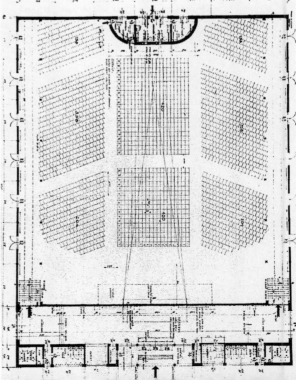

Figure 3.12 *The plan of the cinema – with the largest single span roof in the country* [By permission of Mr Pavel Novák]

greenfield site. At last, Le Corbusier's plans for high-rise flats on the slopes of the hills were taken up and Zlín lost something of its special character. Some of Zlín's original architects survived the transition and adapted to the new context. The original garden city of Zlín was preserved while the new suburbs were built in different ways. The town remains an example of what Ebenezer Howard's Garden City looks like in modern form as developed by pioneering professionals.

Perhaps Howard's greatest legacy for European city planners was threefold. He had wholeheartedly promoted the idea that cities in the future must be planned to avoid the congestion and misery of an overcrowded urban environment. At the same time, he had stood out almost alone in his championship of the needs of the individual, with his emphasis on everything from the individual family home to the demand of a social and cultural environment which people were free to enjoy and anticipate in according to their own wishes. Finally, he had wanted to preserve the quality of both town and country by bringing the two into a symbiotic balance, of mutual advantage to both. European responses to the garden city ideal have varied according to national and regional contexts, especially in the scale of development, its control and finance. The rate of industrialisation and urbanisation has varied dramatically from region to region. Britain and Germany, particularly, had experienced mass urbanisation and a scale of industrialisation before the First World War that was overwhelming in its physical consequences on the environment.

This was the context which had provoked Howard to create his ideas on the cities of the future. The period of the 1930s to the 1960s were to be the heyday of large-scale factory production in Europe which seemed in all cases to bring similar social and environmental consequences in its wake, regardless of ever increasing state powers of planning. Throughout this experience, Howard's ideas have remained a nodal point for those wishing to come to terms with the human consequences of change. The success of the Modern Movement, especially from the 1940s, made the settlements built along garden city lines look irrelevant. But with the passing of time and the ability of these, often small, settlements to retain their quality over decades of change, Howard's message has continued to run as a muted leitmotiv through modern European ideas on planning. The town of Zlín in the ancient historical kingdom of Bohemia, now in the Czech Republic, is a small but living example of the power of Howard's ideas in Europe and how they were modernised and brought up to date for a future age.

NOTES

1. SV Ward (1994) *The Garden City: past, present and future* London, E & FN Spon.
2. D Hardy (1991) *From Garden City to New Towns: campaigning for town and country planning 1899–1946* 2 Vols, London, E & FN Spon.
3. E Lebas, S Magri and C Topalov (1991) "Reconstruction and Popular Housing after the First World War: a comparative study of France, Great Britain, Italy and the United States" *Planning Perspectives* 6, 249–67.

4. E Howard (1898) *Tomorrow: the peaceful path to real reform* London, Swann Sonnenschein.

5. L Rapoutov and MH Lang (1996) "Capital City as Garden City: the planning of post-revolutionary Moscow, in conference proceedings *The Planning of Capital Cities* 7th International Planning History Society Conference, Thessaloniki, 795–812.

6. M Smets (1977) *L'avènement de la cité-jardin en Belgique: histoire de l'habitat social en Belgique de 1830 à 1930* Brussels, Liège. M Smets (ed) (1985) *Resurgam: la reconstruction en Belgique après 1914* Brussels, Credit Communal de Belgique.

7. E Hennaut and L Liesens (eds) (1994) *Cités-jardins 1920–1940* Brussels, Archives dArchitecture Moderne, 51.

8. P Uyttenhove (1990) "The Garden City Education of Belgian planners around the First World War" *Planning Perspectives* 5, 271–83.

9. Hennaut and Liesens (1994) *Cités-jardins*, 55–66.

10. S Meacham (1994) "Raymond Unwin 1860–1940: designing for democracy in Edwardian England" in S Pederson and P Mandler (eds) *After the Victorians* London, Routledge.

11. K Burlen (ed) (1987) *La Banlieue Oasis: Henri Sellier et les cités-jardins 1900–1940* Paris, Presses Universitaires de Vincennes.

12. O Nicoulaud (1987) "De la cité-jardin à la cité moderne" in Burlen, *La Banlieue Oasis*, 125.

13. See Chap 4, note 46.

14. M Rebérioux (1987) "Un milieu socialiste à la veille de la grande guerre: Henri Sellier et le réformisme d'Albert Thomas" in Burlen, *La Banlieue Oasis*, 27–36.

15. See Introduction, pp. 3–7.

16. HE Meller (1995) "Philanthropy and Public Enterprise: international exhibitions and the modern town planning movement, 1889–1913" *Planning Perspectives*, 10, 295–310.

17. D Calabi (1996) "Marcel Poëte: pioneer of 'L'urbanisme' and defender of 'L'histoire des villes'" *Planning Perspectives* 11, 413–36.

18. U Von Petz (1990) "Margarethenhohe, Essen: Garden City, Workers' Colony or Satellite Town?" unpublished paper at Bournville conference.

19. A Schollmeier (1990) *Gartenstädte in Deutschland: ihre Geschichte stadtbauliche Entwicklung und Architektur zu Beginn des 20. Jahrhunderts* Münster, Lit.

20. DF Crew (1979) *Town in the Ruhr: a social history of Bochum 1860–1914* New York, Columbia University Press.

21. BM Lane (1968) *Architecture and Politics in Germany, 1918–1945* Cambridge, Mass., Harvard University Press, 88.

22. D Geary (1991) "The Industrial Bourgeoisie and Labour Relations in Germany, 1871–1937" in D Blackbourn and RJ Evans (eds) *The German Bourgeoisie: essays in the social history of the German middle class from the late eighteenth to the early twentieth century* London, Routledge.

23. Lane (1968) *Architecture and Politics*, 87–124.

24. C Bauer (1934) *Modern Housing* Boston and New York, Houghton Mifflin.

25. N Bullock (1978) "Housing in Frankfurt and the new Wöhnkultur" *Architectural Review* 335–44. See also Lane (1968) *Architecture and Politics*, 90–103.

26. Bullock (1978) "Housing in Frankfurt", 33.

27. CC Collins and M Swenarton (1987) "CIAM, Teige and the housing problem in the 1920s" *Habitat International*, 11, 153–9.

28. A Sutcliffe (1981) *Towards the Planned City* Oxford, Basil Blackwell, 23–30.

29. U Von Petz (1995) "Vom Siedlungsverband Ruhrkohlenbezirk zum Kommunalverband Ruhrgebiet – 75 Jahre Landsplanung und Regionalpolitik im Revier" in *Kommunalverband – Ruhrgebiet Wege, Spuren: Festschrift zum 75 jährigen Bestehen des Kommunalverbandes Ruhrgebeit* Essen, Kommunalverband, Ruhrgebeit, 7–67.

30. R Beevers (1988) *The Garden city Utopia: a critical biography of Ebenezer Howard* Basingstoke, Macmillan, 14–24.
31. P Hall (1988) *Cities of Tomorrow: an intellectual history of urban planning and design in the twentieth century* Oxford, Basil Blackwell.
32. I Bakule (1995) "Riga's Garden Suburb" *Planning History* 17, 2, 6–11.
33. K Kafkoula (1996) "An Out-of-place Utopia? Garden city movement and the planning of capital cities outside the European metropolitan regions" *The Planning of Capital Cities* Proceedings of the 7th International Planning History Conference, Thessaloniki, 160–770.
34. WC Brumfield (1991) *The Origins of Modernism in Russian Architecture* Berkeley, CA, University of California Press, 29.
35. L Rapoutov and MH Lang (1996) "Capital City as Garden City", 795–812.
36. Rapoutov and Lang (1996) "Capital City as Garden City", 805.
37. SF Starr (1976) "The Revival and Schism of Urban Planning in Twentieth Century Russia" and M Bliznakov (1976) "Urban Planning in the USSR: Integrative theories" both in MF Hamm (ed) *The City in Russian History* Lexington, University of Kentucky Press, 230–5 and 243–52.
38. C Cooke (1978) "Russian Responses to the Garden city Idea" in "Garden city Legacy" *Architectural Review* 163, 355–61.
39. E Howard (1904) Published discussion of Patrick Geddes' paper "Civics as Applied Sociology" at the first British Sociological Society Conference, Reprinted in HE Meller (ed) *The Ideal City* Leicester, Leicester University Press, 92.
40. D Brand (1992) "Ullvål Hageby: Engelsk inspirert arkitektur i Oslo" (Ullvål Garden City: English-inspired architecture in Oslo) and "Ullvål Hageby i internationalt perspecktiv" Ullvål Garden city in international perspective in *Byminner* Oslo, 3, 7–17.
41. H Porfyriou (1992) "Artistic Urban Design and Cultural Myths: the garden city idea in Nordic countries" *Planning Perspectives* 7, 263–301.
42. E Mumford (1992) "CIAM Urbanism after the Athens Charter" *Planning Perspectives*, 7, 391–417.
43. V Clark (1990) "The Struggle for Existence: the professionalisation of German architects" in G Cocks and KH Jarausch (eds) *The German Professions* New York, Oxford University Press.
44. S Giedion (1941) *Space, Time and Architecture* Cambridge, Mass., Harvard University Press.
45. Y Cohen and R Baudoui (eds) (1995) *Les Chantiers de la Paix Sociale (1900–1940)* Fontenay-aux-Roses, ENS Editions.
46. WRF Phillips (1996) "The 'German Example' and the Professionalisation of American and British City Planning at the Turn of the Century" *Planning Perspectives* 11, 167–83.
47. S Magri and C Topalov (1987) "De la Cité à la ville rationalisée: un tournant du projet réformateur. Étude comparative France, Grande-Bretagne, Italie, États-Unis" *Revue française de sociologie* 28, 3, July–Sept., 417–51.
48. B Wilpert (1990) "How European is Work and Occupational Psychology?" in R Drenth and RJ Tobias (eds) *European Perspectives in Psychology* Chichester, J. Wiley and Sons, 123–40.
49. J Švácha (1995) "Zlín: Modernism without the avantgarde" in L Ševeček and Zahrádková *The Cultural Phenomenon of Functionalism* Second Conference Proceedings Zlín, Státní Galerie Zlín, 22.
50. FL Gahura (1934) "Building Bat'a's Zlín" *Stavitel* Vol. 14, 11–12, quoted in Ševeček and Zahrádková, *The Cultural Phenomenon*, 26.

148

51. V Šlapeta (ed) (1991) *Bat'a Architektura a Urbanismus 1910–1950* Zlín, Státní Galerie ve Zlíné.
52. P Novak (1993) *Zlínská Architektura 1900–1950* Zlín, Vydala Agentura Čas, 19.
53. J Sedlák (1995) "The Zlín Architectural Phenomenon" in Ševeček and Zahrádková, *The Cultural Phenomenon*, 15 and 18 fn 45.
54. I Gropius (1972) *Walter Gropius, Buildings, Plans, Projects 1906–69* Massachusetts, Catalogue of the International Exhibition Foundation, 9.
55. V Karfík (1934) "Bat'a Architecture in Zlín" in V Šlapeta (ed) (1991) *Bat'a Architektura*, 106.
56. Z Pokluda (1993) "Die Umwandlung einer Landstadt zu einem industriezentrum – die Bevölkerungsdichte in Zlín in 1900–1940" in *Funktionalismus von Zlín* First Conference Proceedings Zlín, Státní Galerie Zlín, 12–30.
57. Z Pokluda (1995) "A picture of Zlín in the Years between the Wars" in Ševeček and Zahrádková, *The Cultural Phenomenon*, 81.
58. J Sedlák (1993) "Die Kleinwohnungfamilienhäuser in Brünn und in Zlín" in *Funktionalismus*, 50–7.
59. Novák (1993) *Zlínska Architektura*, 298.
60. V Šlapeta (1995) "Architect Miroslav Lorenc" in Ševeček and Zahrádková, *Cultural Phenomenon*, 38–46.
61. P Novotný (1995) "Kudlov Barn" in Ševeček and Zahrádková, *Cultural Phenomenon*, 109.
62. A Celzota (1935) *Zlín, Ville d'Activité Vitale* Zlín, TISK one of the multilingual guidebooks published in Zlín in the mid-1930s outlines all the social and cultural "sights".
63. Novák (1993) *Zlínska Architektura*, 295.
64. T Mikuláštík (1993) "Kulturaktivitäten in Zlín in der zweiten Hälfte 30-er Jahre" in *Funktionalismus*, 50–8.
65. P Zatloukal (1995) "Memorial to Tomáš Bat'a" in Ševeček and Zahrádková, *Cultural Phenomenon*, 36–7.
66. A Glogar (1995) "The Study Institute in Zlín: example of a multi-purpose cultural institution" in Ševeček and Zahrádková, *Cultural Phenomenon*, 91–3.
67. V Vašiček (1995) "The Zlín School of Art" in Ševeček and Zahrádková, *Cultural Phenomenon*, 116–17.
68. Some of Gropius' earliest statements on the Bauhaus approach to education seemed to fit the Zlín Institute. He wrote in 1919 "The school is the servant of the workshop, and will one day be absorbed in it. Therefore there will be no teachers of pupils in the Bauhaus, but masters, journeymen and apprentices." Programme of the Staatlich Bauhaus in Weimar April 1919, quoted in HM Wingler (ed) (1978) *The Bauhaus, Weimar, Dessau, Berlin, Chicago* Cambridge, Mass., MIT Press, 31.

CHAPTER 4

HAMBURG AND MARSEILLES: CULTURAL INSTITUTIONS, CIVIC EXHIBITIONS AND CITY DEVELOPMENT 1890–1930

INTRODUCTION

This chapter is devoted to a comparison of two port cities, Hamburg and Marseilles, and the ways in which they demonstrated aspects of European civilisation. The idea of "European civilisation" is an elusive subject, difficult to define and impossible to measure. Yet when historians write about international economic relations in the late nineteenth century, they do not hesitate to suggest that the world multilateral economy which emerged in these years was "Euro-centred". With economic supremacy went a cultural hegemony. Europeans felt themselves to be the most civilised people in the world, which, in the purely practical terms of the proportion of population in Western European countries living in cities, they were. In a Euro-centred world economy, major port cities such as Hamburg and Marseilles were at the centre of world trade and economic development. They may not have been the largest or most important ports in Europe, but they were, respectively, the largest port of Germany (the second greatest economy in the world after the USA) and France (which had the second largest empire after Britain). The question is, if these cities were at the heart of the globalisation of trade and industry, what kind of European civilisation did they represent? Were they at the cutting edge of a global transmission of European culture? What kind of "civilised" values did they espouse? The period 1890–1930 was, in many ways, a turbulent time for both Hamburg and Marseilles. A comparison and contrast of their civic cultural institutions, civic events and the plans put forward to control and direct their physical growth gives some insight into the "quality" of life in these great ports.

One of the first questions is the "quality" of life for whom? Perceptions of what European civilisation was, were obviously dominated by class, race and gender. One of Hamburg's leading citizens at this time was the great art historian, Aby Warburg (1866–1929). He came from a patrician, Jewish family of bankers, industrialists and merchants. In the highly "civilised" social context within which he moved it seemed reasonable to him to seek an answer to questions about the nature of European civilisation through the visual arts and history[1]. He devoted his

Figure 4.1 *Aby Warburg (1866–1929)* [By permission of the Warburg Institute, University of London]

life to creating a library in which it was possible to study the history of human civilisation. He lived his life with great intensity in pursuit of this objective and he became increasingly and desperately depressed. He was deeply affected by the First World War and suffered a complete breakdown. He recovered briefly in the early 1920s when Germany was in the grip of post-war hyperinflation. Then he was to be found giving papers at the Hamburg Chamber of Commerce on how Baroque art, once cut loose from its roots and emptied of content, became like an inflated currency, dispossessing the heritage on which it had drawn. He became ill again but recovered enough to work feverishly in the last five years of his life, 1924–29, on his library.

Four years after his death, with the onset of the Nazi regime, Warburg's family and friends packed up his library and sent it in boxes to London where it survives in a purpose-built building in the University of London. Did Warburg's life and death represent the end of civilisation as it was known? The Victorians believed

that civilisation was based on science and art, activities which are greatly promoted by the growth of cities. Warburg's pessimism has to be offset by the fact that
cities are polyglot entities and the cultural life of a city can transcend prejudices of
class, race and politics, through the continuity of civic institutions designed to
benefit all citizens (whether or not they always achieve their goals). The quality of
life in Hamburg during this period of violent change, will be explored through an
analysis of its cultural institutions, especially its art gallery, the Kunsthalle. As
Hamburg had no university until the 1920s, the Kunsthalle was the most important
cultural institution in the city and its directors, during Warburg's lifetime, became
increasingly concerned with reaching out to the citizens of Hamburg regardless of
class, race and gender.

In Marseilles, on the other hand, the defining moments of its cultural history
during the period 1890–1930, had less to do with institutions and more to do with
events. Twice in the period, in 1906 and 1922, Marseilles played host to two
International Exhibitions, representing France and, at the same time, boosting its
own image. The role of international exhibitions in creating civic identities has
been explored in an earlier chapter dealing with Barcelona. In Marseilles, the
priorities were different as the port was already the largest in the Mediterranean.
For Marseilles the prime issue was defining itself in relation to Paris and asserting
its cultural status. All international fairs were concerned with boosting trade and
industry and in the case of the two exhibitions in Marseilles, promoting the Empire
to the home country[2]. In such an Imperial setting, cultural responses to race, class
and gender become distorted. The very concept of "European civilisation" became
defined within a narrow framework of an Imperial nation, defining its culture
against the "barbarism" that was presumed to exist in the economically under-
developed countries.

Cultural institutions and events are only symbols of a city's sense of civilisation. A more general approach to the quality of life in a city, and a test of its
"civilised" values, can be found in the ways in which its physical environment was
shaped and the responses made to the problems of expansion. During the period
1890–1930, both Hamburg and Marseilles were the second cities of their nation
and both grew dramatically. They each grew threefold: Hamburg from around
500 000 to 1 500 000 inhabitants; Marseilles from 275 000 to 750 000. Hamburg
was always twice the size of Marseilles. In France, Marseilles was locked into
competition with Lyons, to the extent that census returns in the early twentieth
century may have been falsified in order to put Marseilles ahead of her rival as
France's second city. In fact, only between 1910 and 1930 did Marseilles receive
this accolade as Lyons asserted its supremacy in numbers both before and after
this period. Marseilles may have been only half the size of Hamburg but both cities
had to cope with dramatic expansion. They did so at the time that professional
town planning was becoming established and both were to call on talented
practitioners to help them. In Hamburg, it was Fritz Schumacher and in Marseilles,
rather late in the day in the early 1930s, it was Jacques Gréber.

Figure 4.2 *Poster advertising the 1906 Exposition Coloniale, Marseilles* [By permission of the Chambre de Commerce et d'Industrie Marseille-Provence]

Figure 4.3 *Poster advertising the 1922 Exposition Coloniale, Marseilles* [By permission of the Chambre de Commerce et d'Industrie Marseille-Provence]

Planning, however, is not simply about controlling public health hazards, it is also about objectives. To decide on objectives and priorities, Schumacher and Gréber had to be sensitive to the context within which they worked. Their training had made them aware of the national and international developments in their discipline. What they could achieve in the cities in which they worked, however, was determined by the cultural consensus they found there. This chapter will focus on how "civilised" values helped to influence the manipulation of the physical environment of these cities and how they were "improved". These great port cities may have been based on trade, industry and finance, but they were, nevertheless, arbiters of a European civilisation with a long historical perspective. In the early twentieth century, the world may have been altering dramatically with the rise of America and Japan in the world economy and the economic and political chaos produced by the First World War. But the futures of both Hamburg and Marseilles depended on how they accommodated their past and present in the new conditions. Cultural institutions and events brought past and present together. Yet the most obvious legacy of the past is the built environment. City extension schemes were a test of their perceptions of quality. How did Hamburg and Marseilles, major port cities in communication with the world, fare in the global competition to be at the forefront of modern civilisation?

HISTORICAL PERSPECTIVES OF HAMBURG AND MARSEILLES

Between 1890 and 1930, Hamburg and Marseilles shared many similar problems. Keeping the ports busy and their industries flourishing was increasingly difficult before the war and, after it, economic circumstances had changed dramatically. Both cities experienced a rapid increase in the organised labour movement and both were rent with industrial strife and, in Hamburg's case after the war, a brief period of revolution. The First World War had undermined the world of merchants and bankers, the stability of the Gold Standard, the expectations that things could only get better. Yet both faced all these exceptional changes from very different starting points. Hamburg was an ancient port, a member of the Hanseatic League, a virtually independent city–state for many centuries. Marseilles, although it had had ancient origins and a medieval core and had been a significant city in French terms in the eighteenth century, had only really grown to world status in the nineteenth century[3]. Furthermore, it had never even been the capital of its local region, nor, in terms of church and state, head of an ecclesiastical province or a parliamentary city. What difference did it make that Hamburg was an old-established world city and Marseilles the relative parvenu?

The short answer is that this historical legacy had important consequences on the ability of each city to adjust to new challenges. It permeated every part of the cities' existence, their national status and local autonomy. When the new

Figure 4.4 *Hamburg in the inter-war years showing the Alster Lake and parkland* [Map drawn by Chris Lewis]

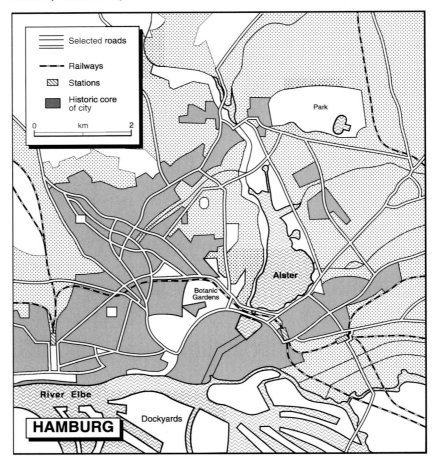

Germany was created in 1870, Hamburg was given *Land* status and treated as a separate region on a par with former kingdoms and princely states. The city remained a reluctant member of the new Germany for a couple of decades, a key problem being the imposition of tariffs on trade. Hamburg only joined the German Customs Union, which fully integrated it with the Wilhelmine Reich, in 1888. Even then, the outer harbour of Hamburg could be used for unloading and loading of cargoes for immediate re-export without the payment of tariffs. These concessions were recognition on the part of national government of Hamburg's desperate bid to

Figure 4.5 *Marseilles in the inter-war period* [Map drawn by Chris Lewis]

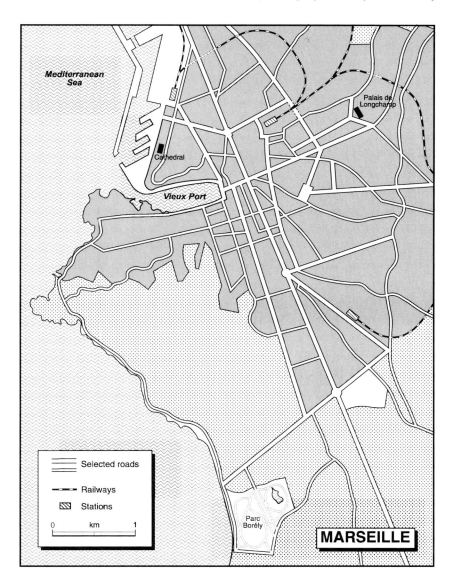

Mediterranean
Sea

Palais de
Longchamp

Cathedral

Vieux Port

Selected roads

Railways

Stations

0   km   1

Parc
Borély

MARSEILLE

increase the volume of its trade against stiff competition from London and Antwerp[4]. For example, Hamburg had not only been a major channel for German exports, it had also been well placed to deal with the Baltic trade and Russia. In the 1870s, American wheat flooded Europe and the historic grain trade of the Baltic suffered irreversible decline. From primary products to manufactured goods, Hamburg was beginning to feel a shift as America surged forward as the greatest economy in the world. The collapse of Russia into revolution after the First World War and its withdrawal from world trade were further blows to this great northern European entrepôt[5]. Fortunately for the great Hamburg shipyards, the German government had begun to invest heavily in developing the German navy during these years.

Thus, despite trade difficulties, Hamburg was still better placed than Marseilles. Marseilles was well located for the Mediterranean trade, yet it had had to develop its own industrial hinterland over the second half of the century. For a brief moment in the Second Empire, with Napoleon III's ambitious desire to put France at the forefront of the new economic order, money had been poured into Marseilles to make it a world port and a financial centre. Such ambition, however, could not be sustained in view of the location of the port and the lack of an industrial hinterland. Competition from the northern European ports, London, Hamburg and Antwerp, was too great. Marseilles turned towards the role it was to foster for the next half century: to become the contact point between France and her colonies in Africa and Asia. The colonial trade helped to sustain the enlarged port and provided the raw materials for industrial development to the north of the city. Soap manufacturing, oil processing and sugar became staple industries. Marseilles ceased to look towards a global horizon, although it still remained the largest port of the Mediterranean[6], and instead, concentrated on colonial markets. The dislocation of these during the First World War and their decline in the 1920s left Marseilles in a state of economic crisis from which it had not recovered by 1930. The economic context within which Marseilles had to forge new standards of civilised life in the early twentieth century was decidedly difficult.

LOCAL POLITICS AND CITY DEVELOPMENT

There were three ways in which city development could take place: by national edict, local initiatives from the town council, or private philanthropy. In both cities, leadership was provided at a local level by a well-established, male, upper bourgeois elite. Paradoxically, women had even less social influence in these port cities than in the capital cities or the former princely states in Germany where aristocratic women at least had some social influence. In Marseilles and Hamburg, trade, industry and finance were supreme and the elites were confident that what was good for business was good for their cities. Over the course of the nineteenth century and the development of the world multilateral economy, the elites of both cities had risen magnificently to the challenges of developing the potential of their cities. In the 1840s, Hamburg had suffered a disastrous fire which burnt down the centre of the city. City fathers immediately engaged the services of an English railway engineer, William Lindley, to use the opportunity to enable the city to install a modern water supply and sewage system as the city was rebuilt. An English engineer was chosen as England was the world leader at that time in the technology of urban public health[7]. Marseilles, on the other hand, was beset with problems of port development and communications. The city fathers there put in hand a project to build a canal from the port to the waters of the Durance at the cost of 40 million francs[8]. For both cities, these were high points in local initiatives.

By the second half of the century, both were more deeply integrated with national government and drew on capital resources well beyond the local business elite. Investment had poured into the city of Marseilles during the Second Empire as well as into the port. Following the example of Paris in the 1850s under Baron Haussmann, Marseilles had been similarly modernised[9]. This meant not only the acquisition of grand boulevards and public buildings in the Beaux-Arts style but also the division of the city into specific areas: heavy industry to the north; in the centre were commercial offices and the stock exchange; to the west and south west, the elegant suburbs of the rich. Marseilles gained the form and feel of a large French city. Little was done for the poor except for improvements in the water supply which had been undertaken in fits and starts since the great plague of 1720 which had killed half the inhabitants. Outbreaks of cholera in the 1830s had reinforced the message while also highlighting the connections between badly serviced areas of the city and the likelihood of disease. New water supplies were sought by bringing water from the River Durance by canal and storing it in a new reservoir. Between 1862 and 1870, the Palais Longchamp was constructed as the *pièce de resistance* of the Haussmannisation of the city, on a plateau overlooking the reservoir. To complete the image of municipal vigour, the two wings of the Palais were devoted to municipal institutions, the left wing housed the Art Gallery and the right wing, the Natural History Museum. The Art Gallery was one of the first purpose-built galleries in France[10].

This development in Marseilles, however, had been largely controlled by central government. In his study of the French urban system between 1740 and 1840, Bernard Lepetit has demonstrated how central government, through a mass of legislation, took control of the framework of city life in terms of layout of roads and communications, parks and open spaces, institutions and public buildings. He suggests that through these measures, the central government was able to impose an organisational order on civic life and on society as a whole[11]. In French culture since the Revolution, there had been a bifurcation between *l'urbanisme* and the development of social and educational institutions for all citizens, which had become marked by the Second Empire[12]. On the one hand, *l'urbanisme* referred to all the activities relating to the conception, organisation and management of cities and urban space; on the other, it was the name given to a professional

activity of urban management called, in the English-speaking world, town planning. What it did not encompass were the kinds of cultural activities, and connections between them and the physical environment which early British town planners, under the influence of Patrick Geddes, referred to as "city development"[13]. The latter was a bringing together of the social development of citizens with the physical development of city. Contemporary French social scientists such as Maurice Halbwachs were equally intrigued as their British counterparts with the question: "What is the connection between the structure of a town and the life of its inhabitants?" They began a distinguished tradition of social and urban studies which yet left *l'urbanisme* distinct and unconnected. Only recently has a modern study tried to bridge the gap fully. Marcel Roncayolo has achieved a stunning geographical analysis of the transformation of urban structures in Marseilles and their social consequences[14].

In Hamburg, a different political system produced very different results. The city's long tradition of self-government was allowed to continue after the unification of Germany. Although the German government built up a considerable volume of national legislation on urban government, the onus was still on city councils to develop their own systems of administration and civic culture. Hamburg had followed its own idiosyncratic path from city–state to city province in the course of the nineteenth century. Richard Evans' study *Death in Hamburg*, uses the 1892 outbreak of cholera in the city to argue that Hamburg had been given the freedom to hang itself, in that it was the last of the great municipalities to have an "amateur" approach to problems of public health[15]. In the official civic response to the cholera outbreak, the needs of business and trade were put above those of the safety of people. From being in the forefront in 1842, after the Great Fire, Hamburg Town Council had been allowed to become complacent. The disastrous handling of the cholera outbreak of 1892 starkly revealed the incompetence of the public health authorities. Yet the city council recovered quickly from this *débâcle*. The building of the new Town Hall in 1897 was both an indication of its renewed self-confidence and a recognition of the closer links it now had to have with central government.

City government in Hamburg, however, was not a democratic affair. The Hamburg Rathaus was one of the city's most elite male clubs. A combination of a voting system based on wealth and the level of rates paid, together with major shifts in the distribution of wealth on a per capita basis, kept it that way. It was a tripartite system, with the richest citizens electing a third of the councillors; the medium rich, a third; and the lowest rate-payers, a third. In the years before the First World War, this became a tiny very, very rich minority electing a third, the very rich electing the next third, the bourgeois the final third and the majority of citizens disenfranchised as they were too poor. Decisions on what was best for Hamburg was still in the hands of a very small well-established elite. Not surprisingly in view of its industrial strength, Hamburg was also a major centre of the Social Democratic Party, newly legal since the lifting of the anti-socialist legislation in 1890. The socialists, however, had their sights on national, not local, government[16]. From 1890, Hamburg's three seats in the Reichstag (to which it was entitled as a city–state) were held by three Social Democrats including Germany's great labour leader of the time, August Bebel.

Yet the city's problems were not on their agenda. The SPD was interested in creating a counter-culture that would bind their members together. They patronised particular drinking places, organised sport and recreation for their members, but all in the interest of nurturing commitment to SPD ideals[17]. These did not include civic cultural institutions or city government generally, nor even the celebration of national cultural events. In 1905, festivities to celebrate the centenary of the birth of Schiller were actually split between those for the bourgeois and those for the workers[18]. Aware of this bifurcation of city life, the Hamburg Town Council endlessly and acrimoniously debated, from 1900 until the war, the need for the city to establish a university, both to keep the city in the forefront in acquiring necessary skills for trade and industry but also to act as a means of creating some kind of civic cultural unity. The University of Hamburg was finally established in 1920. In the years of the Weimar Republic, the Hamburg Rathaus at last became a stronghold of the SPD. The social issue then, enshrined in the Weimar Constitution, was the demand for better housing for the working classes, though that did not include the poorest who were unable to pay economic rents. It did amount, however, to a demand for an improvement in the quality of urban life for members of the organised labour movement.

CIVIC CULTURAL INSTITUTIONS

In both Hamburg and Marseilles, the management of the city's fabric and the evolution of civic cultural institutions over the period 1890–1930, was seen as the role of professionals. The concept of citizenship did not automatically extend to the idea that citizens had equal rights and equal responsibilities. Since they were both port cities, dependent on pools of casual labour, there was an especially large gulf between the educated bourgeois elite and the poor majority. In Marseilles, the growth of the city depended on immigrants. They came from all around the Mediterranean but especially from Italy. By 1930, about 15% of the total population of the city were Italian[19]. No special efforts were made to integrate them into civic life. Indeed, few concessions were made at all and many Italian origin children were without educational facilities (as there were not enough school places) and failed to learn French, thus perpetuating their position at the base of the social hierarchy[20]. The power of the workers, regardless of strikes and the turmoil of the First World War, was very weak in civic affairs. The idea that workers had a right to a voice in local government was not even fully accepted by the SPD in Hamburg. In 1921, after the revolution and with the SPD now in power, the SPD leader, Otto Stolten, refused the position of First Bürgermeister on the grounds that the position should be held by "a man who also had close connections with the old Hamburg families"[21]. What was good for business and good for the elite, was still good for Hamburg. It was a belief that did not disappear quickly.

Top priority for the Marseilles elite did not include the development of their cultural institutions even though they made sure they had all those considered necessary for a city of the size and rank of Marseilles. Always the major concern was the promotion of industry, transport and communications. Desperate to find new markets after the turn of the century, it was local initiatives which helped put in hand one of the last, great, costly, civil engineering projects of the period: the canal to connect with the Rhône that was opened in 1927. It singularly failed to achieve the goal for which it was built[22]. Another plan for the physical development of the city, in 1928, concentrated on the expansion of the port and the industrial areas. Yet Marseilles was not entirely run by the bourgeois. It had a longstanding reputation for political radicalism which, from time to time, surfaced in political power for the Left[23]. It elected its first socialist Mayor in 1892. This was very different from Lyons, but in fact, it did not mark a turning point in directing municipal policies in favour of the poor. The Socialist Mayor, Dr Flaissières, a doctor who had devoted himself to the care of the poor, found he was completely unable (as he wanted) to use the municipal finances on social welfare programmes. When he cut the municipal subsidy to the Opera House to release extra revenue, there was an outcry and 20 000 people signed a petition against his action. The subsidy was restored[24].

One very minor thing he was able to do, which was symbolic in cultural terms, was that he made entrance to the Marseilles Zoological Gardens free for all citizens[25]. This action came at the end of a long process of private philanthropy, private enterprise and municipal support for this institution. The Zoological Gardens had been established in 1854, one of many private and public institutions of the mid-century years which addressed themselves to the task of helping the people of Marseilles to understand the potential resources of the colonial world and how to exploit them. Always strapped for cash, Flaissières' action in the 1890s was significant as it made this particular institution, once and for all, the responsibility of the municipality. Conviction of the importance of the colonies runs like a leitmotiv through the cultural developments in the city. The Natural History Museum was always more important than the Art Gallery. A Faculty of Science was established in the city again in 1854 and, since surveying was the first step before exploitation, over the next few decades, a maritime station was set up and Marseilles became a centre for the study of oceanography[26].

Law and commerce were also recognised as crucial to successful colonial activities. The first developed during the 1880s and the second reached new importance in 1890 with the setting up of an École Supérieure de Commerce for the children of the elite, to which was added, in 1900, a Section Coloniale. In 1896, the museum complex at Longchamp had gained a Colonial Museum. This was the brainchild of Dr Edouard Heckel, a professor at the Faculty of Science for many years who had worked to establish a Colonial Botanic Garden and a Colonial Institute. In the 1890s, both these received funding and were established in a vast complex at Parc Borely. Like Hamburg, Marseilles did not have a university. Those who wished to study Arts et Lettres went to Aix-en-Provence. Dr Flaissières, for all his socialist commitment, presided over Marseilles' high point of determinedly exploiting the colonies.

Hamburg's support for cultural institutions, especially museums and art galleries unconnected with trade, was always more confident and well established than that of Marseilles. Hamburg's elite had been major patrons of the arts for centuries. In Germany, provision for the arts had developed in a less centralised way in the nineteenth century. German art museums were of several types, the most prestigious being the Kunsthalle and the Nationalmuseum[27]. The Kunsthalle was a hall of art, initially created by the provincial *Kunstvereine* – art unions – of local artists and amateurs. The Nationalmuseum was devoted to objects of national significance though it was not national in an administrative sense. Most German large cities had either one or the other kind of art museum, rarely both. Frankfurt and Cologne each supported a Nationalmuseum. Hamburg had a Kunsthalle. In the context of citizens' access to civic culture, however, there were interesting variations. Mostly both kinds of art museum were elitist institutions, rarely visited by workers. This was to change in the late nineteenth century as the museum movement gained momentum. The system of provincial organisations for local government fed the desire to celebrate regional cultures, and regional museums were soon to be found in most provincial capitals. Hamburg, of course, as a city and a region, was exceptionally well placed to support its own cultural institutions. These institutions and their development in the period 1890–1930 were in the hands of professional civic administrators who were politically "non partisan in promoting their pet projects"[28]. A brief history of one institution, the Hamburg Kunsthalle, in this period, provides an insight into the cultural context within which these professionals worked and how they influenced ideas on the modernisation of the city.

THE HAMBURG KUNSTHALLE

The Hamburg Kunsthalle can be used as a symbol of cultural transition in the city. Perhaps transition is the wrong word because what was happening in civic cultural institutions in the period 1890–1930 reflected changing perceptions of the life of the city on many levels: economic, political and social, in which intersections, confusions, dead ends and new beginnings were as significant as continuities. The history of an institution, such as the Hamburg Kunsthalle, tends to emphasise continuities. Yet there were moments, and the period 1890–1930 was one of them, when the Kunsthalle was more important in the life of the city than before or since. The reasons for this were many. Partly it was due to general factors such as the changing perceptions of knowledge and importance given to art *vis à vis* other kinds of knowledge; partly it was due to the power of a political elite and the power that elite gave to the professionals who served it; partly it was to do with the great crisis in the visual arts, posed by the Modern Movement, emanating from Paris, but affecting all of Europe during this period. Sometimes a civic institution, caught up in the maelstrom of conflicting forces generated by change on all these fronts, rose to the challenge and as it did so, became uniquely influential. This is what happened with the Hamburg Kunsthalle.

How it achieved this important position in the period 1890–1930 requires some historical background. On a general level, a starting point has to be that throughout the second half of the nineteenth century, there was a belief that a specifically defined response to art and science was essential for the future of civilisation. What that was, had been popularly and internationally defined by the Great International Exhibition in London in 1851[29]. It had two elements. The first of these was a popular definition of science and art as, in the case of the former, knowledge of the world, currently dominated by the biological sciences and the concept of evolution; in the latter, Art was visual knowledge, the training of the eye. The second element was a commitment to the dissemination of this knowledge as widely as possible. When the 1851 Exhibition closed, after demonstrating Britain's world leadership in capitalist enterprise, the large profit it produced was invested in the development of science and art classes all over Britain. In the pursuit of applied art, those working in this area, from architects to artisans, were encouraged to think about ways of improving the design quality of their work. In Germany, this aspect of art was taken up by the *Kunstgewerbe* movement that, in the first decade of the twentieth century, was absorbed in the formation of the Werkbund.

Fine Art was the province of the upper classes, who were expected to devote their own resources to the acquisition of art as an indication of their sophistication and culture. With unconscious irony on the relationship between capitalism and art, Hamburg had already created in 1850, its first municipal collection of art in a few spare rooms in the Stock Exchange building. Soon however, there was a spate of new public art museums being built across Europe, especially in capital and provincial capital cities. Vienna, in the wake of its Ringstrasse project of city development, acquired an Kunsthalle in 1863. Berlin followed in 1867, and in France, among others, Marseilles in 1869. Hamburg decided to have a purpose-built Kunsthalle which was opened in 1869. The burghers of Hamburg then proceeded, haphazardly, to endow their new gallery with their private collections[30]. Hamburg institutions then got caught up in the national movement for the provision of museums and art galleries which reached a peak in the last decades of the century. To find out just how substantial the achievements had been in this period, a handbook was compiled and published in 1904 of all the institutions devoted to the visual arts in Germany. Some 600 were listed[31]. Of these, however, the Hamburg Kunsthalle was one of the jewels in the crown.

Figure 4.7 *Portrait of Alfred Lichtwark* [By permission of the Warburg Institute, University of London]

Yet the importance of particular institutions to local communities is not easy to ascertain. It was determined by the local context and the quality of the people involved. In a city like Hamburg with an established elite and a strong working-class movement uninterested in bourgeois cultural activities, it needed people of outstanding vision and talent to see a role for the Kunsthalle which could have an impact on the lives of all Hamburg citizens. The Hamburg Kunsthalle was to find such a man in the person of its first professional director, Alfred Lichtwark. Lichtwark was appointed as the Director of the Hamburg Kunsthalle in 1886. With the backing of his management committee (made up of three members of the Hamburg Senate and three members of the Association of the Friends of Art, founded in 1869), Lichtwark was able to interpret what he saw as the role of the Kunsthalle in his own way. As the first "scientific" director, and untrammelled by specific training in gallery management, Lichtwark addressed the issues as he saw them. Liberal in outlook, enthusiastic by temperament and with huge skills in communication, he pioneered ways of bringing art to the people, all the people, and in so doing, transformed the role of the Kunsthalle in the cultural life of the city. One of his oft-quoted sayings was "Wir wollen nicht ein Museum, das dasteht und wartet, sondern ein Institut, das tätig in die künstlerische Erziehung unserer Bevölkerung eingreift" (We do not want a museum that stands around and waits but an institution that actively the promotes the art education of our population)[32].

His first commitment was to cut through all the distinctions between Fine Art and other art forms, and between those able to appreciate art: upper class and workers, men and women, adults and children. On arrival in post, he quickly sorted the collections into some kind of chronological order, giving special place to the specialities that were strongest. These were medieval art, especially the medieval art of Hamburg which he discovered and promoted; sixteenth-century to eighteenth-century art of the Netherlands (which had special connections with Hamburg); and contemporary art in Germany and France, particularly the work of artists in Hamburg. Already his commitment to his city is clear. His commitment to its citizens was equally forceful. He instituted a series of lecture courses to help people understand art. They were open to the public at large. He realised that the way for a civic institution to operate was through the school system which, with universal elementary education, reached out to all. In 1890, he targeted women elementary school teachers and by bringing them into the Kunsthalle for art appreciation classes, cut across a gender divide. Within a few years, he had instigated an Association of Teachers to foster appreciation of art and offered the Kunsthalle for exhibitions of children's art. He was an outstanding educator[33].

He was equally forceful in dealing with the controversies about what was, and what was not Fine Art. In 1893, he offered the Kunsthalle as a venue for an exhibition of photography. He faced the challenge of the Modern Movement avant-garde artists from a liberal and tolerant standpoint. He bought the work of the French Impressionists. When the Kaiser sacked the Director of the Berlin Museum in 1905 for buying Impressionist works (he did not wish to have what he called the "art of the streets"), Lichtwark went out and bought his first Monet. He had already bought the work of Manet, Renoir and Courbet. He also wanted the best contemporary artists to come to Hamburg and paint the city. In the summer of 1913, he was successful in attracting Pierre Bonnard and Edouard Vuillard. Under Lichtwark's directorship, Hamburg's Kunsthalle was totally transformed and it became hugely popular.

Yet his greatest gift to his city was not confined to his work there. He gave enormous inspiration to his fellow professionals working on behalf of the city. A respect for Fine Art was second nature to the bourgeois elite. Respect for a Director of the Kunsthalle with the kind of personal qualities displayed by Lichtwark was second to none. In a city without a university, he held a unique position in the cultural life of the city at a unique moment. From the early 1900s, Lichtwark had campaigned for a new Kunsthalle which was to be completed shortly before his death in 1914. The new museum was one of a number of social institutions put in hand in the early years of the twentieth century. These included high schools, scientific institutions such as the Botanical Institute (1904–6) and the Observatory (1907–12), museums such as the Museum for Folk Art (1907–11) and the Museum of the History of Hamburg (1914–23). These developments represented a new departure in the evolution of Hamburg's cultural institutions. Lichtwark and his educational work at the Kunsthalle had contributed towards the inspiration of a new ideal of modern civic life. He had been aided by Hamburg's wealth and relative independence with its provincial status. Yet he was at the centre of a group of professionals working for the city.

Lichtwark saw his museum as an institute of higher education in the spiritual life of the people of Hamburg, all the people of Hamburg, regardless of race, class and gender. It was a powerful inspiration. The new Kunsthalle was designed by the City Architect, Albert Erbe, but he retired before the building was complete. In 1909, the building was put into the hands of the new City Architect, Fritz Schumacher. The timing of Schumacher's arrival was crucial. He became a friend of Lichtwark (and Lichtwark's successor, Gustav Pauli), just at a time when he found his job as City Architect expanding with new responsibilities for city development. He was appointed the first Head of Hamburg's Municipal Urban Planning Department in 1914. Schumacher was to develop his work in his new capacity, to achieve a new ideal of civilised life for all the citizens of Hamburg. As for the Kunsthalle in the 1920s, it continued to prosper but its great pioneering

Figure 4.8 *The new Museum for the History of Hamburg designed by Fritz Schumacher between 1912 and 1921* [Reproduced by permission from Schumacher, 1935]

Figure 4.9 *The Volksschule (People's College) in Hamburg designed by Fritz Schumacher in 1928* [Reproduced by permission from Schumacher, 1935]

Figure 4.10 *Plan drawings of the new Kunsthalle*

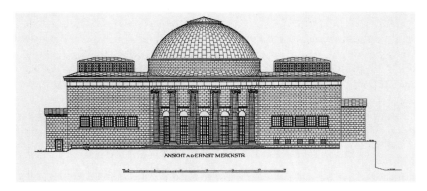

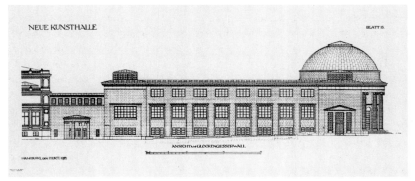

days were over. Pauli struggled to continue Lichtwark's work in ever more hostile conditions[34]. As the post-war German inflation cut away the purchasing power of the Kunsthalle, Pauli did the unthinkable and sold 500 works given to the museum which he considered were not of the first quality, so that he could buy modern works.

In fact, even this drastic action was not enough. The Kunsthalle's leading position in the acquisition of modern art was overtaken by the galleries in Mannheim and Hanover. Yet in one respect, he was successful. The people kept on coming to the Kunsthalle after the war. In 1920, 200 000 visitors were recorded. That was a great achievement but the numbers did not increase over the decade. The activity of art appreciation had to compete with new cultural activities and entertainment, especially commercial entertainment and sport which was attracting the younger generation. Pauli tried to raise the stakes in 1925 by claiming that he now felt that Hamburg's Kunsthalle had become a world institution, not just a civic one. The importance of the tourist, whom Lichtwark had downgraded, was reinserted. Pauli had some success and was invited to be a visiting Professor at Harvard in 1928 to study how the Americans organised their galleries. But the economic and political conditions of the next five years in Germany cut short his ambitions. The Great Depression and the rise of the Nazis personally affected him. He was sacked from his job on the 30th September 1933. Over the period 1890–1930, however, the cultural institutions of Hamburg, especially its Kunsthalle, had played an important role in city development at a time of rapid change. It had been the focal point of a vision of the future, concerned with the well-being of all citizens.

THE CIVIC EXHIBITIONS IN MARSEILLES, 1906 AND 1922

In Marseilles, such a role for the Art Gallery would have been impossible. Traditions, culture and politics dictated otherwise. It did not matter that Marseilles had acquired its first purpose-built Art Gallery in 1869, the same year as Hamburg. The subsequent evolution of cultural institutions in the city took a different path. For all its size and ebullience, Marseilles suffered from the cultural domination of Paris. Paris was simply the centre of French life and culture, the standard against which Marseilles compared itself. The port city did not have the regional identity and cultural independence found in Hamburg. In terms of social development the city had all the institutions, such as schools, hospitals, art galleries, museums and libraries that had been part of French life since the days of the Revolution[35]. In terms of fashion and aspiration, however, Marseilles was at a disadvantage. With increasing dedication since the Second Empire, there was a hidden (or not so hidden) agenda in French cultural life. The French invested their efforts in proving French society and culture was second to none, as first Britain, then Germany, then America, all forged ahead as stronger economies. The glittering centre of French national culture was Paris.

One of the most high profile methods used by the French to project their idea of world hegemony in cultural matters was through the mounting of International Exhibitions in Paris. Four years after the Great Exhibition in London in 1851, there was an International Exhibition in Paris. It was a relatively modest affair, but, with the support of the Emperor, the government took the decision to mount such exhibitions at 11-year intervals thereafter: 1867, 1878, 1889 and 1900. At a stroke, the French had committed themselves to this form of self-promotion for the entire second half of the century and laid a claim to host the Centennial Exhibition decades in advance[36]. It was a universally popular medium. City after city hosted exhibitions. There was a major exhibition roughly every two years in some part of Europe or America in the half century before the First World War. The great International Exhibitions, however, attracted the most resources and attention. The purpose of an international exhibition was gloriously unspecialised. It was a trade fair, an educational programme dedicated to science and art and a source of entertainment. Above all, it was supposed to illustrate the cutting edge of technological progress, social progress and the sophistication of the "civilised" European world[37]. In the Paris exhibitions, this was overlaid with French nationalist aspirations to make Paris the cultural capital of the world. Such an aggressive attempt to dominate encouraged the rivalry of other nations, evident when the Americans mounted the largest and most impressive International Exposition ever, in Chicago in 1893[38]. When Marseilles was chosen in 1906 to host the first French International Exhibition after the Centennial Exposition of 1900, it could not hope to emulate Paris. It had to play to its own strengths which was to represent the image of the Imperial nation and the French colonial empire.

When Marseilles lobbied to take over from Paris the mantle of representing French culture to the world in the major International Exhibitions of 1906 and 1922, its ability to do so was justified in terms of Imperial policy. There was no question that Marseilles would set the new French style or that the exhibitions there would develop knowledge of science, art and social progress for the nation at large. As a Monsieur Bénard wrote in 1906 (in his general report for the Section Internationale d'Océanographie des Pêches maritimes et des Produits de la Mer), the Exhibition made possible: "the gathering of the public gaze of the natural riches of the earth, of our colonies, and of manufactured goods that metropolitan civilisation has sent back in return"[39]. He was naturally a little biased, but the message could have been repeated in reports from nearly all the other sections. Civilisation in Marseilles was defined as the beneficial contact between Europe and the rest of the world.

Social development was focused, not on Marseilles itself, but on what the "natives" achieved under European tutelage. The central exhibit of the 1906 Exhibition were "live exhibits" of native peoples, who were to be seen in the context of their native huts, dressed in native costumes and practising their native skills. The practice of having "live" exhibits of the non-European races of the world had developed in the nineteenth century almost casually. In the 1851 London Exhibition (the British rivalling the French in their love of representing Empire), people were brought from all over the British Empire, but they were not set up as exhibits themselves. That idea was introduced in the Paris 1867 Exhibition when North Africans were exhibited in *tableau-vivants*[40]. In 1889, there was a significant change, due to the growing influence of modern anthropological study. This created a context which reduced human exhibits to zoological specimens, examples of the kinds of "primitive" cultures through which Europe had passed in the far distant path *en route* for its current flowering of sophisticated civilisation. By the time of the Marseilles Exhibitions of 1906 and 1922, this use of native people as exhibits had become "normal" although by 1922, it was a little old-fashioned. The technique was last used at the Paris exhibition of 1931.

Already though, by the First World War, some of the people recruited for these exhibits had learnt, by bitter experience, how to gain more control. The Senegalese and Dahomeyans, two of the most popular exhibits, had formed their

Figure 4.11 *Colonial Exhibition, Marseilles 1906 – Pavilion of the Forests of Algeria* [By permission of the Musée d'Histoire de Marseille]

Figure 4.12   *Colonial Exhibition, Marseilles*
1906 – Pavilion of Tunisia [By permission of the
Musée d'Histoire de Marseille]

own companies to lease themselves out to exhibition organisers. They provided what people wanted to see and they were paid. Greenhalgh in his study of International Exhibitions, quotes (from a guide book of the 1909 London Imperial Exhibition) a passage giving the "accepted" view of the benefits of the French colonisation of Dahomey:

> Order and decency, trade and civilisation, have taken the place of rule by fear of the sword. France has placed its hand on the blackest spot in West Africa, and wiped out some of the red stain that made Dahomey a by-word in the world. Today Dahomey is a self governing colony of France, with a revenue which exceeds its expenditure, a line of railway, rubber and cotton plantations, exporting palm oil and copra, maize, nuts, dried fish, cattle, sheep, pigs and fowls[41].

This was the image of civilisation that the Marseilles Exhibitions wished to portray. The city's livelihood depended on it.

The Exhibitions, for all their national support, were extensions of Marseilles' municipal policy over the last half century. In physical terms, however, they had little impact on the city itself. There were few special buildings or newly landscaped open spaces although a new structure was erected in Parc Chanot for the 1922 Exhibition. In both 1906 and 1922, the major venue of the Exhibitions was the Casino building adjacent to Parc Borely. The Château Borely and its gardens had been a gift to the municipality which had become developed as a social centre from the 1870s[42], when the people of Marseilles suddenly discovered the beach. A tramway, built in 1879 to bring people from the city, confirmed the popularity of this shift and cafés, bars and restaurants followed[43]. The Casino had had a chequered history being closed on occasion for malpractices. The two Exhibitions gave it a short Indian summer. It finally closed for ever in 1926. In style and organisation, the Marseilles Exhibitions were looking backwards to the traditions set by Paris. It could not be otherwise when Paris remained so culturally dominant. The International Exhibitions of Marseilles, both in 1906 and 1922, were not, however, in the business of addressing the whole of French life and culture. The economic context of the city was too strained. The vision of Marseilles' future in these Exhibitions was committed to an Imperial role which was already on the wane by the First World War and markedly so in the 1920s. It was not a favourable context for the introduction of modern town planning and a new kind of socially inclusive civilisation in the city itself, more in tune with modern developments.

CITY DEVELOPMENT IN MARSEILLES AND HAMBURG

Two men were to be responsible for introducing modern town planning in Hamburg and Marseilles in the inter-war years. In Hamburg, it was Fritz Schumacher (1869–1947), appointed as City Architect in 1909 and Director of the Urban Planning Department from 1914; and in Marseilles, Jacques Gréber (1862–

Figure 4.13 *Colonial Exhibition, Marseilles 1922 – Temple of Anghor-Vat and the tower of the Palace of West Africa* [By permission of the Musée d'Histoire de Marseille]

Figure 4.14 *Colonial Exhibition, Marseilles 1922 – view of the Palace of Indo-China* [By permission of the Musée d'Histoire de Marseille]

Figure 4.15 *Colonial Exhibition, Marseilles 1922 – close-up of the Palace of Indo-China* [By permission of the Musée d'Histoire de Marseille]

Figure 4.16 Fritz Schumacher, architect 1869–1947 [Reproduced by permission from Schumacher, 1935]

1962), commissioned to produce a plan for Marseilles in 1931. Schumacher had the great advantage over Gréber in that he had an accredited position in the city administration. Gréber, on the other hand, was the Parisian "expert" called in to produce a plan. Marseilles had instituted in 1924 a Commission Spéciale de Techniciens to plan for urban growth in connection with the development of the new port docks. But its brief was not to deal with the city as a whole. That was to be Gréber's challenge. For Gréber, the timing was unfortunate as 1931 was the year in which the French economy finally succumbed to the international economic catastrophe of the Great Depression, two years or so after Germany and Britain. When Gréber reported in 1933, both the severity of the economic crisis and political instability made it an inauspicious moment and his plan was never implemented. Schumacher, too, had his problems. The First World War was hardly the best moment for starting comprehensive planning projects and revolution and the collapse of the German currency in hyperinflation in the early 1920s, severely curtailed municipal resources. Both men, however, had been deeply influenced by the emergence of the international town planning movement before the war.

Since the 1890s, but with a great quickening in the five years before the outbreak of the war, the modern town planning movement, dominated by Europeans and Americans, had gathered a global momentum. Building and planning capital cities for European colonies, learning the arts of modern city management and, high on the agenda, coping with the rapid expansion of capital cities, all contributed to this. Exchanges of ideas on best practice had occurred informally at the

International Exhibitions and, more explicitly since the turn of the century, in more specialised exhibitions. The Germans, particularly after 1900, favoured focused exhibitions dedicated to specific themes rather than international exhibitions. In 1903, a German City Exhibition was held in Dresden. It was the first to celebrate positively Germany's shift to becoming an urbanised nation. It also celebrated the achievements of municipal governments in handling the transition. It did so in style. There were representations from 128 city governments, exhibits from over 400 manufacturers, occupying 24 buildings including a central hall with 80 rooms. The municipal exhibits were arranged under eight main headings: 1. transport, lighting, street building and drainage; 2. city expansion, building inspection and housing; 3. civic art and architecture; 4. health, welfare and police; 5. schooling and education; 6. care for the poor and sick and various charitable institutions; 7. financial institutions; and 8. record-keeping[44]. Fritz Schumacher was in Dresden for the ten years before he came to Hamburg. He was both teaching and practising architecture. He was also deeply involved in the City Exhibition. The exhibition showed, above all, how city development in Germany was recognised as a concerted effort, tackling social development and the physical environment of the city together.

The speed of German urbanisation, as in American cities, had stimulated municipal governments to think in terms of planning beyond the city to the region, to accommodate future growth. In 1905, the need for a plan for Greater Berlin had been recognised. Two years later, there was a competition. In 1910, an exhibition of the winning plan and plans from many other German cities was held in Berlin from where it moved to Dusseldorf. In the same year, an international town planning exhibition was held in London in conjunction with an international conference organised by the Royal Society of British Architects. It was billed as the First International Town Planning Exhibition. The American and German exhibits dominated the exhibition but the French also sent much material. The British were represented by the collection made over the past two decades by the Exhibition Director, Patrick Geddes, in his Outlook Tower in Edinburgh, in which city development was illustrated as a social as well as an architectural process[45]. This kind of approach had been adopted at the Musée Social in Paris (which did not exhibit in London) over the same two decades. The material collected there was set up as permanent exhibitions at the Musée, where it played a part in influencing the ideas of the French architect planners. Jacques Gréber was a member of the Musée Social and he was to go on to become one of the leading teachers in Marcel Poëte's École des Hautes Études Urbaine set up in 1920[46].

The responses of both men to the modern town planning movement were thus deeply coloured by their own experiences and training. Schumacher was the son of a diplomat and had spent his early life in Bogotà and in New York[47]. He was very receptive to American, British and indeed, other European ideas on city development. Gréber had actually worked abroad. The good luck of being appointed as a landscape architect for a French villa belonging to A.J. Widener, the tramway entrepreneur and millionaire from Philadelphia, led him to be appointed to complete the Fairmount Parkway plan for Philadelphia[48]. Widener put up the money to turn this project of boulevard, park and museum near the centre of the city, a grand "City Beautiful" project, into reality. Ideas for it had first been articulated in the 1870s, rejected in 1894 (regardless of the example of the 1893 White City Exposition) and only gradually put in hand between 1904 and 1917. It was the work which turned Gréber into a recognised architect planner[49]. Schumacher came to the profession by a different route altogether. His most famous early work was a plan, never executed, of a monument for Nietzsche. He had studied art in Munich as well as getting his architectural training at Charlottenburg. He had been a founder member of the national Werkbund in 1907, formed after the 1906 exposition of applied art in Germany of which he had been the principal organiser. The Werkbund had a moral as well as artistic side. Its members were dedicated to using their skills for the benefit of humanity and progress. Schumacher's decision to take up the post of City Architect in Hamburg, rather than other work offered to him, was taken, in his biographer's words: "in the spirit of the Werkbund" in which science and art were brought together for the service of mankind[50]. Schumacher, as his writings show, was always a man with a spiritual as well as material mission[51].

Schumacher was to join a group of professionals at Hamburg. Gréber, on the other hand, like all French architect planners, had no such context within which to work. The problem as always, was actually getting work. Only three French cities: Paris, Marseilles and Lyons, was anywhere near the scale of Berlin, Hamburg and other German cities. This does not mean that French cities were not growing. It was just that the speed of growth had not been enough to force a political decision to create a legal framework for planned urban expansion. The first planning law was eventually passed in 1919, the Loi Cornudet, with ordered all municipalities with more than 10 000 inhabitants to prepare extension plans. The legislation, however, was not strictly enforced because of lack of sanctions for failure to comply. The real problem in 1919 was perceived to be Paris and, not to be outdone by the 1909 competition for Greater Berlin, two competitions were held. The first was for an extension plan for the capital city; the second, for a plan for a new land use of the demilitarised outer fortifications of the city. Léon Jaussely, member of the Musée Social and designer of Barcelona's extension scheme of 1904, won the first. Jacques Gréber won the second[52]. Neither plan was implemented. Gréber had to watch while his plan, which had included large areas of open space being retained as a crucial prerequisite for a healthy modern environment, was destroyed by the sale of land by lots to the highest bidders.

Space in a healthy modern urban environment was not just a matter of giving the city "lungs" as the nineteenth-century sanitationists had believed. Space was seen as essential for recreational and aesthetic purposes as well. Schumacher was more fortunate than his French counterpart. His very first technical challenge, the canalisation of the River Alster, tributary to the Elbe, gave him the chance to develop a full-blown scheme of urban regeneration, creating open space, greenery and recreational facilities in a city where the poorer areas were singularly devoid of such amenities. Schumacher hoped that the State Park would be a key to future city development, offering health and a higher quality of living to all citizens. The excellence of the design he and his department produced, made this an outstanding project. It was completed in 1924. It was the first step in making a new society, transforming the city by means of manipulating the city environment and "by means of social programs, into a collective Heimat"[53]. Schumacher was translating some of the ideological values of the diffuse but pervasive Heimat movement, with its roots in a nostalgia for the old rural way of life, into the modern city. Schumacher was committed to modernisation and change, but like his grandfather, who was the last of the old-style *Bürgermeister* of Bremen who were elected for life, he felt a responsibility to nurturing the people as well as the place. His planning sought new solutions to the relationship between city and country, and between the city and its region.

He was able to develop his ideas on the former, not in Hamburg, but in Cologne[54]. In 1920, the young *Bürgermeister* of Cologne was Konrad Adenauer, anxious to regenerate his city after the war. He attracted Schumacher, under financial constraints in his work in Hamburg, to come to Cologne to create a plan for the whole city as the fortifications were pulled down. Schumacher was seconded there for three years. Cologne was still in the British zone of administration after the war which provided a supportive context for modern planning. Schumacher created the concept of the "green" city, retaining as much as possible of the land for open spaces and making these the connecting links between different parts of the city. From here he began developing his ideas of city and region. In his Cologne plan, he produced ideal diagrams of the point of contact between town and country which "wove" town growth in great zigzag points of development from which it would be possible to look across open spaces of countryside. Back in Hamburg in 1924, he tried to put his ideas for the region and the relationship between town and country into practice. New settlements were located contiguous with open spaces rather than piecemeal on the periphery of the city. With his new political masters in Hamburg, the Social Democratic Party, he was also given a clearer brief: to build new homes for the workers.

Schumacher brought to this task all the weight of his experience and approach. He was in favour of a completely modern, functional approach to the problems of urban growth[55]. When Le Corbusier confronted the architectural world with his drafting of the Athens Charter at the Congrès International d'Architecture Moderne in 1933 in favour of modern architecture and design, Schumacher could have signed up with the avant-garde. That he did not was not an indication of his hostility to the aims of the Charter. It was an indication of his hostility to the architecture that was supposed to best realise those aims. Schumacher was not in tune with the experimental work of the architects of the Dessau Bauhaus. While their design ideas were being taken up by Ernst May in Frankfurt and in urban

Figure 4.17 *The great State Park in Hamburg, designed by Fritz Schumacher, 1910–24* [Reproduced by permission from Schumacher, 1935]

developments in Berlin, Schumacher and his department quietly built more social housing in proportion to the population of the city than was achieved either in Frankfurt or Berlin[56]. This building work had two special features: it was located adjacent to open space if at all possible, near the Alster Park or along the banks of the Elbe, and it was built in red brick. Schumacher's choice of material, against the trend of concrete, glass and steel infrastucture, was not just a matter of design. He had written a pamphlet in 1917 extolling the virtues of the hard-fired Hamburg brick in moral as well as material terms. There was no doubt about his strong streak of neo-romanticism. Bricks had a "dignity" and a warmth. They were akin to the German temperament itself, something which could stand up to the winds and sea mists of Hamburg's climate. They were part of the city's identity and past. His choice was similar to that of other modern architects in northern port cities, especially Amsterdam, where the New Amsterdam School made extensive use of red brick[57].

Schumacher was able to make the kind of impact on Hamburg that Gréber could only dream about making on Marseilles. Not even the bombing of the Second World War could obliterate Schumacher's work. Gréber had to work within a different tradition. The ambition of Marseilles was to be as like Paris as possible. The grim reality was economic and political problems which made large-scale urban planning a virtual impossibility. It made the transition of nineteenth-century ideas of *l'urbanisme* to modern town planning exceptionally difficult. Indeed, Gréber did not try to produce a holistic plan of place and people. His major concern was the infrastructure which conditioned how efficiently the city "worked". What he found in the six months he was given to work on the plan in 1931, was a city which had grown up without overall planning[58]. The Vieux-Port and the New City were quite distinct. The city was moulded by its topography along the coastline from east to west, a line punctured by development emanating from the port which had created industrial areas on the periphery, especially to the north. The social consequences had not been planned and the result was extremely congested and densely populated inner areas. The Vieux-Port had become totally run down. Buildings remained standing only with the help of wooden props which extended into the already limited street space. There was much overcrowding, the worst quarters mostly occupied by immigrants. As for the New City, it had remained relatively unchanged since the nineteenth century. Gréber was conscious of the fact that Marseilles was "old-fashioned", yet neither the municipal administration nor the national framework of legislation gave him the means with which to modernise it. Nevertheless, his appointment was a turning point in the recognition that there was a new expertise developing in town planning which the city needed to utilise.

Gréber, like Schumacher, was a functionalist. His experience of preparing plans for the outer periphery of Paris had made him sensitive to the need to protect the peripheral areas of Marseilles. He envisaged the development of *cités-jardins*[59], open space and recreational areas on the city's outer periphery. As for the centre, he wanted to retrieve the dominance it had had in the past before it had become subject to congestion and overdevelopment. This was to be achieved mainly by widening and extending the major boulevards. At the same time, he sought more efficient ways of connecting the new docks in the north with the industrial areas in the north-east and south-east. Realigning and widening of central boulevards, building new circular routes connecting different parts of the city and planning open spaces on the periphery were his main practical concerns. There was little chance of building working-class housing. When the Marseilles municipality finally put in hand a survey of housing need in 1929 (when the French economy was at its inter-war peak), the shocking extent of overcrowding and poor conditions was revealed. The report recommended the immediate construction of 27 000 housing units and then subsequently, a programme of building 3660 per year[60]. Building on this scale was not carried out, though there was some social housing. It was not part of Gréber's brief. In essence, his commission was to make the city more efficient.

It was an impossible one to achieve. Gréber had seen his plan for Paris destroyed by the force of the private market. Marseilles was no more hospitable to planning practice. He was under no illusions about his chances of success. At the end of his Marseilles report, he wrote: "Chaque fois que cela nous a semblé possible, nous nous sommes contentés de la formule corrective, en améliorant sans bouleverser"[61]. (Each time that something seems possible, we are satisfied in applying some corrective formula in the hope of improving without destroying.) His plan was hailed by Henri Prost, architect planner recently appointed to deal with the problems of the Paris region, as the most complete exposition of the modernisation of French *urbanisme*. This accolade was not only recognition of the quality of Gréber's work, Prost had just produced his own plan for the Paris Region and he had a vested interest in promoting modern planning[62]. The outcomes for the people of Marseilles of Gréber's work were either negligible or actually negative. A decade later, a second plan for Marseilles was produced by Eugène Beaudouin, who tried to build on Gréber's work. It was implemented in the extraordinary circumstances of the early months of 1943 when war and German occupation cut through intractable problems. Some 20 000 people were forcibly ejected from the Vieux-Port to relieve congestion and two-thirds of the area closest to the docks were dynamited[63].

This, however, was during the war. It had not been envisaged by Gréber. War and politics, from its inception, played havoc with the essentially peaceful objectives of the modern town planning movement in its pioneering phases. This chapter began with the despair of Aby Warburg and the outrageous imperialistic behaviour at the International Exhibitions in Marseilles. The quality of European civilisation both appeared to be, and needed to be, challenged. Yet at the same time, in the period 1890–1930, the pioneers of modern town planning, even the less well-known ones, such as Schumacher and Gréber, working in their port cities rather than capital cities in the public eye, were busy giving form to another definition of civilisation. Schumacher was fortunate and Gréber unfortunate in what they achieved on the ground. But in their plans, they were both giving form to a new ideal of modern life in which cities were expected, not just to deliver the traditional elements of urban life, but also the framework of a national life which incorporated rural values of health, well being and morality. When Schumacher helped to organise the 1903 Exhibition of German civic progress, the majority of Germans were living for the first time in cities. By the time Gréber published his plan in 1933, almost 50% of the French population were to be found in cities. What life was to be like in the physical terms in the future was in the hands of these planners.

A major theme in this comparison of Hamburg and Marseilles has been how much the past and its cultural traditions influenced what happened in the future. Yet, in conclusion, it is necessary perhaps, to sound a word of caution. Differences and similarities are matters of degree. On a global scale, in the Euro-dominated world economy in the period 1890–1930, Hamburg and Marseilles shared as many similarities as differences. Even if their respective countries were on opposite sides in the First World War, it was an Euro-centred war in which the two ports played similar roles for their nation–states. The introduction of modern town planning to these cities may have occurred differently for reasons that were economic, political and cultural. But they both responded to the new activity of modern urban planning. Such planning was itself an internationally recognised activity. Its introduction in the first quarter of the twentieth century was part of a major cultural shift as European cities became more self-conscious about themselves, their image and identities. In both Hamburg and Marseilles, this period marked not only a greater awareness about the physical environment but also a growth of societies and institutions celebrating the cities past. There was a blossoming of local historical associations, local civic publications, museums devoted to the history of the city and greater efforts to preserve and enhance both the city's ancient fabric and natural resources[64]. These activities were both supported by the municipal council and by private individuals.

Thus, while it is possible to delineate many cultural differences in the civic consciousness of Hamburg and Marseilles, on a larger scale they shared many similarities. Anthony King has expanded on this point in his discussion of the culture of cities in a global context. He writes:

> When [cities] do *not* have their own historical museums, do *not* have self conscious "cultural policies", do *not* have historically-informed conservation policies . . . is the most accurate and telling comment on the uniqueness of their cultures and sub-cultures: the degree to which cultures are self-consciously "different" is an indication of how much they are the same[65].

For these two great European port cities, the self-conscious nurturing of their individual histories was an indication of the similar experiences they were sharing.

In Hamburg, the Kunsthalle, and in Marseilles, the International Exhibitions, had both been vehicles for articulating the new self-consciousness about civic culture to their citizens. The work of the first professional town planners drew on that inspiration and brought to it, as well, their own responses to the international town planning movement. Aby Warburg was right in one thing: the transmission of civilisation and civilised values from one generation to the next is a complicated process.

NOTES

1. EH Gombrich (1970) *Aby Warburg: an intellectual biography* London, Warburg Institute, University of London.
2. P Greenhalgh (1988) *Ephemeral Vistas: expositions universelles, great exhibitions and the World's Fairs 1851–1939* Manchester, Manchester University Press, 119.
3. M Roncayolo (1996) *Les Grammaires d'une Ville: essai sur la genèse des structures urbaines à Marseille* Paris, Éd. de l'École des hautes études en sciences sociales.
4. W Ashworth (1987) *A Short History of the International Economy* 4th edn London, Longmans.
5. N Ferguson (1995) *Paper and Iron: Hamburg business and politics in the era of inflation 1897–1927* Cambridge, Cambridge University Press, 1–92.
6. WH Sewell Jr (1985) *Structure and Mobility: the men and women of Marseille 1820–70* Cambridge, Cambridge University Press, 1–4.
7. Lindley's plan was amended by a prominent local architect, Gottfried Semper, who transformed it to accommodate aesthetic considerations. BK Ladd (1990) *Urban Planning and Civic Order in Germany 1860–1914* Cambridge, Mass., Harvard University Press, 80.
8. M Roncayolo (1996) "De la croissance libérale aux grands plans d'urbanisme" in J-L Pinol (ed.) *Atlas Historique des villes de France* Paris, Hachette Livre, 184.
9. P Graff (1996) "Les transformations haussmanniennes" in Pinol, *Atlas Historique*, 188.
10. C Georgel (ed.) (1994) *La Jeunesse des Musées: les musées de France au XIXe siècle* Paris.
11. B Lepetit (Eng. trans. 1994) *The Pre-industrial Urban System: France, 1740–1840* Cambridge, Cambridge University Press, 272–3.
12. For a discussion of *l'urbanisme* see F Choay (1965) *L'urbanisme, utopies and réalités. Une anthologie* Paris, Seuil; F Choay (1983) "Doctrines et Théories d'Urbanisme non progressistes" in G Duby (ed.) *Histoire de la France Urbaine*, Vol 4. *La Ville de l'âge industrielle* Paris, Seuil; G Bardet (12th edn 1990) *L'Urbanisme*, Paris, Presses Universitaires de France; J-L Harouel (1993) *L'embellissement des ville. L'urbanisme français au XVIIIe siècle*; J-L Harouel (1991 4th edn) *Histoire de l'urbanisme* Paris, Presses Universitaires de France; H Lefebvre (1970) *La révolution urbaine* Paris, Gallimard.
13. H Meller (1990) *Patrick Geddes: social evolutionist and city planner* London, Routledge, 156–74.
14. M Roncayolo (1996) *Les Grammaires d'une Ville*.
15. RJ Evans (1987) *Death in Hamburg: society and politics in the cholera years 1830–1910* Oxford, Clarendon Press.
16. RA Comfort (1966) *Revolutionary Hamburg: labor politics in the Early Weimar Republic* Stanford, Stanford University Press, 17.

184

17. D Geary (1998) "The Prussian Labour Movement 1871–1914" unpublished paper.

18. D Geary (1998) "Workers and Culture in Germany in the early 20th century" unpublished paper.

19. Faux, Cubells and Moy (eds) (1988) *Les Étrangers à Marseille, 1880–1939* Marseilles, Dir. des archive des Bouches-du-Rhône, 6.

20. Ville de Marseille (1935) *L'Œuvre Municipale, 1929–1935* Marseilles, Municipality, 435.

21. Comfort (1966) *Revolutionary Hamburg*, 61.

22. R Borruey (1992) "Réinventer une ville-port? Le cas de Marseille" in J-L Bonillo, A Donzel and M Fabre (eds) *Métropoles portuaires en Europe: Barcelone, Gênes, Hambourg, Liverpool, Marseille, Rotterdam* Bouches-du-Rhône, Éditions Parenthèses, 127–47.

23. In 1871, while Paris had been held by the Commune, the Marseilles Socialists, radicals and working classes had proclaimed a Communist Revolution. Throughout the 1870s, the extreme left was able to command considerable support in elections, up to 32% of the vote. Marseilles elected the first socialist deputy in France in 1881. C Barsotti (1984) *Le Music Hall Marseillaise, 1815–1950* Arles, Mesclun, 79.

24. E Spiteri (1987) "La permanence de l'opéra à Marseille" *Revue Marseille*, 149, 29–33.

25. P Chatelain (1937) "Le Domaine Communale: le Jardin Zoologique" *Revue Marseille* December, 11–16.

26. E Camau (1905) *Marseille au XXe siècle: tableau historique et statistique* Marseilles, Paul Rivat, 64–88.

27. J Pedro Lorente (1998) *Cathedrals of Urban Modernity: the first museums of contemporary art 1800–1930* Aldershot, Ashgate, 145–99.

28. Ladd (1990) *Urban Planning*, 246.

29. CH Gibbs (1981) 2nd edn *The Great Exhibition of 1851* London, HMSO.

30. V Plagemann (1997) "Die Anfänge der Hamburgischen Kunstsammlungen und die erste Kunsthalle" in U Schneede und H Leppien (eds) *Die Hamburger Kunsthalle: Bauten und Bilder* Leipzig, Seemann 9–20.

31. Prof. Dr Henning Bock (1998) "Provincial Museums in Germany in the 19th Century" unpublished paper for conference, "Art Museums, Past, Present and Future" Royal Academy of Arts, London, March 1998.

32. V Plagemann (1997) "'Wir wollen nicht ein Museum, das dasteht und wartet': Lichtwark al Kulturpolitiker" in Schneede and Leppien, *Die Hamburger Kunsthalle*, 38–40.

33. H Leppien (1997) "Alfred Lichtwark: der erste Direktor der Kuntshalle" in Schneede and Leppien, *Die Hamburger Kunsthalle*, 40–4.

34. O Christ (1997) "Vom Erbe Lichtwarks zum 'Museum einer Weltstadt': die Hamburger Kunsthalle unter Gustav Pauli" in Schneede and Leppien, *Die Hamburger Kunsthalle*, 78–92.

35. An account of all civic institutions is to be found in Ville de Marseille (1935) *L'Œuvre Municipale, 1929–1935* Marseilles, Municipality.

36. RD Mandell (1967) *Paris 1900: the Great World's Fair* Toronto, University of Toronto Press.

37. Greenhalgh (1988) *Ephemeral Vistas*, pp. 3–27.

38. N Harris, W de Wit, J Gilbert and RW Rydell (eds) (1993) *Grand Illusions: Chicago's World Fair of 1893* Chicago, Chicago Historical Society.

39. Rapport Général by MC Bénard (1906) *Exposition Coloniale de Marseille* Marseilles, Section internationale d'Océanographie de Pêches maritimes et des Produits de la Mer, 159.

40. Greenhalgh (1988) *Ephemeral Vistas*, 85.

41. Greenhalgh (1988) *Ephemeral Vistas*, 95.

42. A Musée de Beaux-Arts had been located in this Chateau since 1863. It was later to include the Musée d'Archéologie.

43. Guide to the exposition *Marseille au XIXe siècle* March–July 1993, Éditions Réunions de Musées Nationaux, Paris.

44. A Lees (1985) *Cities Perceived: urban society in European and American thought, 1820–1940* Manchester, Manchester University Press, 240.

45. Meller (1990) *Patrick Geddes*, 175–7.

46. D Calabi (1996) "Marcel Poëte: pioneer of 'l'urbanisme' and defender of l'histoire des villes'" *Planning Perspectives*, 11, 4, 413–36.

47. F Schumacher (1935) *Stufen des Lebens: Erinnerungen eines Baumeister* Stuttgart, Deutsche Verlags-Anstalt.

48. A Lortie (1994) "Jacques Gréber: les plans pour Philadelphie, 1917 et Marseille, 1933" in J Dethier and A Guiheux (eds) *La Ville, art et architecture en Europe, 1870–1993* published on the occasion of the exhibition *La Ville* Feb.–May 1994, Paris, Centre Georges Pompidou, 161.

49. He had also won the competition to provide an extension plan for Lille.

50. H Frank (1994) "Fritz Schumacher 1869–1947: Hambourg et Cologne" in Dethier and Guiheux, *La Ville*, 144–5.

51. He wrote two books with a spiritual approach: *The Language of Art* and *The Spirit of Architecture*.

52. M Steenhuis (1997) "Paris 1934: Plan d'Aménagement de la Région Parisienne" in K Bosma and H Hellinga (eds) *Mastering the City: North-European city planning 1900–2000* Vol II, Rotterdam, NAI Publishers/The Hague, EFL Publications, 226–7.

53. K Bosma and H Hellinga (1997) "German Urban Planning: between urban periphery and region" in *Mastering the City*, 63–4.

54. S Mulder (1997) "Cologne 1923: Generalsiedlungsplan" in Bosma and Hellinga, *Mastering the City*, 192–9.

55. F Schumacher (1932, repr. 1984) *Das Werden einer Wohnstadt: Bilder aus dem neuen Hamburg* Hamburgische, Hausbibliothek.

56. Review of the Schumacher Exhibition, Hamburg in *Frankfurter Allgemeine Zeitung*, 11th June 1994.

57. M Casciato (1996) *The Amsterdam School* Rotterdam, OIO Publishers.

58. R Balhady (1992) "Le Plan Gréber et Marseille: rencontre d'une ville et d'un urbanisme" *Revue Marseille*, 164, 81–5.

59. See Chapter 3.

60. *L'Œuvre Municipale 1929–35*, 266.

61. Lortie (1994) "Jacques Gréber", 161.

62. Steenhuis (1997) "Paris 1934", 267.

63. S Crane (1999) "Deciding when to draw the line: urban strategies and the Vieux-Port of Marseille" unpublished paper, Urban History Conference, Oxford, March 1999.

64. The Musée du Vieux Marseille was housed in the building erected in the Parc Chanot for the 1922 Exposition.

65. A King (1991) "The Global, the Urban, and the World" in AD King (ed) *Culture, Globalisation and the World System*, Basingstoke, Macmillan, 149.

SEASIDE RESORTS BEFORE AND AFTER THE FIRST WORLD WAR: THE SURVIVAL STRATEGIES OF BLACKPOOL AND NICE

INTRODUCTION

Seaside resorts are something of an enigma in the history of European urbanisation. In many respects, they were the "new towns" of an industrialising continent. The successful ones grew rapidly in the wake of the railway. Yet the management of this growth followed patterns unlike that in any other kind of town. Their purpose was to provide leisure facilities and entertainment, not to their resident population, but to the endless waves of visitors, arriving each "season". As they grew, they had to remain attractive. People did not come to the seaside just because it was there. They came to the seaside resort to be amused and entertained. Seaside resorts were thus in the business of raising and meeting expectations. They were particularly sensitive to changes in fashion and taste, the bedrock of popular culture. This had two important consequences. First, the implications of growth on the built environment and the whole relationship of town and its natural setting were of prime importance. Seaside resorts had to pioneer ways of managing urbanisation without destroying the natural features which drew people to them in the first place.

Second, to be successful, resorts had to be in the forefront of cultural change. The latest technology as applied to leisure, the most up-to-date manifestations of popular and mainstream culture were a vital component of their ability to attract. And yet it was not the only one. As they grew, they built their success on an image of their "traditional" role, a role which had been established before the coming of the railways, when their original sources of visitors had been identified. Their survival depended on a reinterpretation: the honing of "traditions" and the trumpeting of "modernity", above all, the need to remain attractive to each new generation. The origins of Nice and Blackpool as seaside resorts could not have been more different. Nice had grown to prosperity as the winter resort of the aristocracy and upper classes of Europe; Blackpool was the favourite summer destination of Britain's northern working class, especially the factory workers of Lancashire, the stormtroopers of the Industrial Revolution. Yet, in practice, both towns had also depended on middle class and bourgeois visitors who provided a degree of stability in the market. Both towns had grown considerably by the end of the nineteenth century. Blackpool's resident population was about 50 000 in 1900 and the number of annual visitors had reached about 3 million. Nice was always larger as it grew to serve as the administrative capital of its region. It had about 100 000 permanent residents in 1900 and about a extra 100 000 living *en villégiature* during the winter season.

Yet despite all these contrasts, both resorts were united by one thing: the challenge of sustaining their success in the greatly different social conditions of the twentieth century. In the period 1900 to 1940, the European world was convulsed by the consequences of world war, economic depression and massive social and political changes. The speeding up of technological change induced by the war and the application of inventions to the pursuit of leisure, combined with social and political change, left the resorts with no option. They had to invest in change or decline. There was, however, a paradox: change for the future had to emanate out of the "traditions" of the past. The most successful seaside resorts, such as Blackpool and Nice, had established cultures and traditions on which their image was based. Many of these were the type of nineteenth-century "invented traditions" which have been identified by Hobsbawm and Ranger. They were both national and international, part of the "spirit of the age", and local and specific. Between the 1880s and the First World War, the cultural hegemony of the Euro-dominated world was a time, Ranger writes "of a great flowering of European invented tradition – ecclesiastical, educational, military, republican, monarchi-cal"[1]. Imperial London and Republican Paris of the Belle Époque were the centres of this universe.

Both Blackpool and Nice drew on these models in the construction of their own images as successful seaside resorts. The Paris Exhibitions of 1889 and 1900 particularly were influential in setting trends, catering for all social levels, with high culture and social events for the upper classes and popular amusements for the masses (in 1889, the Tour Eiffel and in 1900, the massive funfair)[2]. Class, gender and ethnicity were subsumed in an imperialistic European culture which provided the framework which everyone understood. At a local level, both Blackpool and Nice had established their own traditions which supplemented this European framework. Blackpool was geared to a mass market and invented a tradition of endless sources of amusement and entertainment which could be enjoyed at will by passers by, at any time[3]. To prolong the season, the idea of Blackpool's illuminations of the seaside esplanade was invented, a new tradition which, invented just before the First World War, depended on the new technology of electricity[4]. Nice had had a similar aim in the last decades of the nineteenth century of keeping visitors for as long as possible, but with a different market in mind. The higher social classes, wintering in Nice, needed more personal service. The Nice Carnival, the *mardi gras*, a sequence of organised entertainments for the boring months after Christmas, was reinvented in 1873. A committee of Fêtes was set up which planned various activities to give the Nice Carnival an attractiveness to affluent visitors and this "tradition" worked very well for subsequent decades.

In the first half of the twentieth century, however, certainties about the continuing appeal of such "traditions" were disappearing. The market for seaside resorts was changing, especially in the inter-war period. Annual holidays as opposed to day trips became the norm for the working classes and more of them than ever before became entitled to annual leave[5]. The numbers and wealth of European aristocracy, on the other hand, were much depleted particularly after the First World War. Here, Blackpool was winning and Nice losing. But there were other factors. The inter-war period particularly, marked the beginning of a new fashion for the sun, sea swimming, outdoor exercise and relaxed social behaviour[6]. This was to transform Nice into a summer as well as a winter resort, serving a different market. What united both resorts was their determination to stay abreast of fashion, even to shape it. In doing so they had to address head-on those factors transforming urban life everywhere. Walter Benjamin, working and writing in the 1920s, has given us some of the most significant insights into cities and the processes of cultural change. His great, fragmented work, *Passagenarbeit* was focused on Paris, but, in 1924, he visited Naples. Here he was to make those observations of place and people which, some commentators assert, inform the basis of his theories on cultural change and modernity[7]. Naples was more than a seaside resort, but it shared some of the characteristics, at least, of Nice. It is hard to imagine Walter Benjamin visiting Blackpool. The high seriousness of Benjamin's quest for understanding modern society seems alien to Blackpool's image of a town dedicated to the pursuit of raucous good humour. That, however, is merely an indication of the power of image. Benjamin's insights into the social consequences of modernity provide a corrective to the image of all seaside resorts, especially the successful ones such as Blackpool and Nice.

The power of national and international, mobile capital, invested in any profitable enterprise, was to transform not only work patterns but leisure provisions as well. The fragmentation of leisure pursuits, the alienation of the individual, the "porosity" of city life as "modern" forms of exploitation were filtered through the flotsam and jetsam of the old[8], were all aspects of the urban experience of seaside resorts which were exaggerated by their very nature. From the 1890s, if not before, the capitalisation of amusements in both Nice and Blackpool drew on sources well beyond the confines of the towns themselves. Both resorts experienced rapid and intensive development from the 1880s, regardless of their former histories. The turning point for Nice was the international exposition it mounted in 1884. In the previous decade, new efforts had been made to turn Nice from a *villégiature* for the rich and health conscious, wishing to winter peacefully in the sunshine, to an attractive venue for the *beau monde* who came to see and be seen[9]. The Promenade des Anglais gained greater significance as the location of more and more facilities and, of course, itself was remodelled to provide the backdrop for the endless strolling of the leisured classes at the key moments of the day. The 1884

Exposition, however, was even more ambitious. It was a claim by the Niçois to regional status, national importance and high culture. Located in a huge building and containing pavilions from many places in the Mediterranean, including one from Algeria, the exposition had a twofold purpose. It was used to promote the city as an elegant and attractive venue for visitors and at the same time, emphasised its regional significance by displays of industry and agriculture. It was in the business of maximising all profitable enterprise[10].

Blackpool, for all its differences in climate and regional significance, was going down the same path. The acquisition of its famous Tower in the 1890s, in imitation of the Tour Eiffel, was an enterprise which required external capital. By the turn of the century, the capitalisation of its hotel accommodation had led to the need to find markets outside that of the holiday-makers. Blackpool became a conference centre. By the turn of the century, it was attracting a long list of regular conference visitors, which sustained the larger hotels, themselves the fruit of inward invest-ment in the town. The interaction of economic and social factors in both Blackpool and Nice had produced complex results. The process of "modernising" to meet new demands was confusing. In both places there is a jostling between "image" and "reality", which defies simple analysis. Both were full of the marginal people whom Benjamin used to illustrate his insights: the street performers, musicians, organ-grinders, puppeteers, street vendors, billboard men, the purveyors of ice cream. In both, there were dramatic fluctuations between survival and destitution for those people dependent on the whims of passing visitors.

Both places were also in the grip of powerful lobbies. In Nice, an Italian mafia appeared to coexist with another strand, politicians of outstanding calibre (in the inter-war period, Jean Médecin) dedicated to public service and the town's welfare. In Blackpool, public and private enterprise co-existed and worked in a complicated fugue of activity, sometimes co-operating, sometimes antagonistic. Again, hints of corruption surfaced from time to time Thus both places shared, for all their differences, similar challenges in the period following the First World War. They had to sustain a heavily capitalised economic base or fall into dramatic decline. They had to sustain growth without destroying the quality of the physical environ-ment. They had to find the administrative will and skill to steer their towns, heavily dependent on fashion and popular culture, through a period when both were changing fast. This chapter is devoted to an analysis of how they did it.

The Natural Environment of the Seaside Resort

The place to start, perhaps, is with the natural environment. The *raison d'être* of a seaside resort is its natural location. The contrast between the natural endowments of Blackpool and Nice could not have been more extreme. In the very origins of the town of Blackpool in the late eighteenth century, visitors may have come for the quality of the air and the hardy (or indeed, the sick) for a little

Figure 5.1 *Blackpool in the inter-war period* [Map drawn by Chris Lewis]

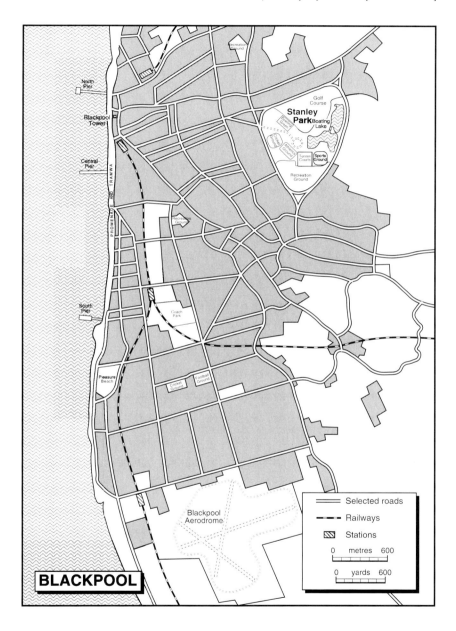

Figure 5.2 *Expansion of Nice in the inter-war years* [Map drawn by Chris Lewis]

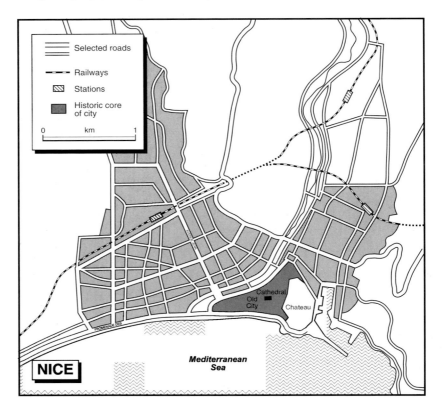

sea bathing for health reasons (with the use of bathing machines). However, John Walton in his work on the town, has no illusions about the importance of Nature to the town's subsequent success.

> The coastline lacked scenic grandeur . . . The Fylde countryside nearby, too, was flat and lacked objects of interest for the cultivated visitor . . . In most respects, then, Blackpool was disadvantaged by its lack of natural amenities . . . What it did have, however, was a lively and boisterous sea, which came right up to the houses on the front; and once it had been safely contained behind sea defences, it was an unalloyed boon in attracting working class visitors. Spray blew across the promenade at high tide even in the centre of the amusement district, and provided an added entertainment for the growing band of late-Victorian visitors who would not have dreamed of bathing, but who derived enormous pleasure from watching the sea in dangerous mood[11].

Blackpool's summer season was short. It varied between six to nine weeks, depending on the timing of the holiday periods allowed to the Lancashire workers. Yet even in the shortest season, the weather could not be guaranteed to be either sunny or warm. The 6 miles of sandy beach were a special resource on the sunny days. Blackpool was bracing. It depended on its location to survive but its natural environment had a wildness which the frequent incidence of high winds in the winter months merely underlined. The challenge for the town and its entrepreneurs was to construct the attractions which would supplement the meagreness of nature. By the late Victorian period, there were three piers, the Raikes Hall Gardens and the Winter Gardens, and the Tower as major attractions, and many smaller ones besides[12]. These facilities offered holiday-makers a refuge where they could spend the day, or part of a day, an essential requirement for their pleasure since many stayed in the cheap accommodation of boarding houses which was not available to them during the day. Yet not all the holiday-makers were working class. Blackpool had a loyal following among the middle classes, especially those born and brought up in Lancashire. T.H. Mawson, landscape architect and town planner, who was later to be commissioned to work on the town, was among these. He wrote of all his commissions, Blackpool appealed to him most. "The fact that I am a Lancashire man may account for this preference. Blackpool's unbroken stretch of golden sand, its bracing air, and the kaleidoscope gaiety of its mile of promenade, combine to weave a spell of attraction"[13].

The contrast with Nice is absolute. Practically every writer or visitor to the Côte d'Azur waxes lyrical about the natural beauty of its location. "Nice," wrote one nineteenth-century commentator,

> et c'est là charme suprême, Nice n'est point une ville, c'est un grand parc, où les plus splendides palais disparaissent dans des bosquets d'orangers, sous des touffes de roses. Nice n'est pas plus dans ses rues ombragées que sur la pente de ses collines ou dans l'ombre de ses vallées; on ne voit ni où elle commence ni où elle finit; c'est un immense jardin où chacun semble avoir planté sa tente au hasard, sûr de trouver, sur n'importe quel point de ce paradis terrestre, la santé et le bonheur[14].
>
> [Nice, and that is its supreme charm, Nice is not a town, it is a great park, where splendid palaces disappear in orange groves, beneath clumps of roses. Nice is not more in its shady streets than on the slopes of the hills which give shade to its valleys: one cannot see where it begins or where it finishes; it is an immense garden where everyone seems to have sited his tent by chance, certain of finding, no matter where in this earthly paradise, health and happiness]

Nice, gushed the guidebooks, was an earthly paradise, overwhelmed by the superabundance of a gentle Nature. The 1884 Exposition building was specially located on an elevated site so that visitors could appreciate the view of the whole city, surrounded by its magnificent ring of mountains. Then one could see the number of villas at different levels in the midst of their orange groves and flowers and finally, at the end of the view, the huge expanse of sea and the sky which was always blue[15]. The climate was the final gift: warm, sunny and pleasant in the winter months. In place of Blackpool's fiery promenade was the balmy Promenade des Anglais, its lines of palm trees barely swaying in the lightest breeze; the sea, a shining azure blue. Here, though, Blackpool did have a tiny advantage: the golden sand instead of the stony shingle of Nice's town beach, but then Nice was not geared to the needs of children. Preservation of the natural environment was to become an ever greater problem with urban growth. By the turn of the century, the areas devoted to hotels and facilities for visitors had created new urban areas well beyond the "Old" Nice of the fishing port and the hillsides had become the sites for some of the largest hotels.

Such contrasts would appear to make the comparison of these two resorts unfeasible. Yet both were united by a realisation that they had to preserve the "natural" elements of their environment in such a way as they would continue to attract visitors. Only towards the end of the twentieth century have European cities, far away from the seaside, begun to find, in the wake of de-industrialisation, that their survival in the future depends on establishing the image that they are pleasant places to be. Nice and Blackpool have been doing this for two hundred years. It was a process though, that had to be learnt. As in all growing towns of the nineteenth century, the first tasks were the problems of public health and the provision of essential services. Here the different traditions of Britain and France influenced what was done. The legislative framework in Britain, the Public Health Acts of 1848 and 1875 had encouraged an awareness of the need for local authorities to provide a pure water supply. Blackpool acquired, in the 1870s, that watchdog of the nineteenth-century city, a Medical Officer of Health. He was to fight a long battle raising standards of public health in order to avoid epidemics, such as the smallpox epidemic in nearby Southport in 1876, which ruined "the season" there[16]. The institution of compulsory local bye-laws for the notification of infectious diseases and, in the 1890s, the institution of better drainage systems and a pure water supply provided the basic modicum of modern standards of public health[17].

In Blackpool, the key issue of building regulations, though, was another matter. There had been national legislation since 1875 defining standards of building and regulating levels considered to constitute overcrowding. In a seaside resort like Blackpool, with its short season and need to accommodate large numbers of working-class visitors, dividing lines between what was healthy and what was not, were difficult and interpretation of regulations was brokered by economic and cultural parameters. Blackpool's special feature was to provide working-class holiday-makers with large numbers of cheap boarding houses, serviced by a formidable army of landladies. Boarding houses were ordinary homes which housed visitors in the summer months as if they were lodgers (a well-established nineteenth-century method of finding the money for the rent). The landladies' own families had to be accommodated in odd places, enduring the worst conditions, while the rest of the house, in the season, was turned over to providing bedspace for visitors[18]. While these visitors were also prepared to put up with great discomfort, often groups of strangers sharing the same room (divided by a sheet hung on a line across the room) and multiple occupancy of beds were commonplace, no public regulations proved effective. But by the twentieth century, cultural shifts and growing expectations of comfort put an end to these ruses for maximising income. Visitors were no longer prepared to "make do" for the duration of their holidays. Many with greater sources of income had already made the move to better appointed lodging houses or hotel accommodation before the war, though the boarding house landladies were still an important resource for the town as a whole.

In Nice, the move to greater levels of public health administration was slower. The legal framework was centrally developed but much depended on local initiative to improve the quality of local services. Baron Haussmann, fresh from his labours in modernising Paris in the 1850s and 1860s, retired to Nice. He did not, however, live in the old town[19]. He moved to a villa in the hills, away from sources of contamination in the environment. Nobody expected the town to invest heavily in public services (and raise local taxes to do it), least of all the Niçois themselves. There were actually two water supplies instituted: one for the rich visitors and one from the local river, known to be contaminated, for the residents of the old town. In Nice, there was never enough water and this remained the case until the First World War. Only in the decade before the war had the local authorities instituted a new drainage system, essential with the growth of the town, especially in summer. In fact, the conditions in Nice in the summer, when the heat exacerbated the problems caused by an insufficient water supply and inadequate drainage system, made it a most unsuitable place to be on health grounds. Haug's study of Nice catalogues the challenge facing the local authorities as the numbers of visitors mounted but also, crucially, the numbers of permanent residents grew at the end of the nineteenth century.

Managing growth without destroying the attractiveness of the urban environment was thus an activity which both Blackpool and Nice had approached in a somewhat desultory fashion, guided by the framework of national legislation in their different countries. This cavalier approach became impossible in the twentieth century with increasing legislation, some directly concerned with a new awareness of the need for town planning and the growing expectations of visitors who wanted higher standards of hygiene and comfort. The war, in many ways, produced a cultural turning point. All "normal" expectations of social life, including the taking of holidays, were suspended and even if, as in the case of Blackpool, people did manage to escape for a short break there and the resort actually thrived during wartime, there were few imperatives to develop new attractions. There was a muting of aggressive image marketing and both resorts did what they could for the war effort[20]. Endowed with large hotels and situated a long way from enemy action, both were used for the accommodation of troops on training exercises and especially for the recuperation of invalided troops. The end of the First World War and the prospect of restoring the holiday trade to its former importance made both towns more self-conscious of the quality of public services and the amenities they offered. The war had had particularly adverse effects on Nice and its region. It was hit by severe shortages of vital necessities, including food, as the French economy crumbled under the strain of sustaining the war effort and many of its local industries, such as the perfumeries, which were luxury trades, suffered dramatic decline in demand. On the return to peace, both resorts needed to readjust and realign to a post-war world.

This realignment was multi-faceted. It included categorical imperatives such as new legislation emanating from central government on public health, transport and the management of the growth of towns; the rising aspirations of the working classes and the changes in technology and fashion. Just as Nice had suffered more than Blackpool during the war, it was also forced to confront the changed post-war circumstances more immediately. Blackpool was able to coast back to peace-time circumstances, full of happy holiday-makers from the North West enjoying the restocking boom after the war which brought much employment. For Blackpool, the moment of truth was to come in 1921 with a national slump and the first signs of the collapse of Britain's basic staple industries: coal mining, ship building and textiles, which was to be the dominant social experience of Britain in the inter-war period. Nice had to face the immediate problems of its large luxury hotels in dire need of refurbishment after use as troop accommodation, yet with little hope that the former visitors, who had once enjoyed their luxuries, coming back in great numbers. At the same time, the depression of local trades and industries led to industrial unrest and a wave of strikes. For Nice there was no similarly large cushion of post-war holiday-makers eager to enjoy the peace right away.

In the 1920s both resorts had to face the vicissitudes of the economic fortunes of their regions. Yet in the face of these difficulties, they both recreated their image as centres of pleasure and entertainment and sustained their ability to draw ever more visitors. They were to do this guided by the self-conscious transmutation of their cultural image to include a sense of modernity. The old "traditions" were recast. In the 1920s, both resorts developed the institutions and images to replace those which had served them so well in the preceding half century. By the end of the decade, both had acquired the new image for the next half century. In Blackpool's case, it was a refinement and development of the mass entertainment industry and a concerted effort to improve the physical appearance of the town. For Nice, there was the major transformation of emphasis from winter to summer with the beginning of a summer holiday season from 1920 and the orderly development of the town which grew rapidly in this period, acquiring many examples of Modernist architecture in apartments and villas. The framework for both towns was the post-war legislation on urban development. In Britain, the "Homes for Heroes" election campaign of Lloyd George was followed by the Housing and Town Planning Act of 1919 and the Housing Act of 1923. In France, there were the laws of 1919 and 1924 which encouraged all towns to draw up "un plan d'aménagement, d'embellissement et d'extension". Neither Blackpool nor Nice leapt into action to do very much at first, since much of this legislation depended on availability of resources and administration which needed to be developed. There was, however, a shift in perception of what was required, and as seaside resorts needing to attract people, both towns began a much more directed process of growth. The next sections of this chapter will be devoted to exploring how the municipal governments of Blackpool and Nice responded to the challenges.

BLACKPOOL AND ITS MUNICIPAL GOVERNMENT IN THE 1920S

On the 2nd January 1920, the key figure of Blackpool's local administration, the Borough Treasurer, William Bateson, made a speech on the prospects of a new era at Blackpool. He said:

> Blackpool cannot afford to settle on its lees; it must either go forward or go back. There is no such thing as standing still in the life of a town so pre-eminently constituted to afford life, health, vigour and pleasure to millions . . . Progress is its motto as well as a law of life, and the supreme aim of our Governors should be to initiate, stimulate and carry out a broad and statesmanlike scheme of development on the best possible lines[21].

These were astonishing words from a treasurer, especially one answerable to the ratepayers, in a municipal borough. Blackpool's municipal council was to embark in the 1920s on a period of remarkable entrepreneurism. In the course of the 1920s, the physical environment of the town was to be transformed and the money was borrowed to pay for it. The town council took on a greater role in resort development, both of the physical environment and social activities.

While elsewhere in Britain, the inter-war period is seen as a moment of hesitation, if not decline, in the role of local government in many municipalities, in Blackpool, there was little faltering. The revolution in attitudes to local government in the late Victorian period, epitomised by the business man politician, Joseph Chamberlain in Birmingham and the professional city manager, Sir James Marrick in Glasgow, had depended on charismatic figures at the head of powerful middle-class political lobbies in major provincial cities. Blackpool's modest scale and local entrepreneurship meant that the local council essentially, in the half century before the First World War, acted as a back-up authority to initiatives coming from elsewhere. In the 1920s, this was all to change and Blackpool has its town council to thank for the efforts which were put into modernising and controlling the future development of the resort[22]. There was no one particularly outstanding personality responsible for this achievement. Of key importance were the councillors and aldermen drawn from the ranks of local entrepreneurs, and the professional and permanent borough officials, particularly the leading officials: the Borough Treasurer, Surveyor and Engineer, and the Borough Landscape Gardener. Above all, there were the officials in charge of the municipal services of local government established in the late Victorian period: gas, water and electricity, transport and roads, public health and housing, education and leisure.

In all these areas, the experience of the First World War, and the rising expectations after it, led to a quantum leap in the role of Blackpool's Town Council, even though resources were still limited and administrative structures undeveloped. What reinforced this was the relative lack of importance of class politics at the local level. The needs of sustaining an attractive resort took priority over the needs of the residents. The Labour Party might have held its conferences in Blackpool annually, but the local labour movement did not fight for control of the local council. Unemployment and pay and conditions for those in work were the main targets of the movement and as an employer, in its municipal services, the town council faced strikes from its workers over the decade. Yet the council itself could credibly sustain the belief that it was the voice of the people of Blackpool. In 1920, the *Blackpool Gazette* and the *Blackpool Herald* were merged to become the *Blackpool Gazette and Herald*. In its new guise, it became the mouthpiece of municipal Progressivism and the major propaganda machine of local government. Its reports presented an upbeat version of Blackpool's corporate identity. A seaside resort was a business[23].

What the town council wanted to do required the framework of national legislation for its implementation. Lloyd George's "khaki" election of 1918 and the "Home for Heroes" campaign got a mute response from the Blackpool Town Council. Homes were capital-intensive and did not bring in great rewards. Yet the far less publicised Housing and Town Planning Act of 1919 was something much more useful. Under the very first Housing and Town Planning Act of 1909, town extension schemes (the first objects of town planning legislation) were regulated by the Local Government Board. By 1919, there was a new Ministry of Health established with a full-time Chief Planning Inspector, George Pepler. Pepler was closely in touch with Patrick Abercrombie, Professor of Civic Design at Liverpool, the Chair especially funded in 1908 by Lord Leverhulme for the promotion of town planning[24]. It was still not altogether clear what town planning actually was at this time. Pepler and Abercrombie had the idea that it was the pursuit of the coherent manipulation of the physical environment in pursuit of efficiency and beauty.

Such an interpretation exactly suited Blackpool. An article appeared in the *Blackpool Gazette and Herald* in 1920 by a Mr Ernest Lawson entitled "Town Planning for Blackpool". Lawson suggested a complete redevelopment of the town. While other town councils discussed it, Blackpool's decided to act. Lawson had also named one of the most successful English firms able to carry out town planning work: T.H. Mawson and Sons. Mawson was the founder of the new discipline of Landscape Architecture, a subject he had laid out in his influential book, *Civic Art: studies in town planning, parks, boulevards and open spaces* (1911) and a member of the Department of Civic Design at the University of Liverpool[25]. He was at the end of a long and illustrious career that had started in the Potteries redesigning the public parks of the Five Towns. His fame had grown and he had been given commissions all over the world. A recent demand for his services had come from Canada where he was employed to design public areas for the government and plan at least five university campuses in different towns. Most prestigious of all, he had been employed by the King of Greece to work on parks, gardens and the town development of Athens, the ultimate test for a twentieth-century planner trained in the classical school. Blackpool had to have the best.

Mawson recounts in his autobiography that the prospect of planning the future of Blackpool was, in all the town planning work he had dreamed of, the project that excited him most[26]. The town was expanding more rapidly in the first two decades of the century than most towns in the UK and a vast residential population was settling within the boundaries of the town. The Mayor and town council all agreed that a new physical layout of the town was a top priority. Canvassing support for this in 1920, the Mayor was reported in the local press as saying:

> to his mind Blackpool was on the threshold of greater prosperity than it had hitherto known. If the council was indifferent to the prospects ahead it would be criminal to remain idle and not take action . . . They saw the higgledy piggledy condition of the town today, the narrow streets and lack of recreation grounds . . . They [council and ratepayers] must widen their streets, prepare a park and look to the future. They must not only prepare for the visitors but look to the residential portion of the borough [hear hear][27].

His last comment was significant. It was new for Blackpool Town Council to worry about the provision of services for the resident population. The Mayor had also mentioned two projects, the provision of open space for recreation and the infrastructure needed for urban expansion, which were potentially the most costly. He was able to take the council and the people along with him in these plans as careful preparations had been made to make sure that these developments would be income earning, at least the development of the open space. Blackpool's Town Council prided itself on having the lowest rates in the country since its services were mainly income earning. It became one of the first British towns to adopt modern town planning. It was certainly the first seaside resort to do so.

There was a degree of serendipidity in Blackpool reaching this point, a "modernisation" of an established role. The town council recognised that there needed to be more facilities available to visitors than those conceived of in the late nineteenth century. Essentially, the late Victorian form of the town had been established by a combination of private enterprise and public investment (especially in the decade preceding the granting of municipal status to Blackpool in 1876) and the rate-payers did not suffer as the investment paid off, relieving the rates of the debt burden. What was different in the 1920s was the scale of the proposed changes and the guidance offered by a framework of national legislation. What was also different was the growing recognition of the need to serve the local community of Blackpool residents as well as the visitors. The numbers of residents

Figure 5.3 *Photo of main entrance of Stanley Park* [By permission of Blackpool Borough Council]

was growing rapidly in the 1920s as the expansion of the municipal boundaries brought the developing retirement settlements within the town's jurisdiction. Municipal progress was not now just a matter of keeping the punters happy and the coffers of the entrepreneurs full. The town needed to respond to an ideal of urban life which was being articulated elsewhere. Modernising Blackpool was thus a more complicated business than developing the latest entertainment facilities.

It was in this context that the town council turned to the prospect of modern town planning. Typically Mawson got the contract for Stanley Park in July 1922, through the good offices of his most influential client, Lord Leverhulme. Leverhulme invited Blackpool's Town Clerk and the Borough Engineer to spend a weekend at his bungalow at Rivington Pike, situated in climatic conditions very similar to those of Blackpool (especially the strong winds) which Mawson had successfully landscaped for him. Blackpool's Stanley Park was an area of 256 acres, strategically located less than 2 miles from the seafront. Mawson knew then that his foot was in the door for gaining a commission for the redevelopment of the whole town. As he put it: "because it was inevitable that the periphery of the park and the sub-division of the residential areas would call for the application of town-planning principles, and this proved to be the case"[28]. He was asked to plan a new South Shore extension, which included recasting the shape of the Promenade in this direction and developing a small building estate (which he liked to think had

Figure 5.4 Drawing of the Rose Garden, Stanley Park [By permission of Blackpool Borough Council]

Figure 5.5 Drawing of the Italian Garden, Stanley Park [By permission of Blackpool Borough Council]

the appearance of a "garden city") to pay for the improvements. He laid out the new settlement with the fronts of the houses facing the railway track, each framed by its little garden so that visitors would see what a paradise they were coming to. As always, Blackpool's town planning was geared both to its image and the need to be self-supporting. Even Stanley Park was divided into five sections for development, the town council offering £20 000 a year for the work and gaining revenue from the completed sections. (It made more money from the start than expected.)

With such a compliant authority, Mawson let his imagination soar and he produced a plan for the redevelopment of the town centre as a magnificent square, in a Beaux-Arts classical style, though to build it would necessitate the removal of the gas and electricity works and the setting back of the Central Railway station. The Town Council could not countenance that. Yet by the end of the 1920s, Blackpool had become one of the most highly planned urban environments in Britain. A further Extension Bill was launched in 1928 with an estimated cost of a further £505 000[29]. By this time, millions had been spent on the Promenade and South Shore improvement schemes, recreation grounds and parks, open-air and covered swimming baths, golf courses, an aerodrome, street improvements, infrastructure (gas, water, sewerage, electricity) for new residential development and much more, including public transport and Blackpool's tram and bus services. To take the ratepayers along with them, the Town Council kept to business principles for new developments, thus keeping the rates low. They also had to sustain the flow of visitors. Here was the other challenge of "modernisation": how to sell the new attractions to potential visitors. Once again, well-established traditions were to be completely recast. Blackpool depended on the textile towns of Lancashire for its major support. These towns still had their "Wakes Weeks" when the mills closed down and the whole town decamped to Blackpool[30]. Yet the massive expenditure on urban redevelopment made it vital to attract even more visitors. Blackpool set about applying new technology to its well-established forms of entertainment.

Over the decade, images of the Paris Exhibition of 1900 became very faint and in its place, was the model of America. In 1928, the Great Wheel was dismantled to be replaced by funfair-style entertainment (there was an amalgamation of the Tower and Winter Gardens Companies)[31]. But the transition was not total and, in any case, Blackpool developers always had a clear understanding of their local market. France still led the world in terms of film production, cars and the development of the aeroplane. Blackpool acquired nine cinemas to supplement the theatres and live pier entertainment which still continued. It made sure that new crazes such as dance halls were prolifically provided while still looking at older forms of cultural expression. In 1924, the town council embarked on the organisation of Blackpool's first carnival which, in many respects, gives a flavour of Blackpool's cultural transition to its version of "modernity". Thus, 1923 had seen the first Minority Government of the Labour Party and in the summer of 1924, the great Empire Exhibition in London. Would the Lancashire working classes start looking further afield for their holidays? Most working-class people of either sex

Figure 5.7 Photo of Blackpool's Carnival 1923 (damaged on right) [By permission of Blackpool Borough Council]

went to the cinema every week, sometimes more often, where they were fed with make-believe images of the luxurious lifestyles of the very rich. Paradise became, not Blackpool, but the Côte d'Azur. Why not bring the attractions of Nice to Blackpool? Why not replicate the Nice Carnival? Blackpool municipality arranged for artisans from Nice to come to Blackpool to advise and help build the floats for Blackpool's Carnival. Nice's Carnival was the most famous in Europe. Nice had the image of the resort of the rich and famous. Blackpool was in the business of creating fantasy[32].

Yet the town council was also building on well-established Lancashire traditions. Street processions at holiday times or to mark particular occasions were a nineteenth-century practice well understood by the crowds[33]. In Blackpool's Carnival procession, the Mayors of many local towns (Preston, Wigan, Widnes, St Helens, Accrington, Southport and Oldham) were given a special role and the Lord Mayor and Lady Mayoress of Manchester were presented to King Carnival (Doodles). There were also deputations from Scarborough, Bridlington, Morecambe and elsewhere to see if Blackpool had invented a new tradition which could be emulated. M. Auguste Guano, manager of the Nice firm hired to construct the tableau, saw a business opportunity. He was reported as saying:

> I could have fancied myself in Nice. I was astonished. I never thought English people could have so captured the spirit of revelry. Already the carnival is very good – equal

to Nice, I think. By the end Nice may be outrivalled. We have no trades processions there and our King Carnival is not a living Jester – he is just a colossal effigy round whom carnival centres[34].

The anxious coach owner (also a town councillor) who hired 600 Pierrot costumes to attract custom need not have worried. The crowds turned out and had a good time, too good in view of the level of drunkenness and disorder which followed.

The idea of carnival, though, did not last. But it was not the disorder which killed it off. Much more evident was the tiresome disruption of daily life with the blocking of roads bringing the town to a standstill[35]. There were, in fact, only two carnivals. One in 1923 and the second in 1924 (the latter washed out by the weather). However the town council went into celebratory mood in 1926 on the occasion of its golden Jubilee. There was a formal opening of Stanley Park, though the town was only able to get Lord Derby K.G. to do the honours. Royalty in the form of H.R.H. the Prince of Wales had visited Blackpool in 1921 and was to do so again in 1927, though the main purpose of his visit on the latter occasion was to open the Miners' Convalescent Home at Bispham. Indeed, social institutions such as new secondary schools were as likely, by the end of the decade, to get publicity as the opening of the greyhound track. Blackpool's municipal council finished its decade of modernisation by removing from its old building (rebuilt as a 2000 capacity Conference Hall by the amalgamated Tower and Winter Gardens Co) into a new town hall.

The great spending era, however, was over. The last extravaganzas of the 1920s, the air pageants at the new Municipal Aerodrome, lost money. The effects of the Great Depression dampened the will of the council to borrow. There were natural disasters. Storms in the winter of 1927 had destroyed Blackpool's new South Shore Promenade and led to extensive flooding. There were social disasters. The problems of the unemployed surfaced. In the winter months, the level of unemployment in the town was much greater simply because there were now more people involved in sustaining the season who were left unemployed in the winter months. The season had been extended as far as possible. From the Jubilee Year, the Blackpool Illuminations in September had reached new heights of inventiveness which was to continue throughout the 1930s. The limitations of mass travel kept Blackpool going. A train journey to the resort was still possible despite the privations brought by the Great Depression. People came in good times and bad to get away from it all. Blackpool became a symbol of modern popular culture, earnestly investigated by Mass Observation[36].

What is progress? What is industrial civilisation? Were the answers in Blackpool? What the researchers found, however, was seen through the prism of class: middle-class researchers investigating the ways (unknown to them) in which the working classes enjoyed themselves. They failed to notice that what they were looking at was a nineteenth-century new town, built on service industries, which had remade itself in the 1920s. The introduction of paid holidays for those in

Figure 5.8 *Poster of Blackpool for 1922 (hinting at a Nice image with the carnival jester and the long dress of the carnival queen)* [By permission of Blackpool Borough Council]

Figure 5.9 *Poster of Blackpool for 1925 (the thoroughly modern miss in short skirt dancing to the gramophone with the image of the old pleasures in the background)* [By permission of Blackpool Borough Council]

employment had helped it weather economic depression. Its importance as a conference centre and a place of retirement augmented that. It had specialised in transforming its old-established culture of entertainment and recreation by adopting a more vigorous style of municipal government and a modern attitude to its physical environment. By the end of the 1920s, the administrative structures of government were undergoing investigation, with some hints of maladministration requiring further management rationalisation[37]. The age of unfettered municipal dynamism was over but not before Blackpool had been set on the road to survival for another quarter century.

NICE AND ITS MUNICIPAL GOVERNMENT IN THE 1920S

In the decade after the war, Nice was to be as transformed as Blackpool. Its initial transformation was, though, the result of private entrepreneurship, working alongside a quiescent local government. Nice had to survive as a tourist resort in very different circumstances from those of the Belle Époque. It was to do so with *élan*, entering a new "golden age" of tourism, with its winter season going from strength to strength while its new summer season, instituted in 1920, slowly gained in importance[38]. In terms of selling itself to tourists, Nice managed to create a new glamour, based on fashion and culture, art and the avant-garde. Artists such as Matisse, who had gone there in 1917 to escape the exigencies of the war in Paris, returned frequently. Raoul Dufy was also to paint intoxicatingly lovely pictures of the city in the 1920s. Writers, especially North Americans such as Ernest Hemingway sojourned for the winter in Nice. Isadora Duncan, the modernist dancer, met her untimely death on the Promenade des Anglais, strangled by her long scarf fluttering behind her in the breeze, which caught on a lamp post as she was passing in an open car[39]. Intrigue, glamour, wealth (especially from North America) and even a local film industry which produced romantic films set in Nice, were the ingredients of the new image[40]. Yet behind the image, the realities of city development for the rapidly expanding numbers of permanent residents were very different. Recovery from the First World War was painful and long drawn out and the expansion of the town demanded a new degree of planning and control if the major attractions of the resort for tourists were not to be killed off by unplanned development.

Nice needed a saviour. She found one in her most charismatic leader of the twentieth century, Jean Médecin (1890–1965), who became the Mayor in 1928 and was to remain so until his death in 1965 (apart from a brief interlude between 1944–47 when he fell out with the Vichy régime and was imprisoned)[41]. His ability to remain in power was extraordinary. He did so outside the main divisions of local and national politics, outmanoeuvring both Left and Right in all elections. He stuck to a principle of political administration which was unusual: it did not matter how many votes particular candidates got, they were not included in his

Figure 5.10 *Jean Médecin with girls dressed in traditional Niçoise costumes – still keeping distinctive traditions while developing modern approaches at an exhibition in 1954* [By permission of the Musée d'Art et d'Histoire, Palais Masséna, Nice]

administration of the city. While he had an overall majority, he ran the show. His political talents were to take him into national politics. He was elected to the General Council as the representative of the canton of Sospel in 1931 and a year later had become a deputy. In 1938, he was made a member of the Senate. This he did while retaining his independence from any party, though his political convictions were clear: liberal and republican, against dictatorship, yet an advocate of order and an anti-communist. He was a unique figure and consummate politician. What made his career possible was his power base in Nice. The position of the city as a tourist resort, its proximity to Italy (which during the First World War had aspirations to reclaim it), its rapid growth in the 1920s and its dire economic problems, were well understood by Médecin. The initiatives he put in hand to help the city survive were the bedrock of his career[42].

In the 1920s, Nice was a town of dramatic contrasts. The season was restored and new tourists came but the war and its aftermath had produced high unemployment in the town and the region and the sufferings of the poor were compounded by a high rate of inflation in the first half of the decade. On the one hand, there were bitter strikes of those in work, especially in 1919, the tramway workers and gas workers[43]. On the other, there was a restoration of the Comité des

Figure 5.11   Jean Médecin with potential benefactors on the terrace of the Palais de la Méditerranée in 1929 [By permission of the Bibliothèque de Cessole, Palais Masséna, Nice]

Fêtes who began to organise events to attract the rich middle classes to the town, beginning with a Paris to Nice motor race (a development of the races organised before the war along the southern coast as far as Marseilles). The Nice Carnival was reborn in 1922 but now the *carnavaliers*, the artisans who made the floats for processions (such as M. Guano who had gone to Blackpool in 1923), had organised themselves into an association to protect their interests[44]. Poverty in juxtaposition to ostentatious wealth was nothing new in Nice. What was new was the scale and determination of the workers' struggles to improve their lot. What was also new was that the efforts which had been made to develop local industries and agriculture alongside the tourist industry, especially since the International Exposition in Nice in 1884, were now in ruins. Agriculture in the region was in dramatic decline from which it did not revive until the end of the decade. Industries in Nice and the immediate hinterland, mainly devoted to luxury trades, were at a standstill. These factors contributed to a high inflow of immigrants to the city which produced the fastest rate of population growth in its history to date: an increase of from around 100 000 in 1914 to 177 180 in 1931.

In this hiatus, with high rates of inflation, the answer for private investors seemed to lie in property. Borrow, build and sell. Profits were assured. The bourgeois Niçois set about this with enthusiasm. One historian has estimated that there were 93 housing developments in the town between 1921 and 1929, 72 of them in 1925 and 1926[45]. These developments were unfettered. The open spaces and gardens, the orange groves and hill slopes of olive trees all disappeared. By the end of the 1920s, Nice was no longer a "city of gardens". This was the context in which Jean Médecin came to power. He had a vision of how to modernise Nice and to save it. He worked with passion to achieve this objective which is what endeared him to the Niçois voters. He had two immeasurably powerful forces on his side: the development of new legislation on the government of cities emanating from the centre but with an emphasis on local initiatives; and his own personal record in the First World War as a much decorated war hero. The first gave him the framework for action, the second the respect necessary to introduce new ways of controlling and modernising the city. His war record was exemplary: twice wounded, cited four times in *ordre du jour* of the army, fought at Verdun, promoted to captain in 1916 and awarded the *Légion d'Honneur* in front of his troops and later, the *Croix de Guerre* and the *Médaille Militaire*. At the end of the war, still only 28 years old, he enrolled for the bar and began a career as a lawyer which was to stand him in good stead in interpreting statute law relating to city development in a situation complicated by the relationship between national and local government and local politics[46].

Three pieces of legislation were particularly useful to him. The French government, in the midst of reconstructing the devastated areas in the war zone, had been made freshly aware of the need to develop the legislative framework of the practice of *l'urbanisme*. The law of 14 March 1919, known as 'Le Plan Cornudet' after the politician who authored it, encouraged all municipal councils to take on a new role in managing and beautifying their towns and controlling their extension. Expertise and resources to carry out such schemes were as scarce as they were after the 1919 Town Planning Act in Britain. In France, there were at least two more pieces of central legislation, however, which could be used by Nice's municipal council. The first was the law of 24 November 1919 which was directed to those towns which were centres of health and beauty and thus of importance to the tourist trade. This law placed these towns under the regulation of the National Office of tourism and allowed them to levy special local taxes to pay for improvements. The problem, however, remained the relationship between central and local government. Central edicts were all very well, but who was going to determine on the ground in the locality what should be done? The final piece of legislation which addressed this to some extent, was the decree of 5 November 1926 on the decentralisation of communes and departments. It was an invitation for Nice as the major city of the Alpes-Maritimes to have a greater degree of responsibility for its own development[47]. It was in the wake of such legislation that Médecin was able to build his own power base.

As far as the revival of tourism was concerned, this could not wait for changes in legislative frameworks. From the early 1920s and the revival of the Comité des Fêtes, local entrepreneurs and international businessmen had worked together to recreate Nice as a modern, fashionable resort. Initially the prospects did not look all that good. The demand for a winter resort for the European aristocracy had been annihilated by the First World War. As Nice got larger and more crowded, the very rich went elsewhere to buy their villas, to Antibes, Cannes or even further afield, to other *grandes stations balnéaires françaises* such as Biarritz and Deauville. The large hotels, away from the centre, never recovered from their war use as convalescent homes for the troops and in the course of the inter-war years, 15 out of the 22 largest hotels (including internationally famous ones such as Le Majestic, le Grand Hôtel de Cimiez, le Palace, L'Edward's) all closed down. There were, however, new international visitors, often rich and sometimes famous, especially from America and also the faithful British. Motor cars, casinos and the ostentatious displays of wealth were now the strongest attractions. All had been present before the war. What was different now was the style. Here Nice, like Blackpool, reinvented its old traditions. Nice even looked to Paris, as had happened in the Belle Époque, for inspiration. It came in the form of the last International Exposition in Paris in 1925 in the old nineteenth-century mode, the Exposition that launched the style of Art Deco. Nice became the quintessential location of the style. Overnight the posters advertising the town were transformed. Traditional posters had shown a flower girl against the background of the Baie des Anges. Now the female figure wore a bathing costume, arms outstretched to the sun: the modern woman seeking pleasure and relaxation[48]. The best winter season of the decade was 1929. It was supplemented by the best summer season of the 1920s as measured by the holiday tax taken by the town[49].

Relaxation in the "modern" style was easily followed by boredom. The Nice entrepreneurs were quick to recognise the need for some new form of entertainment. They invented the idea of Le Palais de la Méditerranée. It was to contain restaurants and bars, cafés and meeting rooms. It was large enough to also contain a theatre and dancehall and various boutiques. Situated on the Promenade des Anglais, it was designed to be the focal point of the wealthy holiday-maker, a place where you could guarantee to run into friends at certain times of the day without all the fuss of making specific arrangements. The plans for its construction were headed by Frank Jay Gould, a descendant of the family of American railway millionaires. He was well known as an entrepreneur in the development of seaside resorts such as Juan-les-Pins and ski resorts in the Alps. He headed an organisation which had all the vested interests in Nice on his side, including,

la Chambre de commerce, le Syndicat d'initiative, la Fédération des associations industrielles et commerciales des Alpes-Maritimes, la Chambre syndicale des hôteliers, l'Automobile-club de Nice, le Syndicat des restaurateurs et des limonadiers. Le syndicat des chauffeurs de taxi et la fédération des spectacles notamment.

By the time it came to be built in 1928, the style had shifted from Art Deco to a neo-classicism (a style which was to be displayed at the Paris Exhibition of 1931). It was stylish, modern, ill-fated. It was built in reinforced concrete faced in stone,

Figure 5.12 *Poster of Nice in the 1930s designed to reinforce its luxurious image in a new modern style* [By permission of the Musée d'Art et d'Histoire, Palais Masséna, Nice]

proclaiming its modernity. It was decorated by one of France's leading sculptors, Antoine Sartorio[50]. Just three years later, it was to suffer a disastrous fire and Frank Jay Gould pulled out. It was restored, but by then, the years of economic depression had begun to bite in France as they had done earlier in America and Northern Europe. Tourism was a fickle business for sustaining a growing town.

No one understood this better than Médecin. Very astutely, he decided on a three-pronged attack on the problems of the city. He was always at the forefront in promoting any project which might improve the chances of attracting tourists; but this was backed up by a determination to build up the town as the capital city of the Alpes-Maritimes, with attention to principles of *urbanisme*; and finally, he wanted to encourage the social and cultural life of the city of permanent residents to counteract the idea that Nice was just a frivolous seaside resort. The latter objective had occurred almost by accident. At the end of the war, Prince André Masséna had donated his large villa (built by his father between 1898 and 1901) to the city. The first idea of what to do with it was to create an art museum, dedicated to the Beaux-Arts and to the history of the region. It was opened in January 1921 with grand receptions and an exhibition of "Nice à travers les âges". Here an idea was born. This was an additional tourist attraction (especially the chance to see the interior of the Villa Masséna) and at the same time, a point of departure for generating an interest in Nice: its past, present and future. This was a "tradition"

Figure 5.13 *Drawing of main façade of the Palais de la Méditerranée* [By permission of the Bibliothèque de Cessole, Palais Masséna, Nice]

Figure 5.14 *Façade sculpture by Antoine Sartorio* [By permission of the Bibliothèque de Cessole, Palais Masséna, Nice]

which had been established before the First World War by the Academia Nissarda, which was founded in 1904 with the purpose of encouraging a vigorous pursuit of local history. With its separate dialect of Nissart, the identity of town and region was especially well defined, the first prerequisite for generating loyalty and dedication to local endeavours.

Médecin had entered local government for the first time in 1925. His first post was a joint one: "l'Instruction publique et aux Beaux-Arts". His predecessor as Mayor, Alexandre Mari, had also been responsible for education. When the Hôtel du Parc Imperial closed its doors (one of the first of the big hotels to do so), Mari persuaded the municipal council to buy it and turn it into a school. Again there was still an eye on the needs of those living *en villégiature* and foreign residents, who would be able to send their children there. Médecin had spotted as early as 1923 that the Villa Cocconato had, in its grounds, a large part of the site of the earliest settlement in the region. As Mayor, he set about trying to buy the Villa and he succeeded eventually almost 30 years later, setting up Nice's Archeological Museum in the 1950s. There were many other such purchases and projects. A further impetus was given to this method of saving the grand urban fabric of the past and encouraging social regeneration at the same time, when Médecin had to face the economic decline of the 1930s, produced by the central government's attempt to beat depression by deflation. In 1933, he inaugurated a new cultural institution: Le Centre Universitaire Méditerranéen. It had all the ingredients of his style of urban regeneration: housed in unused buildings, devoted to the study of the activities of the region, an attraction for foreigners. As Médecin said at the official opening in June 1937:

> Dans la grande œuvre qui s'impose à tous aujourd'hui, les collectivités, comme les individus, ont leur tâche à remplir. Devant les difficultés de l'heure, la cité prend une conscience nouvelle du rôle qui lui incombe. L'administration municipale de Nice poursuit, dans tous les domaines de l'urbanisme moderne, un effort qu'elle veut aussi clairvoyant et hardi que possible[51].
> [In the great challenge that faces us today, the community, like the individual, must try to succeed. At this difficult time, the city has a new consciousness of the role that the civic administration of Nice takes in all activities of modernising the city, an effort in which one has to be as far-sighted and as strong as possible.]

Médecin had a clear perception of *l'urbanisme moderne*. As Mayor from 1928, his first act was to put the Plan Cornudet into action. The public roads of the town were in a parlous state. There was the delicate issue of who was responsible for the roads to the new private housing estates and there was a need, which was becoming ever more pressing with the development of the town, for a network of roads to be established, to facilitate movement from one area to another. Médecin put in hand the building of the great boulevard which acts as the main artery of the town and has been named after him. His political skills were vital to the promotion of the work on the urban network and the upkeep of new roads. But the project

which was well known as the "marotte" of the Mayor was the modernisation of the Promenade des Anglais[52]. As in Blackpool, the Promenade was the heart of the tourist industry and the showpiece of the whole town. In the 1920s, the Promenade des Anglais became ever more important as the focal point of the tourist experience of Nice as the larger private villas and grand hotels, away from the seashore, were sold or closed down. James Thurber wrote a piece on the experience of being in Nice in the inter-war period in which he suggests that one of the key features of the town was that you could always be sure you would meet friends and acquaintances as they all moved around the hotels, casinos, the Palais and other entertainments which were all located very close to the Promenade des Anglais[53]. Since 1921 and the restarting of the great car races of the pre-war years, all the races started or finished at Le Promenade. By 1931, it had become the fashion to have motor races in the city. Médecin had undertaken the modernisation of the Promenade (widening both road and pavement, adding adjacent gardens) just in time. The Nice Grand Prix became a major tourist attraction.

In some ways, though, the image of the great cars roaring around the Promenade des Anglais, was less an image of modernity and had more resonance with the past than the future. Médecin's survival depended on his appreciation of this. Another project he put in place in 1934 was the Haulage Depot for large trucks to encourage the town's role as an entrepôt of trade. Left-wing politicians were never able to oust him even in 1936 as there was a strong right wing too. He was able to play one off against the other. The national government of the Popular Front of 1936 did have one unexpected effect on Nice. Parisian workers were given holidays with pay and their unions organised fleets of trains to take them to the Côte d'Azur. They arrived in the summer at the station in Nice in their own carnival mood, singing, processing, playing musical bands, much to the astonishment and disapprobation of some of the Niçois. For the communist workers, however, this was a signal for the future. Lamenting the high unemployment and the closing of the big hotels, a communist pamphlet of February 1936 suggests that the hotels should be taken into public ownership and used for workers' holidays. That would create the beautiful tomorrow, with workers creating work for others through seeking holidays themselves. The introduction of paid holidays for workers in France was to do just that. Nice and Jean Médecin would survive into another era.

CONCLUSION

What both Blackpool and Nice had done in the inter-war period was to recast themselves in a new form. Urban regeneration had been based on recreating their "traditions" with modern images and on a revolution in municipal administration. In both cases, while the dominant theme had been the need to attract visitors, the needs of the resident population had come to play a much greater part in the prioritising of projects. Successful seaside resorts were better at fighting off

economic depression and unemployment. Nice and Blackpool were nothing if not successful, but their struggles with the latter helped to fuel their revolution in municipal administration. This was perhaps the most important element in their survival. Both Blackpool and Nice embraced town planning on a scale which was quite remarkable for the time in established towns. With a weak or non-existent industrial base, public works created employment as well as made the towns more attractive. Both towns were also very conscious of the need to *appear* modern. Modern technology (electricity and the internal combustion engine supplementing gas and steam power), and modern methods of communication – film, radio and modern methods of advertising – were all of supreme importance. The consequences of these developments had to be contained within the urban fabric without harming its attractiveness. Open spaces needed to be retained, pollution kept to a minimum and the "natural" environment of the city unharmed. How Blackpool and Nice tried to achieve these outcomes has been the major theme of this chapter. Blackpool and Nice were totally different resorts, with totally different physical and cultural environments. Yet the method of regeneration they both employed, based as much on their history and culture as the economic parameters of the day, were very similar. What was attempted was determined by cultural factors, especially the understanding of what creates a sense of personal well being. City and citizen, or in the case of seaside resorts, city, citizen and visitor, were changing together.

NOTES

1. T Ranger (1983) "The Invention of Tradition in Colonial Africa" in E Hobsbawm and T Ranger (eds) *The Invention of Tradition* Cambridge, Cambridge University Press, 211.
2. *Exposition Universelle de 1889: Catalogue illustrée des beaux-arts, 1789–1889* New York, Garland, 1981; *Catalogue officielle illustrée de l'Exposition decennale des beaux arts de 1889 a 1900* New York, Garland, 1981; P Greenhalgh (1988) *Ephemeral Vistas: a history of the expositions universelles, the great exhibitions and world's fairs, 1851–1939* Manchester/New York, Manchester University Press/St Martin's Press.
3. JK Walton (1988) "The World's First Working Class Seaside Resort: Blackpool Revisited 1840–1974" *Transactions of the Lancashire and Cheshire Antiquarian Society* 88, 1–30.
4. Blackpool's electricity works were opened in 1893 by Lord Kelvin (the president of the Royal Society), A Clarke (1923) *The Story of Blackpool* Blackpool, Palatine, 257. The illuminations were introduced in Blackpool in 1912, JK Walton (1996) "Leisure Towns in Wartime: The Impact of the First World War in Blackpool and San Sebastian" *Journal of Contemporary History* 31, 4, 607.
5. J Walvin (1978) *Beside the Seaside: a social history of the popular seaside holiday* London, Allen and Unwin, 110–17.
6. J Urry (1989) "Cultural Change and Contemporary Holiday Making", *Theory, Culture and Society* Vol 5, 9(i), 33–55. I Ousby (1990) *The Englishman's England: taste, travel and the rise of tourism* Cambridge, Cambridge University Press.
7. W Benjamin (1925) "Naples" *Frankfurter Zeitung* 19 August 1925.

8. G Gilloch (1996) *Myth and Metropolis: Walter Benjamin and the city* Cambridge, Polity Press, 21–36.
9. CJ Haug (1982) *Leisure and Tourism in Nineteenth Century Nice* Kansas, Regents Press, 48.
10. See Chapters 1 and 4 for more discussion of civic exhibitions.
11. JK Walton (1978) *The Blackpool Landlady: a social history* Manchester, Manchester University Press, 43–4.
12. Raikes Hall Gardens appeared in the 1860s, the Winter Gardens were created in 1875 and the Tower in 1894. A Clarke (1973) *Story of Blackpool*, 176, 209, 215. JK Walton (1975) "Residential Amenity, Respectable Morality and the Rise of the Entertainment Industry: the case of Blackpool, 1860–1914", *Literature and History* 1, 62–78.
13. TH Mawson (1927) *The Life and Work of an English Landscape Architect* London, BT Batsford, 340.
14. VA Malte-Brun (n.d.) *La France illustrée: Alpes-Maritimes* Paris, Rouff, quoted in *Nice Historique* 98ᵉ année 1995, 21.
15. "L'exposition of Nice 1884" in *Lou Sourgentin* March–April 1984, 6–19.
16. JK Walton (1983) *The English Seaside Resort: a social history 1750–1914* Leicester, Leicester University Press, 128.
17. In 1910 and 1911 Blackpool's board obtained Parliamentary powers to construct a new waterworks. The war held up this project but by the early 1920s it had been constructed in the Hodder Valley, while the New Grizedale reservoir was completed in 1922. A Clarke (1923) *Story of Blackpool*, 257.
18. Walton (1978) *Blackpool Landlady*, 80–99.
19. Haug (1982) *Leisure*, 102.
20. Walton (1996) "Leisure Towns", 603–18.
21. *Blackpool Gazette and Herald* "Blackpool's New Era", 3 January 1920, 7.
22. According to Walvin, Blackpool exemplified the process of inter-war building in seaside resorts. The municipality spent £1.5 million on promenade and gardens, £100 000 on an open air pool, £1.25 million on a park and the Winter Gardens etc. Walvin (1978) *Beside the Seaside*, 117.
23. The columnist using the *nom de plume* "Zephyrus" was especially prominent in this. He underlined the hard-nosed business line when in 1924 he declared "for goodness sake don't let us pretend any more, it is the holiday makers' money we want in Blackpool", *Blackpool Gazette and Herald* "Another View of the Carnival", Saturday 28 June 1924, 9.
24. G Dix (1981) "Patrick Abercrombie, 1879–1957" and G Cherry "George Pepler, 1882–1978", both in G Cherry (ed) *Pioneers in British Planning* London, Architectural Press, 103–49.
25. TH Mawson (1911) *Civic Art: studies in town planning, parks, boulevards and open spaces* London, BT Batsford.
26. TH Mawson (1927) *Life and Work*, 340.
27. *Blackpool Gazette and Herald* "The £800,000 Bill", 6 January 1928, 8.
28. Mawson (1927) *Life and Works*, 341.
29. *Blackpool Gazette and Herald* "More and More a Town of Residence", 12 May 1928, 9.
30. G Cross (ed.) (1990) *Worktowners at Blackpool: mass observation and popular leisure in the 1930s* London, Routledge.
31. T Bennett (1986) "Hegemony, Ideology, Pleasure: Blackpool", in J Wollacott (ed.), *Popular Culture and Social Relations* Milton Keynes, Open University Press.
32. JK Walton (1998) "Popular Entertainment and Public Order: the Blackpool Carnivals of 1923–4", *Northern History* Vol. XXXIV, 170–88.

220

33. RD Storch (ed.) (1982) *Popular Culture and Custom in Nineteenth Century England* London, Croom Helm, Chaps 5 and 6.
34. *Blackpool Gazette and Herald* "Carnival Items", 12 June 1923, 12.
35. *Blackpool Gazette and Herald* "Another View of the Carnival", 28 June 1924, 9.
36. Cross (1990) *Worktowners*.
37. In the review of municipal activity in 1929 it was suggested that there should be rationalisation of municipal adminstration by taking the responsibility for electricity away from the Tramways Committee (which had been the subject of a special sub-committee investigation) and the setting up of an Electricity Committee. Reported in *Blackpool Gazette and Herald* "Review of Municipal Activity in 1929", 28 December 1929, 11.
38. E Pastorelli (1964) *Le Tourisme à Nice de 1919 à 1936* Aix-en-Provence, D.E.S. Histoire.
39. J Bergamasco (1993) "Une Étoile s'éteint sur la Promenade: vie et mort d'Isadora Duncan", *Nice Historique* 96e année, 71–5.
40. R Schor (n.d.) *Nice et les Alpes-Maritimes de 1914 à 1945*, Nice, Publications du Centre Régional de documentation pedagogique de Nice, 40.
41. M Derlange (1988) *Les Niçois dans l'histoire* Toulouse, Privat, 142–3.
42. See catalogue of exhibition *Jean Médecin. Un homme, une ville*, 16 Dec. 1990 to 19 Feb. 1991 Musée d'Art et d'Histoire, Palais Masséna, Nice.
43. Schor (n.d.) *Nice et les Alpes-Maritimes*, 35–9.
44. A Sidro (1979) *Le Carnaval de Nice: et ses fous* Nice, Éditions Serre, 120–5.
45. M Bordes (ed) (1976) *Histoire de Nice: et du pays niçois* Toulouse, Privat, 366.
46. H Charles (1990) "Jean Médecin et le développement de la ville de Nice", *Nice Historique* 93e année, July to Dec, 47–65.
47. P Lavedan (1960) *Les Villes Françaises* Paris, Éditions Vincent, 189–217.
48. See the posters in the catalogue of the exhibition, *Jean Médecin. Un homme, une ville*. Musée d'Art et d'Histoire, Palais Masséna, 16 Dec. 1990–10 Feb. 1991, 48–53.
49. Schor (n.d.) *Nice et les Alpes-Maritimes*, 42; Bordes *Histoire de Nice*, 365.
50. A Rouillier (1995) "Antoine Sartorio: poète de la pierre" and "Histoire d'un malentendu. La façade du Palais de la Méditerranée" both in *Sourgentin* Vol 115, Jan–Feb, 16–18 and 19–20.
51. M Carlin (1990) "Nice, Ville Universitaire" *Nice Historique* July–Dec, 83–91.
52. G Le Breton and A Nission (1993) "Nice 1930: de la Promenade au Palais" *Nice Historique*, 14–29.
53. J Thurber (1963) "la Grande Ville de Plaisir" in *Vintage Thurber: a collection in 2 Vols of the best writings and drawings of James Thurber* London, Hamish Hamilton, 66–71.

CHAPTER 6

KINGSTANDING AND VILLEURBANNE IN 1934: THE TALE OF TWO HOUSING ESTATES IN BIRMINGHAM AND LYONS

INTRODUCTION

Most of the examples used for comparison in this book have been whole cities. In this last chapter, a different scale has been chosen. The micro scale of the new housing estate, a key feature of the "modern" city offers a chance to ask a fresh set of questions about the quality of civilisation in early twentieth-century European cities. Large, coherently planned, housing estates in the inter-war period tended to be public housing schemes, that is, housing development controlled by the local government authorities, designed to rehouse those living in slum conditions. This, however, was not a straightforward activity. If public money was to be used for re-housing, should not the new developments aim at higher standards than ever before? Could a new kind of environment be created which would not deteriorate? What are the requirements of modern urban living and who decides what they are? When do the *diktats* of public health finish and choice begin? What choices were there? What about the issues of community values nurtured and funded by public expenditure versus the choices of individuals and their own life achievements?[1] These questions go to the heart of the challenge of creating a modern urban environment designed to promote new ways of urban living. They were at the heart of the debates at the meetings of the Congrès d'Architecture Moderne which promoted Modern functionalist architecture[2]. In the 1930s, new currents in public housing policies and architecture were coming together to create a new kind of urban environment, but the legacy of history and culture was equally strong.

Kingstanding in Birmingham and Villeurbanne in Lyons were both completed in 1934. They are not particularly well known among all the examples of 1930s' housing estates to be found in all the large cities of Europe. In fact, the great experimental days of public housing in European cities, which had gained the most publicity, were almost over. The enormous apartment blocks in Vienna, the experimental housing in the new Frankfurt, the expansion of public housing in Berlin and Hamburg, the great brick-built apartments of public housing in Amsterdam, were all products of the 1920s[3]. Yet coming after these pioneering days, Kingstanding and Villeurbanne can reveal more about the cultural assumptions which determined their physical form. The provision of public housing, recognised since the earliest days of industrialisation when employers used housing as a means of getting and keeping a stable, loyal and skilled labour force[4], has always involved more than putting a roof over some family's head. Mid-Victorian housing schemes by philanthropists such as Thomas Peabody in London had aimed at reforming the social behaviour of the poor. Philanthropic apartment blocks were built like fortresses against a wicked world and there were strict rules governing the behaviour of tenants[5]. Anyone who defaulted on the rent was immediately evicted. The First World War had encouraged a new set of parameters. Public housing was the reward for the sacrifice of the masses and to ward off the prospect of communism and revolution. The home was the refuge of the family and the family was the key social unit in a democratic state.

The two developments of Kingstanding and Villeurbanne offered diametrically opposite physical interpretations of what this meant. Kingstanding was built on a greenfield site, at relatively low densities, in a style which owed a great deal to the work of Raymond Unwin and Barry Parker, architects of Howard's Garden City in Letchworth[6]. There were many crucial differences, however. Kingstanding, as a public housing project, could not aim for "social mix". It continued instead the nineteenth-century tradition of social segregation in suburban development. Its identity was determined by that. Villeurbanne, on the other hand, introduced the concept of a different kind of modern urban living. It was the first major modern development in a Lyons suburban area which aimed at producing an integrated urban community with a communal sense of identity. Like Kingstanding, there was not much "social mix", since Villeurbanne was an industrial commune. The new estate was built on a brownfield site in this rapidly expanding industrial hinterland of Lyons. In the facilities it provided for inhabitants, it was an exemplar of what modern technology and aspiring cultural values could do to improve the comfort and education of the respectable working classes. The two ideals behind these estates, were, however, not just the products of different architectural designs. They were the products of a whole range of economic, social and political factors which had shaped the histories of Birmingham and Lyons. This chapter will try to unravel what some of these were.

PUBLIC HOUSING STRATEGIES IN BRITAIN AND FRANCE, 1890–1930

The first context which needs to be sketched in is the national response of Britain and France to the problem of working-class housing[7]. In the period 1890–1930, both nations, in common with the rest of Europe relied on private market forces to provide an adequate housing stock in the growing cities. What forced national governments to change their minds was the public health movement and political expediency. Public health legislation in Britain relating to the sanitary condition of large cities had brought the death rate down each decennial period since 1870. Housing, however,

Figure 6.1 *Kingstanding in the inter-war period* [Map drawn by Chris Lewis]

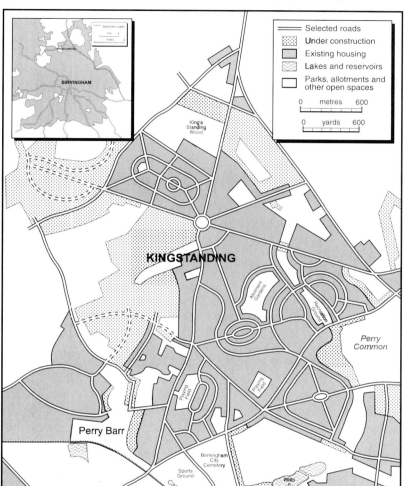

was another matter. It affected the owners of urban properties and their inhabitants. The cause of overcrowding, one of the prime indicators of a major public health hazard, was found, by the Royal Commission on Working Class Housing which sat from 1884–1885, to be the result of poverty[8]. An additional pressure on the British government, which had helped it to decide to call a Royal Commission in the first place, was greater publicity about moral concerns, mostly related to sex, in

224

Figure 6.2 *The new civic centre of Villeurbanne of 1934* [Map drawn by Chris Lewis]

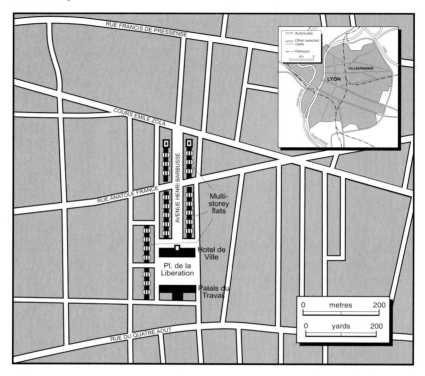

overcrowded and unregulated housing[9]. The result was the 1890 Housing Act which flagged up the problem but provided little guidance on how to finance it[10].

In France, where cities had grown much more slowly and small-scale landlords had more political power, there was less concerted pressure on government on this issue[11]. In 1890, the social reformer and former mayor of Le Havre, Jules Siegfried organised a philanthropic society, La Société Française des Habitations à Bon Marché, to provide capital for projects to build cheap housing. In 1894, the French government backed this initiative with further promises of financial assistance, though HBM housing was still a matter for private enterprise. The second factor pressing both the French and the British governments to change their views on this issue was political expediency. The fear of revolution during and after the First World War was a strong incentive. Neither government, however, felt itself to be on the front line in this respect. Lloyd George famously promised "Homes for Heroes" in his election campaign of 1918 but when the programme of house building ran into the sands of an economic slump and a lack of expertise among municipal administrators, little effort was made to rescue it[12]. In France, the cost and effort of reconstruction of the devastated areas, the battleground of the war itself in the north east of the country, absorbed all available finance and energy.

In these circumstances, in the inter-war years, even in Paris, two main outcomes followed. With great effort and dedication, and using the HBM legislation to the full, it was just about possible for enterprising mayors, such as Henri Sellier of Suresnes, to build homes for those of the working classes who could pay the rent[13]. For the poor, especially the 1 100 000 recent rural immigrants flocking to the Paris region, there was very little and many were forced to the shanty towns on the outskirts of the city[14]. London, which also grew by 1 000 000 during the inter-war years, was a paradise for the speculative builder. There was also, however, the London County Council, which experimented, and among other schemes, built "cottage" estates in the surrounding countryside and decanted East Enders into them[15]. Many slums still remained[16]. Generally, until 1930, neither British nor French governments produced any permanent solutions to the problem of working-class housing. Even large-scale schemes such as those of Henri Sellier or the LCC were sustained only for relatively short periods. The complexities of providing working-class housing remained, both on an ideological and practical level.

Who benefited from public housing schemes? What kind of life faced the rehoused and was it sustainable in economic and social terms? What balance was kept between cost and the pioneering of modern conveniences? In practical terms, there were the problems of the scale and organisation of the building industry, the implementation of new technology, the availability of land and its ownership, existing housing structures and the ways in which the provision of working-class housing had been handled in the past[17]. Fresh legislation, the Loi Loucheur in France, passed in 1922 but not put into effect until 1928, which set specific housing targets and was directed more closely towards the rehousing of the poorer working classes; and the Greenwood Housing Act of 1930 in Britain, which again placed greater emphasis on rehousing the poor, opened a new chapter. The Greenwood Act offered subsidies for slum clearance. The Loi Loucheur made possible loans from the Caisse des Dépôts et Consignations[18]. Both countries had upped the stakes in the fight against substandard housing and overcrowding. By the end of the inter-war period about 15% of the new housing in both countries had been provided with state aid. Yet legislation and the national context only provided the framework for this achievement. What actually was built on the ground owed a great deal to local circumstances.

HOUSING AND THE HISTORICAL CONTEXT OF BIRMINGHAM

The economic and social history of the "second" cities of Britain and France was a determining influence. Birmingham and Lyons had become industrial giants in the nineteenth century. In 1700, Birmingham only had 15 000 inhabitants. By 1801, it was 74 000, 233 000 by 1851, 523 000 by 1900, and by the mid-1930s, it had reached 1 000 000. Lyons had been a far more important medieval and early modern city than Birmingham and had a population of 110 000 in 1800. Its growth in the nineteenth century, however, was far less spectacular, by British (though not by French) standards. By 1850, it had a population of 177 000. There was massive growth in the 1860s to 268 000. Thereafter, growth continued so that by the mid-1930s, the city had reached about 500 000, only half the size of Birmingham. (At that time, it did not, of course, contain Villeurbanne.) Both cities harboured many different industries but Birmingham was dominated by the metal trades and engineering, Lyons, by textiles, especially silk, and the manufacture of textile machinery. Both were situated close, on the one hand, with thriving industrial hinterlands and coalfields; on the other, with fertile agricultural land, supplemented, in the case of Lyons, with the proximity of important vineyards. These are bland comparisons. Birmingham, as arguably the first industrial city in the world, and Lyons, the dominant city in France, apart from Paris, during the Belle Époque, had both been experiencing, for almost a couple of centuries, radical change, new technologies, and the social aspirations of those formerly outside the mainstream of political and cultural life[19].

Social change and political developments in these cities were to have nationally influential outcomes in many ways, not least through the careers of their two most famous mayors, Joseph Chamberlain in Birmingham and Édouard Herriot of Lyons. These men put their stamp on city and nation and directly, and indirectly, influenced decisions which affected the built environment of their home cities. Responses to the problems of working-class housing stemmed from a political context they helped to create. This is not to say there were not many other factors at work which will be reviewed later. But working-class housing is a political issue if it is caused by poverty and lack of regulation. Chamberlain (1836–1914) and Herriot (1872–1957) were certainly not profoundly interested in the provision of working-class housing. Yet they were responsible at a local level for the political environment in which this issue was to be worked out. The impact these men had on their respective cities lasted for decades, more than half a century in the case of Édouard Herriot, who was Mayor from 1905 to 1942 and from 1945 to 1957[20].

Chamberlain's great Mayoralty had been a mere three years from 1873–76 but the municipal debt he accumulated lasted for decades, as did his political influence. In the early 1870s, he gained a reputation as a municipal reformer, willing to use the expertise he had acquired in business to the task of running and improving the city of Birmingham. The municipalisation of gas and water, the improvement of the city centre by the demolition of existing buildings and the construction of a major new thoroughfare in the manner of Haussmann's treatment of Paris, gave Birmingham a new sense of its civic identity[21]. It was paid for largely by increasing Birmingham's municipal debt and relying on future growth of the city (and its rates) to absorb the task of repayment. His subsequent career on a national level (he was made an MP in 1876) was chequered as he switched political allegiance on the issue of Irish Home Rule, leaving Gladstone's Liberal Party to join the Conservatives. The driving force behind his political career was less party politics and more a conviction of the need to ally business experience and social reform. He reached the apogee of his political influence as Secretary of State for the colonies at the end of the century. For him, the colonies were Britain's vital power structure within the world multilateral economy. As world competition in trade became ever fiercer, Britain could develop a special relationship with her colonies which would bring prosperity to British industrial cities and to trade through the erection of tariff barriers. Chamberlain was a modern Imperialist[22]. The political legacy he left to Birmingham in ideological terms was a belief in a market economy which worked through domination and control.

Already by the mid-1870s, this stance had generated resistance in the city, not just from political opponents and those concerned with the economic outcomes of Chamberlain's policies, but also on an ideological level. Curiously, this resistance was drawn from the same social strata as Chamberlain, from the successful manufacturing class with strong links with the British Empire. George Cadbury, the chocolate manufacturer, had to seek space on the city's periphery for the expansion of his business. His Quaker beliefs led him to a different, more paternalistic view of how business could serve social reform. The cocoa plantations in Africa were carefully managed to keep the subservient natives in what were considered, in days of rampart racism, "decent" conditions. In Birmingham, Cadbury had a different, though equally paternalistic, ideal for his workers. He built a new estate, Bournville, to house his workers. It was to stand as a model against Chamberlain's "wicked city", a place where the forces of nature would counteract evil urban influences; where people of different social classes would live adjacent to one another; where the workers for his factory would be strongly encouraged to live clean, healthy and sin-free lives; and where a plethora of educational institutions would encourage self-improvement[23]. There was a strong effort to create a village atmosphere, where face-to-face contact would develop community identity and loyalty. The physical model was an old Warwickshire village and a Tudor manor house was bought and relocated in the village centre to reinforce the message. Being a Quaker, Cadbury believed in self-discipline and he created the Bournville Village Trust as an independent body, on which residents served, to manage the estate outside the control of the factory (although a member of the Cadbury family was elected Chair until well after the Second World War).

Physically, beyond the village green, the settlement was dominated by linked parks and walkways which enabled inhabitants to reach village or factory without going along roads. The housing was low density and mixed to accommodate different social classes. Much of the development only took place from the late 1890s when the chocolate factory was more profitable and Raymond Unwin, the Letchworth Garden City architect, was brought in to plan the expansion of the village[24]. It presented a strong model of an ideal, improved environment for the working classes, taking its place in the tradition of factory settlements built by canny and paternalistic employers since the early Industrial Revolution. Before the First World War, it played a key part, locally and nationally, in establishing the garden suburb ideal as the best form of urban environment for the future. Government settlements for war workers in Scotland in the First World War, at Gretna and Rosyth, were built on these lines[25]. Suburbs in Hull, Liverpool, Leicester, London, York, Doncaster, Bristol, Caerphilly, Coventry, Datchet, Guildford, Hereford, Manchester, Merthyr, Oldham, Sevenoaks and Wrexham had been built on garden suburb lines before the war. A British model of an ideal modern suburban development had been strongly identified. Its main physical features were housing for independent family units at low density, gardens, open space, and the retention of trees. Cadbury had his factory in Bournville, but in other suburbs, factories were strictly excluded. Inhabitants needed to use public transport to get to work and, for social facilities, to use those already provided by the city to which their suburb was attached.

In Birmingham before the war, the influential Chairman of the Housing Committee, Councillor J.S. Nettlefold had believed that the provision of such "garden" suburbs could be best achieved through a combination of public control and private enterprise. He was totally against the provision of council housing[26]. The municipality could control the land and provide the legal framework. Private enterprise must build the houses. The Harborne Tenants Association, set up through Nettlefold's initiative, created one of the most successful suburban environments to prove his point. Birmingham's belief in private enterprise only became dented after the First World War. There was a complete *volte face*, however, in 1924, after the passing of Wheatley's Housing Act, one of the few pieces of legislation achieved by the first Minority Labour Government. When the town council changed its mind, it did so on a massive scale. Labour members of the Housing Committee were able to persuade a Conservative-led town council to follow the new direction, indicating a common cultural consensus on the matter. From being one of the largest cities with the smallest commitment to public housing, it became the largest provider of such housing in the country[27]. The peak year for council house building before the Second World War was 1930, in the midst of the Great Depression. Birmingham built 6715 houses in that single year. Arthur Greenwood, Minister of Health for the Labour Government and architect of the 1930 Housing Act came to Birmingham on 25 July 1930, to open Birmingham's 30 000th council house. The house he opened was in Greenwood Place, Kingstanding.

Kingstanding was built on the land of Kettlehouse Farm, bought by the council in 1930 and was to house more than 30 000 inhabitants just two years later. On completion, it had 4802 housing units and was the largest municipal estate in England outside the London area. By the Second World War, it was one of 15 individual estates with more than 1000 houses built by the city, providing altogether, a total of 31 800 houses[28]. The building of this estate thus came at a particular point in the history of public housing in Birmingham. It was part of the first wave of massive investment in such housing which had become a hallmark policy of the city. But it was before the appointment in 1935 of Sir Herbert Manzoni as City Surveyor, the man with a mission to demolish the old and build the new Birmingham[29]. With its conversion to the idea of municipal housing, the city council started out on its new role with all the vigour of a dedicated Imperialist annexing territory. The city bought up greenfield sites and used land lavishly in low density, low-rise housing, reminiscent of the Bournville ideal but reducing it to a low-cost formula, without the social and community development elements. Symbolic of its attitude was a metal version of the city motto "Forward" which was to be found sunk into concrete in the middle of the vast, grass covered traffic island in the centre of the Kingstanding estate. The spirit of Joseph Chamberlain was abroad even in a mode he would not have recognised! Yet it was Cadbury's ideal of the future which had the firmest hold. The Birmingham ideal of the democratic state was a dominant, strong local authority that mitigated against its authoritarianism with a paternalistic outlook.

HOUSING AND THE HISTORICAL CONTEXT OF LYONS

The municipal housing estate was very much a British response to the problem of poverty and working-class housing. In Lyons, the national and local context was completely different. When Herriot became the Mayor in 1905, he was not given the choice of transforming administrative structures. He was a professional politician and his Mayoralty was a stepping stone to national prominence which he very ably took. He was fortunate that he set out on his career at a point when the problems of the Third Republic seemed to be abating. In 1905, the Act was passed with formally separated Church and State and the Dreyfus affair was drawing to a close. Herriot was to prove a dynamic mayor and a major figure in the Radical Socialist Party. The skill with which he bridged these two roles: bourgeois Mayor of the great city of Lyons and leader of the Radical Socialists caused him to earn the sobriquet in his old age of the "personification of the Third Republic"[30]. He was elected to the Chamber of Deputies in 1919; became premier of France in the Cartel des Gauches government of 1924 (France's first Left coalition government); and had two further brief periods as premier in 1926 and 1932. With the victory of the Popular Front in 1936, he became the President of the Chamber of Deputies, a post he held until 1940. He was famously imprisoned for his opposition to Pétain and refusal to collaborate. In Lyons, in the inter-war period however, his radicalism did not extend to the question of working-class housing.

Herriot, like Chamberlain, wanted to put his mark on the city in the grand manner. He wanted to build a great monumental staircase linking the basilique de Fervière, built on the hill above the old city, with the cathédrale Saint-Jean, destroying most of Vieux Lyons in the process[31]. Fortunately he was unable to do this because of cost. But he put much energy in building new institutions such as

Figure 6.3 *A large grass-covered traffic island in Kingstanding* [Author's photo]

schools and hospitals, institutions which had formerly been provided by the Church. In this activity, he was able to engage the services of one of Lyons' foremost architects, Tony Garnier (1869–1948). Garnier has gained even greater fame since his death as one of France's leading modernist architects[32]. During his lifetime, the fact that he lived and worked in Lyons kept him out of the national limelight. Herriot was an enthusiastic supporter of his work and he was commissioned to build new city abattoirs (1906–14), the Lyons stadium (1913–19) the Hospital of Grange Blanche (1909–30) and the École Supérieure du Textile (1930–33). The only housing he was able to work on was a small project in the quartier of États-Unis where he built several blocks of flats (1920–35)[33]. One of the best of the six war memorials he designed was located in the Parc Tête d'Or, a parkland purchased from the commune of Villeurbanne in 1884. Garnier was not directly responsible for the design of the new estate in Villeurbanne but he was appointed the judge of the competition for the winning design and he gave the prize to one of his students from the School of Architecture in Lyons[34]. The physical form of Villeurbanne was thus to owe a considerable debt to Garnier.

Tony Garnier had published the series of drawings he made of the Industrial City of the future in 1901, the year that the Garden City Association in Britain held its first congress in Bournville, attended by municipal administrators from all over the country, as well as housing reformers. Garnier's vision could not have been more different[35]. It was rooted in industry and an urbanisation transformed by new technology[36]. Raymond Unwin, the Garden City architect, was a middle-class Englishman, inspired by the Arts and Crafts movement of William Morris. Garnier was the son of a pattern-maker in the silk industry and had spent his early youth in the ancient crowded textile quartier of Lyons, the Croix-Rousse. The buildings of this quartier are perched against the hillside, very tall for medieval buildings, and the area is dissected by a labyrinth of passages rather than roads. These *taboules* proved very helpful as escape routes for the Resistance in the Second World War[37]. Garnier's Cité Industrielle which he was dreaming about at the turn of the century, was the antithesis of this. His work at the École des Beaux Arts in Paris had won him the Prix de Rome and it was in Italy, studying ancient civilisations, that he began his drawings of the city of a future civilisation. Buildings were light, airy and modern. Views of the city, often drawn as if the artist was in an aeroplane, displayed an organised, dense and coherent plan, in total contrast to the wide-open spaces of land within which they were located. It was a distinctly urban dream[38].

Garnier's vision was far ahead of his time. Le Corbusier was making his drawings of the Modern City two decades later. Modern architecture roused little interest in Lyons in the 1920s[39] and it was really the project for Villeurbanne which made the greatest impact with the new style in the region. Why this was so, however, had to do with far more than an architect's vision. The prospects for Villeurbanne grew out of its relationship with Lyons, its past history and structure, its political complexities, the speed with which it was growing and the leadership of its Mayor, Lazare Goujon[40]. The dense tissue of experience these factors produced ensured that Villeurbanne was, in its cultural impact on its inhabitants, the very reverse of Kingstanding. Kingstanding was a product of Birmingham's expansionist imperialism but this was not so in Villeurbanne. One of the most influential factors was the fact that it was an established commune outside Lyons[41]. For most of the nineteenth century it had been a rural commune but gradually small workshops and industries moved out of the large city to find cheaper space for expansion. The trickle of industrialisation became a flood from the 1880s. Villeurbanne became a centre for the development of finishing industries for silk textiles, especially dyeing. This introduced the need for chemicals and chemical plants were built. As the silk industry collapsed, artificial silk became a leading sector and again new factories were built in Villeurbanne.

Villeurbanne grew from 8000 inhabitants in 1880 to 44 000 by 1914. From the war to the completion of the new buildings, it gained a further 30 000 people, some of them immigrants from North Africa, Italy and Spain. Thus an old-established commune with administrative structures suitable for a rural society became thrown into the task of creating a new identity for itself as it was transformed. Bonneville's study of the metamorphosis of the suburb is a highly complex work which illustrates how the process of urbanisation was led by industrialisation[42]. The outcome was determined by a social structure formed by economic activity and given its voice through local political articulation. While unskilled workers from the larger factories were growing in numbers, they still lived alongside those who had longer roots in the suburb: the agricultural workers, gardeners, artisans, shopkeepers, café owners, small industries and trades, even some professional groups such as lawyers, doctors and schoolteachers needed by the commune. The built environment of the commune was largely unplanned except for the axial roads which connected it to Lyons and neighbouring communes. Housing was extremely varied. It included everything from small speculative developments to self-help housing and single-storey structures. In the two decades before the First World War, the commune became socialist and the local commune was in support of the workers in strikes against the large industrialists[43].

In some senses, Villeurbanne was an embattled little commune, struggling to absorb the changes within itself but keeping a united front against the hostile forces from outside. In 1906, the city of Lyons made moves to take it over, as had already happened in a number of communes on the outskirts of the city. Villeurbanne resisted and Herriot dropped the plan on the grounds of cost. Dealing with the administrative problems of the commune might cost the city more than it would gain in revenues. In 1924, in the exciting national elections which brought the Cartel des Gauches to power and Herriot to the premiership[44], Dr Lazare Goujon was elected the socialist mayor of Villeurbanne, beating the communists by about 1000 votes[45]. It was the response of the commune to the historic split of 1920, when French communists and socialists had parted company on the issue of how to work for future revolution. Goujon's platform of moderate and practical social reform appealed not only to the huge majority of the industrial working class but also to the other minority interests to be found in the commune. Goujon was a doctor and high upon his list of priorities was high quality housing for all. His election at this time was a challenge: to work out on the ground the practical social reform promised by the socialists.

However, 1924 was not a good time to try and achieve a massive housing programme with a major financial crisis influencing national government. Because of it, the Cartel des Gauches fell from power and was followed by a succession of weak governments, each less able than the last to deal with the financial crisis. Goujon turned his attention to two projects for which he could hope to raise finance, a new town hall and a Palais du Travail for the people. Both were signals of his intent to create a new kind of urban civilisation in Villeurbanne. The former indicated the new status of the enlarged commune. The latter was a manifestation of the social and cultural programme which Goujon wanted to initiate to bring about social revolution. He was dedicated to a programme of popular education for the workers[46]. The Palais du Travail was a concrete example of his intentions. When he opened the subscription list for the building in 1927, he gave a fiery speech outlining his vision. It was for a centre which would give space to all local groups: mutualists, syndicalists, co-operators, philanthropists, artists, sports people. There were to be facilities for conferences and exhibitions. It was to empower the working classes and to help them create their future.

> La création d'un véritable Temple laïque, centre d'activité intellectuelle, artistique et morale est indisponsable au développement démocratique de la Cité, ainsi qu'à l'éducation intégrale de la classe ouvrière, condition essentielle d'une amélioration véritable de son sort[47].
> [The creation of a very secular Temple, a centre of intellectual, artistic and moral activities is indispensable to the development og democracy in the city, as much as to the full education of the working classes, the essential element in the true amelioration of their condition.]

Raising the money for these projects took years. Suddenly, however, on 1 August 1930, the whole campaign was transformed. A local large engineering firm closed down, leaving a huge unoccupied site in a central location. Goujon realised that this could be used, not only for the Mairie and the Palais du Travail, but also for working-class housing. He managed to secure a loan through the HBM mechanism just one week before the government closed it down, as the financial crisis of the Great Depression began to bite. Over the next four years, the new centre for Villeurbanne was to take shape. In conception, form and outcome, it was to be a total contrast to Kingstanding in Birmingham which was coming to completion over the same years. The physical environment which each created and the social and cultural context experienced by inhabitants provide two very different models in the development of modern urban living.

THE PHYSICAL AND SOCIAL DEVELOPMENT OF KINGSTANDING

Asa Briggs, in his *History of Birmingham*, referred to a local survey made in 1932 between Kingstanding and an old-established county town, Shrewsbury, with a slightly smaller population. Kingstanding had a population of 30 000, Shrewsbury slightly fewer. "Shrewsbury had 30 churches, 15 church halls and parish rooms, 5 other halls, and 2 public libraries; Kingstanding had 1 church and 1 hall"[48]. The contrast not only emphasises the scale of Kingstanding, it also points up the role played by churches and the voluntary sector in producing the facilities needed for

Figure 6.4 *The Palais du Travail (the Palace of Work)* [Author's photo]

communal activities. In Kingstanding, there was little prospect of public funding for social facilities. The problem was cost. Also, Birmingham Town Council's conversion to providing council housing embodied a new democratic ideal but not one which encompassed new ideas about social development[49]. Who would define what the latter meant? What say had the people moving to Kingstanding, or local authority officials responsible for the project? What about the views of local philanthropists and those working for social reform? Did political parties have a role? Or even the architects and builders responsible for the new built environment? Only the latter had a clear brief. Their task was to build conventional two-storey homes, at the lowest possible price and density, according to government regulations (TW) and to the principles of best practice adopted in British public housing since Raymond Unwin's days at the Local Government Board during the First World War.

It did not amount to a new manifesto in urban living. However, there was some political dimension in Birmingham's conversion to council housing. While there was broad cross-party agreement on the need to clear slums and provide better standards of housing for the working classes, it was the minority Labour Councillors who were fiercest in their demands for action. They campaigned for better housing alongside other objectives such as better educational facilities for the disadvantaged and better health care. But the new housing estates were not seen as a brave new world, heralding the birth of new opportunities across a broad front, which could, collectively, be seen as a new cultural ideal for the working classes. Kingstanding, like other estates in Birmingham, was a matter of providing decent homes, no more and no less. Birmingham's Labour Councillors were particularly vociferous in their demands for homes, not flats. Flats for the working classes, in their experience, were those to be found in unpopular tenement blocks. Sometimes, these had been built by philanthropists whose ideas of improved housing for the working classes were constrained by cost and a belief that a communal water tap on each floor of a tenement block constituted an improvement on a slum house.

Birmingham, as a progressive local authority, decided to send a delegation, including some Labour Councillors, on a fact-finding mission to Germany, Austria and Czechoslovakia, to look at the working-class housing there, especially the blocks of flats. It was the first British local authority to do this, and the councillors came back enthused with what they had seen, especially the huge public housing programmes such as those in Vienna[50]. But they were unable to convince their colleagues. In any case, the argument was somewhat academic as the cost of building flats did not fall below that of other forms of building until 1934[51]. Kingstanding, thus, presented Birmingham's Public Works Committee with the challenge of building in a conventional manner at lowest cost, though some effort was put into prefabrication of standard units. The greenfield site land was relatively cheap but each house had to incorporate new standards of public health and hygiene. There had to be an indoor lavatory and purpose-built bathroom. All

Figure 6.5 *Different housing designs in Kingstanding: model one* [Author's photo]

Figure 6.6 *Different housing designs in Kingstanding: model two* [Author's photo]

Figure 6.7 *Different housing designs in Kingstanding: model three* [Author's photo]

Figure 6.8 *Different housing designs in Kingstanding: model four* [Author's photo]

houses were to be supplied by gas and electricity. All that could be sacrificed to cut cost was space. First to go was the front parlour, the status symbol of the respectable working class. This did not represent a huge saving in building costs and the financial implications of the development determined that the council would have to charge a level of rent beyond the means of the poor.

Kingstanding's new population was therefore, drawn largely from the skilled and respectable working classes. It was not a slum clearance project. The fact that it was completed during the period of the Great Depression, however, inevitably meant that many inhabitants were unemployed and living on public assistance. Kingstanding was meant to be a paradise in comparison with the physical conditions of inner city Birmingham but it still had a strong undertow of poverty. The experiences of the new inhabitants, were nothing less than dramatic. There was a complete contrast between the old urban environment and the new. The new inhabitants left behind them their extended families and their friends. They left behind the everyday contacts of the crowded streets of the inner city. Instead, there were long empty streets of new housing with few focal points. There was some provision for a couple of rows of small shops, mainly located either side of the central traffic island. When the development was completed, the most that could be expected were food shops, newsagents, a post office, possibly a co-operative store, a haberdashery and hairdressers. Gone were the second-hand furniture shops, the pawnbrokers, the corner shop. Residents were expected to do their other shopping in the city centre.

Commercial entertainment was provided by a small cinema, the Mayfair, opened in 1931 and the much larger Odeon, a grand modernist building, opened by a local MP in 1935, which could seat 1346 people[52]. There was also an extremely large public house. Birmingham Council had long tried to cut down on the excessive number of public houses in the inner city. Local brewers were bribed, by offers of large suburban sites, to close down smaller pubs in the city centre. Kingstanding became the beneficiary of a large establishment. An important social facility was the local school, a focal point for meeting friends and community activities. But in the early days, the reaction of the inhabitants was one of shock. A local history of the estate says that:

> In 1929, Kingstanding was a hopeless sea of mud. There were no amenities, not even buses. There was no church, no meeting place, and for many residents at that time who were "on the dole" there was a long and, for those days, expensive journey to collect their small allowance. Consequently there was a need for the residents to combine together in their own interests and those of their neighbours[53].

Life could be bleak and lonely compared with the bustle of the inner city. For those who could afford one of the new wireless sets, the programmes of the BBC Midland region were uniformly dominated by a middle-class view of the world[54].

Those first on the scene were, unsurprisingly, the philanthropic social workers who had worked previously in the inner city districts from which the new tenants

Figure 6.9 *The new urban design feature:*
the cul-de-sac to stop through traffic
[Author's photo]

Figure 6.10 *The original Odeon building in*
Kingstanding [Author's photo]

Figure 6.11 *Front façade of the major Kingstanding public house, "The Trees"* [Author's photo]

Figure 6.12 *The local school, a low-rise building for maximum light and airiness* [Author's photo]

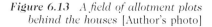
Figure 6.13 *A field of allotment plots*
behind the houses [Author's photo]

were drawn[55]. A Kingstanding Settlement was started in the early 1930s, "as a direct result of approaches made by people who had been re-housed from the Aston area of the city. These people had already experienced the companionship of the Settlement in Summer Lane and wanted to see a similar project in their new environment." The churches were next. The Congregationalists actually closed down and sold their chapel in Steelhouse Lane, Birmingham, and used the proceeds to build a new chapel in Kingstanding. The new chapel, which included a large meeting room, was opened in 1934. The Methodists, supported by the Birmingham Methodist Central Mission, did the same[56]. Gradually, a number of denominations, including the Catholics, found their way there. Secular groups based on shared enthusiasms began to develop. Kingstanding was close to Perry Common, a housing estate which slightly predated it. A number of activities, including a drama group, the British Legion, sports teams and even an opera group, were shared by the two estates. A local magazine, *The Kingstanding and Perry Common Review*, was eventually launched in the mid-1930s, as an information sheet for tenants.

By then, the editors had a remedy for the new tenants still coming onto the estate who were finding Kingstanding a dull place to be. "The houses are very nice, and so are the gardens, the roads are wide and there is plenty of light and air"[57]. But new tenants found a poverty of social life. Now, however, community associations were springing up to organise events all the year around. The main emphasis though, remained the private home and garden. There was a strong gender and age bias to the kinds of activities which were supposed to fill the time the tenants spent at home. For the men, digging the garden was a top priority. The pages of *The Kingstanding and Perry Common Review*, were full of articles on gardening, with seasonal programmes and special tips[58]. Many of the tenants were beginners, never before having had a garden. The women's domain was the home. With internal plumbing and a supply of hot water, regular chores such as the household's laundry, could be accomplished within the home. In inner city areas, extensive use had been made of the municipal baths and washhouses. Now, in every home, women were expected to cope with the bedlinen, towels and clothes of all members of the family, with the only mechanical aid perhaps being a boiler and mangle. The time it took to do the washing was less than it had been in the old houses, but the labour was still heavy and the cost of the hot water expensive. Household bills often led to the women cutting down on their own food to stretch meagre resources to pay for them[59].

New houses also encouraged new standards of cleanliness[60]. The inter-war period saw an explosion in the launching of new women's magazines, aimed at entertainment but also full of household "tips" for the ideal housewife[61]. In cultural terms, it was the woman's role to create and sustain the home. Higher standards of cleanliness and new technology meant that the housework became more onerous. The women of Kingstanding were experiencing what was a total transformation of home and family life, regardless of levels of poverty[62]. Family size among the working classes had dropped dramatically since the First World War although contraceptive devices were neither free nor widely available. Patterns of marriage and relationship with kin were changing, accelerated by the physical move to Kingstanding[63]. The age group expected to gain most from the new environment, were the children. *The Kingstanding and Perry Common Review* devoted a whole page each issue to children's activities. There were numerous voluntary groups such as Boy Scouts and Girl Guides, Cubs and Brownies, and sports teams. The climax of the outdoor activities was the annual gala which had competitions and cake stalls, vegetable produce and musical bands.

From 1934, the Community Associations of Kingstanding, Glebe Farm and Weoley Castle had organised summer camps, the tents and equipment having been donated by a member of the Cadbury family. Initially, these camps were for men and boys only. In 1936, the first camp was held which also included the women and children. It poured with rain but the pages of *The Kingstanding and Perry Common Review* were jubilant that it had taken place at all and had actually been a success. The cooking had been done by the women and the food was the best so far achieved at the summer camp. It was a public demonstration of the new family "ethos" and the determined efforts being made at community building[64]. Savage and Miles have suggested in their recent study of change within the British working class that by the First World War, "the decline of elite middle-class civic involvement and the rise of working-class associational activity had turned many towns and cities from middle-class to working-class environments". There were, however, exceptions. The example they cite is the one of Birmingham, "where the Chamberlain family remained dominant in local politics down to the Second World War"[65]. The evidence from Kingstanding suggests that, even with all the physical transformations of the new estate, that cultural hegemony remained unbroken.

THE PHYSICAL AND SOCIAL DEVELOPMENT OF VILLEURBANNE

Over the past decade, there has been an explosion of interest in the development of Villeurbanne in the 1930s[66]. This has been generated above all, by the physical form of the town centre. With modernist designs for the new Mairie and Palais du Travail already in place, the decision was taken to build a grand central avenue leading to the central square. The end of the avenue was to be marked by huge *gratte-ciel* (skyscrapers). Lesser blocks punctuated the continuous building on either side of the avenue up to the Mairie. In one fell swoop, the Mayor, the Chief Engineer of the Municipality, M. Fleury, and the architects, Giroud and Leroux, were to achieve a new urban identity for the commune, a new concept of a modern urban environment and 1500 new housing units for workers. It was the first attempt to do such a thing on this scale in Lyons and its immediate hinterland. It was bold, experimental and new. It was not planned, however, as a single project from the start. The planning and design of the new city centre took place in a piecemeal fashion over a number of years as fresh opportunities arose, in terms of the availability of land and finance[67]. There was no preconceived model. Villeurbanne was unique.

The imagination and, equally important, the expertise required to carry out the rebuilding schemes came from a new element in the public life of the commune: the growth of professionalism[68]. The Mayor, elected from 1924 to 1935, Dr Lazare Goujon, was not only a passionate socialist, he was also a doctor, dedicated to finding ways of helping the working classes find new ways of healthy living in an urban environment[69]. But Goujon's plans would have come to nothing without the back-up of a whole range of municipal services which were developing fast in the inter-war period. A key figure in the realisation of the city centre development was the professional municipal engineer, M. Fleury. He was invited in 1934 to address a conference of technical experts in Marseilles on the subject of Villeurbanne. What he gave them, though, was not a review of the technical problems of development. Instead, he offered a discourse on a new relationship between the municipal bureaucracy and the people, a new professional ideal. It was symbolised by the buildings themselves and their internal arrangements. He used the example of the interior layout of the new Mairie to emphasise his point. He said:

> L'intérieur est bâti sur un plan très simple, très clair qui traduit bien l'intention qui fut celle de l'Administration communale, de mettre tous les organismes municipaux

"au service" de chaque contribuable de la cité, de chaque "citoyen"[70].
[The interior is built to a very simple plan, very obvious, which strongly indicates well the intention of the communal Administration, to put all the elements of municipal organisation at the service of each ratepayer of the city, to each citizen.]

He was giving new substance to the idea of citizenship.

On the ground floor were all the offices which needed direct access to the street: the Tax Office, Police Headquarters, Technical Services, Registration and Stamp Office. On the first floor, accessed by two large staircases from either side of the building, were the administrative services, located in two vast halls which were

Figure 6.14 *The central square between the Mairie and the Palais du Travail* [Author's photo]

light and airy. On the second floor were the reception rooms and offices of the Mayor and his officers, the marriage room and the library. Everything was coherently located and easy to find. There were no long corridors and mysterious doors. The whole aim was to dispel the fears of citizens that they would not find what they wanted. Remarkably, the Chief Municipal Engineer did not dwell on the techniques used in the construction of the building. What he wanted was to emphasise the new ideology of the modernist building, what it represented in social and cultural terms. His comments on the Palais du Travail were similar. He was totally enthusiastic about its role as the social and cultural hub of the commune. He barely mentioned the technical problems and new solutions that

Figure 6.16 *The façade of the Mairie opposite the Palais du Travail* [Author's photo]

had been used in its construction. It was a huge modern-styled building with two wings, the left wing was devoted to the Public Health office and the public dispensary, the right wing to meeting rooms and offices for local societies.

The centre of the building was used for mass meetings and public services. There was a large conference room for meetings of all kinds, a theatre which could seat 1300 spectators, a huge brasserie-restaurant and, right in the basement, a swimming pool. There had been a technical problem with the lighting of the pool. A unique solution had been found of putting projectors under the water which provided light, enabled the safety of bathers to be monitored and maintained the privacy of swimmers from public view. Fleury barely mentioned it. He, Goujon and the architects were on a crusade to create a new working-class culture and way of urban living. The skyscrapers and flats in the central boulevard were built in the same spirit. There were a number of technical achievements. All the flats were placed in such a way that they caught the sun. Each was equipped with a balcony to maximise the access to light and air of the residents. Further, a totally innovative plan was put in place to supply the flats with hot water and heating from a local power plant, recently built to supply local factories. The flats were equipped with lifts and stairs. Yet the way these innovations were publicised was in terms of their social benefits, not their technical achievements. The lifts and stairs were considered to be good meeting places, enabling tenants to get to know each other. The hot water and heating were of benefit to women, helping to reduce greatly the burdens of domestic housekeeping.

There is no doubt that the men responsible for the construction of Villeurbanne were in the grip of a strong and well-identified ideology. In a working-class commune, they were creating new ways of urban living that had little reference to nearby Lyons. It had two clear dimensions: the first, an emphasis on improving the private family home and encouraging family life; the second, a shared communal identity based on the communal facilities provided by the municipality. It was possible to think in these terms as Goujon, Fleury et al. were building on past experiences. Villeurbanne was not totally new. It had been transformed from a rural to an industrial commune in a very short space of time and by the 1920s was a thriving industrial area. Since the First World War, the question of working-class housing had been high on the agenda. There had been an extensive growth in the use of the HBM machinery in new initiatives to build homes. Among the many associations involved in this, the three largest were La Société Coopérative des HBM "Jardins and Foyers" of 1921; le Domaine du Combattant érigé à Cyprian; and, at the end of the decade, la Société Villeurbannaise du HBM of 1929. In form at least, this model of a combination of public and private initiatives for housing was used even by the municipality in the *Gratte-ciel* project. A Société Villeurbannaise d'Urbanisme was set up in 1931 as the mechanism for promoting the development of the real estate. The most important social consequence of this approach was that it precluded the poor. Rents had to be paid to service loans. The municipality had no funds for subsidies.

Figure 6.17 *The careful detailing on an entrance door* [Author's photo]

The result was thus inevitably patchy. In Croix Luizet, one of the poorer quarters of Villeurbanne with a high immigrant population, there were some outstanding small achievements with societies using HBM support, but this was small scale. As more people packed into the quarter in the 1920s, drawn by the large-scale industries offering relatively unskilled jobs, the little *cité-jardin* built there showed strong signs of the social intentions of those that developed it. Roads were named after French pioneers of social reform, such as the Rue Jean Zuber, Alfred Ribot, George Picot, Emile Cheysson. Or sometimes the roads were named after the social objectives themselves, such as Rue du Foyer, Rue de la Famille, Rue de la Jeunesse[71]. But by the early 1930s, France had been belatedly drawn into the international crisis of the Great Depression. As the British economy began to make a recovery (in which house-building played a part), the French sank further and further into depression. In Villeurbanne, the ranks of the unemployed, or the strikers. striking against the lowering of wages below subsistence levels merely to keep firms in business, were growing in number (there were 4000 with voting rights in 1935). For them, the activities of the socialists were an irrelevance.

Goujon and his supporters had staked everything on their urban programme. In a brave, but possibly foolhardy, bid to achieve their social goals, Goujon had

Figure 6.18 *The urban texture of the grand avenue* [Author's photo]

negotiated a loan of 50 000 000 francs in 1931[72]. He wanted to complete his public works programme by the building of a huge sports stadium and undertake the *Gratte-ciel* project. In the economic circumstances of a failing national economy, with governments trying to beat depression by deflation, such a loan proved to be crippling. In the elections of 1935, Goujon lost power to the Communists who immediately halted the urban programme. The foundations of the sports stadium, laid by Goujon, were never built upon. But the Mairie, the Palais du Travail and the grand avenue of workers flats, marked by the two massive skyscraper blocks, were all completed by 1934. Goujon had the satisfaction of inviting the Prefect of the Rhône Département and Édouard Herriot, the Mayor of Lyons to the offical opening in 1934. Both warmly congratulated him and the commune on its achievement, conveniently forgetting their roles in the past, trying to take over and control the commune. That, at least, must have been a satisfying moment for Goujon. The historian Bonneville suggests that the success of the municipal urban programme in Villeurbanne was to bring standards of bourgeois comfort and urban living to the working classes in a new form, a modern architecture. The elegance and style of the development gave dignity and a certain grandeur to the objectives of a socialist municipality.

KINGSTANDING AND VILLEURBANNE: MODELS OF THE FUTURE?

Kingstanding and Villeurbanne were created in totally different political, economic and cultural contexts. Yet they were not produced in a vacuum. The provision of working-class housing had become an international issue which governments of every political persuasion were bound to have to tackle as the speed of mass urbanisation continued. Neither Kingstanding nor Villeurbanne proved to be lasting models[73]. By 1935, Birmingham had completed 15 large public housing estates on greenfield sites on the city's periphery. These were cheek by jowl with private developments, on similar lines in similar styles to public housing, which were also built in the inter-war period. Collectively, this building was to transform totally the physical environment of the city into one with many large relatively low density suburbs. In 1935, with the appointment of Sir Herbert Manzoni as the City Engineer, a new phase opened. Manzoni was intent on the urban regeneration of central areas. Held up by the war, nevertheless Manzoni managed to institute a major reconstruction of the inner city built environment, developing a new and gigantic transport system for the private motor vehicle. This redevelopment brought the problem of housing for the poorest classes once more to the fore as their inner city homes were demolished.

By that time, the costs of public housing forced local authorities to build flats with lower specifications in terms of space per family. In the skyscraper apartment blocks built in Birmingham in the 1950s, however, there was little attempt to construct balanced communities with clear guidelines to modern urban living as had been offered to the flat dwellers in the centre of Villeurbanne. Nor was the network of voluntary associations and social clubs, which had made such a difference to Kingstanding's early tenants, able to operate as effectively in a different social and environmental context. It was not just a matter of scale. The cultural norms which had determined Birmingham's housing policy in the years before 1930 were no longer there. The whole political and social environment of city government had changed. As always, the provision of working-class housing provided a barometer of current cultural values. What happened in Birmingham, was mirrored in Lyons a decade or so later. France's second city was no more able to benefit from the example of the little socialist commune of Villeurbanne, than Birmingham had been when it began to build its municipal flats[74].

The economic and political problems of France in the late 1930s and the Second World War period precluded many large initiatives in Lyons to promote working-class housing. After the war, the ancient Herriot was invited back to the city to be once more Mayor, a tribute to his stance in the war, but also an indication of the doldrums within muncipal government as Lyons began to grow and develop its industrial base. Eventually, by the end of the 1950s, plans were afoot to regenerate the physical environment of the city with new transport schemes, echoing the schemes in hand in Birmingham. Like Birmingham, Lyons was too large a municipality to be able to stamp an identity on a particular project such as had happened in Villeurbanne. Le Corbusier, not Tony Garnier, became the guiding standard for modern architects and the International Style, devoid of local politics, ceased to represent social values beyond those dictated by the architects[75].

The history of Kingstanding and Villeurbanne in the early 1930s does give, however, some insights into the very different responses which could be made to creating new modern urban environments for the working classes. Both aimed at achieving new standards of health and hygiene; both were beset in these aims by the existence of poverty. Both tried to achieve a new kind of urban environment which would not decay in the same way as unplanned crowded inner city districts. Both offered a particular compromise to the potential clash between public authority responsibility and private choice. Both put their faith in encouraging family-centred values. In the aftermath of the First World War, there was a reaffirmation of family values, of gender roles within marriage and the importance of achieving new standards of childcare and mothering. These were very much products of a particular moment. But the huge difference in the physical environments created in Kingstanding and Villeurbanne emphasises one thing: there were many ways of achieving a new social ideal. With improved communications in Europe, ideas could be shared on a national, even international basis. However, this did not lead to any kind of uniformity of response. The utter contrast between Kingstanding and Villeurbanne demonstrates the importance of history, the cultural context and politics in determining the outcome.

NOTES

1. A Rapaport (1981) "Identity and Environment: A Cross-cultural Perspective" in JS Duncan (ed) *Housing and Identity: cross cultural perspectives* London, Croom Helm.
2. See Chapter 4, p. 178.
3. C Bauer (1943) *Modern Housing* Boston, Houghton Mifflin.
4. SD Chapman (1967) *The Early Factory Masters: the transition to the factory system in the Midland textile industry* Newton Abbot, David and Charles, 157–9; S Pollard (1965) *The Genesis of Modern Management: a study of the industrial revolution in Great Britain* London, Edward Arnold.
5. J Tarn (1973) *5% Philanthropy: an account of housing in urban areas between 1840–1914* Cambridge, Cambridge University Press.
6. See Chapter 3, pp. 119–21.
7. N Bullock and J Read (1985) *The Movement for Housing Reform in Germany and France 1840–1914* Cambridge, Cambridge University Press; C Pooley (ed) (1992) *Housing Strategies in Europe 1880–1930* Leicester, Leicester University Press; MJ Daunton (ed) (1990) *Housing the Workers: a comparative history 1850–1914* Leicester, Leicester University Press.
8. AS Wohl (1977) *The Eternal Slum: housing and social policy in Victorian London* London, Edward Arnold.
9. A Mearns (1883) *The Bitter Cry of Outcast London* London, Frank Cass reprint 1970.
10. The Act codified and extended the powers of local authorities to build both replacement and additional housing. But the legislation was permissive; finance was not forthcoming and few local authorities had the managerial competence on hand to undertake house-building directly. J Morton (1991) "The 1890 Housing Act and its aftermath: the era of the 'model dwellings'" in S Lowe and D Hughes (eds) *A New Century of Social Housing* Leicester, Leicester University Press, 13–32.
11. RH Guerrand (1987) *Propriètaires et Locataires: les origins du logement social en France (1850–1914)* 2nd edn Paris, Quintette, 345; Bullock and Read (1985) *Movement*.
12. M Swenarton (1981) *Homes for Heroes: the politics and architecture of early state housing in Britain* London, Heinemann Educational.
13. Sellier gave an address on this subject to the General Council of the Seine in 1913, published in B Marrey (ed) (1998) *Henri Sellier: Une Cité pour tous* Paris, Édition du Linteau, 63–93.
14. A Power (1993) *Hovels to High Rise: state housing in Europe since 1850* London and New York, Routledge, 38.
15. JA Yelling (1992) *Slums and Redevelopment Policy and Practice in England, 1918–45 with Particular Reference to London* London, UCL Press.
16. JA Yelling (1990) "The Metropolitan Slum: London 1918–51" in SM Gaskell *Slums* Leicester, Leicester University Press, 186–223.
17. CG Pooley (1992) "Housing Strategies in Europe, 1880–1930: towards a comparative perspective" in Pooley, *Housing Strategies*, 325–48.
18. Power (1993) *Hovels to High Rise*, 231–2.
19. For Birmingham, see E Hopkins (1998) *The Rise of the Manufacturing Town: Birmingham and the Industrial Revolution* Stroud, Sutton, and A Briggs (1952) *History of Birmingham: borough and city* Vol II, London, Oxford University Press. For Lyons, J-L Pinol (1980) *Espace Sociale, espace politique: Lyons à l'èpoque du Front Populaire* Lyons, Presses Universitaires de Lyons.
20. S Bernstein (1985) *Édouard Herriot, ou la République en personne* Paris, Presses de la Fondation Nationale des Sciences Politiques; M Balfour (1985) *Birmingham and Joseph Chamberlain* London, Allen and Unwin.

21. A Briggs (1963) *Victorian Cities* London, Odhams, Chap 5, 185–244.
22. EHH Green (1999) "Gentlemanly Capitalism and British Economic Policy, 1880–1914: the debate over bi-metallism and protection" in RE Dunett (ed) *Gentlemanly Capitalism and British Imperialism* London, Longmans, 52–4.
23. The Cadbury family strongly encouraged adult education. The first George Cadbury Memorial lecture was given in the Selly Oak Adult Education College, endowed by the Cadburys, in 1927 by Albert Mansbridge, founder of the Workers' Educational Association in 1902.
24. M Harrison (2000) *Bournville: Model Village to Garden Suburb* Chichester, Phillimore.
25. R Rodger (1995) "Scottish Housing and English Cultural Imperialism c 1880–1940" in S Zimmerman (ed) *Urban Space and Identity in the European City 1890–1930s* Budapest, CEU History Dept, Working Paper Series 3. 73–94.
26. JS Nettlefold (1908) *Practical Housing* Letchworth, Letchworth Garden Press.
27. C Chinn (1991) *Houses for People: 100 years of council housing in Birmingham* Exeter, Birmingham Books, 49.
28. GE Cherry (1994) *Birmingham: a study in geography, history and planning*, Chichester, John Wiley and Sons, 115.
29. A Sutcliffe and R Smith (1974) *Birmingham 1939–1970: History of Birmingham* Vol III London, Oxford University Press.
30. See title of Bernstein's biography (1985) *Édouard Herriot, ou la République en personne* Paris, Presses de la Fondation Nationale des Sciences Politiques.
31. J-L Pinol (ed) (1996) *Atlas Historique des Villes de France* Barcelona and Paris, Hachette Livre, 164.
32. C Pawlowsky (1967) *Tony Garnier et les débuts de l'urbanisme fonctionnel en France* Paris, Centre de Recherche d'Urbanisme.
33. M Bonilla and D Vallat (1987) *Les Immeubles d'Appartements Modern. Saint-Étienne 1923–1939* St Étienne, École d'Architecture de Saint-Étienne, 119–20; *La Cité de la Création* (1991) Musée Urbain Tony Garnier, Lyons, Centre de Recherche Esthétique et Cités. The housing project contained 1567 flats for 4000 tenants.
34. N Pierrou (1989) "Tony Garnier et l'école lyonnaise" in P Gages *L'Avenir Enterprise Cooperative. 70 ans de l'histoire d'une métropole* Liège, Pierre Mardaga.
35. D Wiebensen (1969) *Tony Garnier: the Cité Industrielle* London and New York, Studia Vista: for Garden City Association meeting in Bournville, see D Hardy (1991) *From Garden Cities to New Towns: campaigning for Town and Country Planning, 1899–1946* Vol I, London, E & FN Spon, 46–7.
36. AS Travis (1977) *The Evolution of Town Planning in France 1900–1919, with Special Reference to Tony Garnier and Planning in Lyons* Birmingham, University of Birmingham, Centre for Urban and Regional Studies.
37. M Ruby (1979) *Le Résistance à Lyons: 19 juin 1940–3 septembre 1944* Lyons, L'Hérmes, 48.
38. R Jullian (1989) *Tony Garnier: constructeur et utopiste* Paris, Philippe Sers Editeur.
39. Bonilla and Vallat (1987) *Immeubles*, 119.
40. M Bonneville (1978) *Villeurbanne: naissance et métamorphose d'une banlieue-ouvrière: processus et formes d'urbanisation* Lyons, Presses Universitaires de Lyon.
41. Meurat (1982) *Le Socialisme municipal: Villeurbanne 1880–1962 – une histoire d'une différenciation* Lyons, Presses Universitaires de Lyon, 103–10.
42. Bonneville (1978) *Villeurbanne*, 45–68.
43. Meurat (1982) *Socialisme municipal*, 50–75.
44. M Agulhon (1993, English edn) *The French Republic 1879–1992* Oxford, Blackwell, 189–203.
45. At the first round of the election, Goujon got 4405 votes, the communist leader got

4034. In the second round, the Radical Socialists threw in their lot with Goujon and he polled 5915 votes to the communists' 4958.

46. Meurat (1982) *Socialisme municipal*, 146–8.

47. Meurat (1982) *Socialisme municipal*, 147.

48. Briggs (1952) *History of Birmingham*, 235.

49. The "garden suburb" was still the ideal for the physical form, see Chap 3, but it did not incorporate a vision of independent social development.

50. City of Birmingham (1930) *Report . . . of the deputation Visiting Germany, Czecho-slovakia and Austria in August 1930, for the purpose of studying the system of tenement or flat dwellings erected in various towns* Official Publication of the Municipality of Birmingham.

51. A Sutcliffe (1974) "A Century of Flats in Birmingham 1875–1973" in A Sutcliffe (ed) *Multi-Storey Living: the British working class experience* London, Croom Helm, 194.

52. C and R Clegg (1983) *The Dream Palaces of Birmingham* Birmingham, privately published.

53. *Kingstanding Past and Present* (1968, 3rd edn 1984) Birmingham, Birmingham Public Libraries, 18.

54. The Birmingham Council of Community Associations was the week's "Good Cause" on the Midland BBC programme in Aug 1936. Sir Barry Jackson, supporter of the Birmingham Repertory Co. and cultural life in the city, gave the address.

55. These were Settlement workers, clerics and philanthropic women, engaged in voluntary social work. This kind of activity was well established before the First World War. HE Meller (1976) *Leisure and the Changing City 1870–1914* London, Routledge and Kegan Paul, Chaps 6 and 7.

56. *Kingstanding Past and Present* 18–25.

57. "A Page for New Tenants" *Kingstanding and Perry Common Review* May 1937, 3.

58. A whole page in each issue was entitled "Gardening Notes for (month)".

59. A 1939 social survey of Kingstanding revealed low levels of nutrition among inhabitants at a time of plenty elsewhere. Cherry (1994) *Birmingham*, 116. Similar results were found in Wythenshawe, Manchester's prestige model estate of the inter-war years. J Greatorex and S Clarke (1984) *Looking Back at Wythenshawe* Timperley, Willow Publishing.

60. It was officially estimated that the housewife would find her workload reduced by 50%. Such estimates did not take poverty into consideration. See A Ravetz (with R Turkington) (1995) *The Place of Home: English Domestic Environments 1914–2000* London, E & FN Spon, 216–19.

61. P Tinkler (1995) "Women and Popular Literature" in J Purvis (ed) *Women's History: Britain 1850–1914* London, UCL Press.

62. L Davidoff, M Doolittle, J Fink and K Holden (1999) *The Family Story: blood, contract and intimacy, 1830–1960* London, Longman, 185–220.

63. M Young and P Willmott (1957) *Family and Kinship in east London* London, Routledge and Kegan Paul; H Jennings (1962) *Societies in the Making: a study of development and redevelopment within a country borough* London, Routledge and Kegan Paul.

64. *Kingstanding and Perry Common Review* Sept 1936, 7.

65. M Savage and A Miles (1994) *The Remaking of the British Working Class 1840–1940* London, Routledge, 68.

66. J Bourgin and C Delfante (1993) *Villeurbanne: une histoire de gratte-ciel* Lyons, Éditions Lyonnaises d'Art et d'Histoire, 5–10.

67. Meurat (1982) *Socialisme municipal*, 153.

68. Y Cohen and R Baudouï (1995) *Les Chantiers de la Paix Sociale (1900–1940)* Fontenay/ St Cloud, ENS Editions, 15–22.

69. A Lagier (1989) "Les Gratte-ciels de Villeurbanne" in P Gages *L'Avenir Enterprise Coopérative*, 63–75.

70. Meurat (1982) *Socialisme municipal*, 160.

71. B Meurat (1980) *Croix Luizet: quartier de Villeurbanne* Lyons CNRS, Centre Régional de Publication de Lyon, 41.

72. Meurat (1982) *Socialisme municipal*, 155–7.

73. A British book on design, A Bertram (1938) *Design* London, Pelican, actually uses a photograph of Villeurbanne and juxtaposes it with an English style estate (very similar to Kingstanding) to illustrate the possibilities of what planning could and had achieved. I am indebted to Dr Mervyn Miller for this reference.

74. For redevelopment of Lyons in the 1960s, see J-L Pinol (ed) *Atlas Historique*, 170–1.

75. An account of how Le Corbusier wanted to change people to fit his designs is given in R Fishman (1977) *Urban Utopias in the Twentieth Century: Ebenezer Howard, Frank Lloyd Wright and Le Corbusier* New York, Basic Books, 163–264.

Select Bibliography

This bibliography has been organised to relate to each chapter in the book. Fullest bibliographical details are given in the footnotes. The most useful general works or bibliographies on European cities and the themes that are pursued in this book are as follows:

Introduction

Benevolo, L (1993) *The European City* Oxford, Blackwell.

Bosma, K and Hellinga, H (eds) (1997) *Mastering the City: North-European city planning 1900–2000* Vols I and II, Rotterdam, NAI Publishers/The Hague, EFL Publications.

Burtenshaw, D, Bateman, M and Ashworth, G (1991) *The European City: a western perspective* London, David Fulton Publishers.

Dethier, J and Guiheux, A (eds) *La Ville, art et architecture en Europe 1870–1993* published on the occasion of the exhibition *La Ville* Feb–May 1994, Paris, Centre Georges Pompidou.

Geddes P (1915) *Cities in Evolution* London, Williams and Norgate.

Hall, P (1988) *Cities of Tomorrow: an intellectual history of urban planning and design in the twentieth century* Oxford, Blackwell.

Hall, P (1998) *Cities in Civilisation: culture, innovation and urban order* London, Weidenfeld & Nicolson.

Handlin, O and Burchard, J (eds) (1966) *The Historian and the City* Cambridge, Mass., MIT Press.

Hohenburg, PM and Hollen Lees, L (1985) *The Making of Urban Europe 1000–1950* Cambridge, Mass., Harvard University Press.

Lampard, EE (1976) "The Urbanising World" in Dyos, HJ and Wolff, M (eds) *The Victorian City: images and reality* Vol. I, London, Routledge and Kegan Paul.

Lawton, R (ed) (1989) *The Rise and Fall of Great Cities* London, Belhaven Press.

Lees, A (1985) *Cities Perceived: urban society in European and American thought 1820–1940* Manchester, Manchester University Press.

Meller, H (ed) (1979) *The Ideal City* Leicester, Leicester University Press.

Meller, H (1990) *Patrick Geddes: social evolutionist and city planner* London, Routledge.

Mumford, L (1938) *The Culture of Cities* New York, Secker and Warburg.

Mumford, L (1946) *City Development* London, Secker and Warburg.

Mumford, L (1961) *The City in History: its origins, its transformations, and its prospects* London, Secker and Warburg.

Olsen, DJ (1986) *The City as a Work of Art: London, Paris and Vienna* New Haven, Yale University Press.

Reulecke, J (1985) *Geschichte der Urbanisierung in Deutschland* Frankfurt am Main, Suhrkamp Verlag.

Rodger, R (ed) (1993) *European Urban History: prospect and retrospect* Leicester, Leicester University Press.

258

Rodgers, DT (1998) *Atlantic Crossings: social politics in a progressive age* Cambridge, Mass., Harvard University Press.

Schorske, CE (1966) "The Idea of the City in European Thought" in Handlin, O and Burchard, J (eds) *The Historian and the City* Cambridge, Mass., MIT Press, 95–114.

Slater, TR "Urban Morphology in 1990: developments in international cooperation" in Slater, TR (ed) (1990) *The Built Form of Western Cities: essays for MRG Conzen on the occasion of his eightieth birthday* Leicester, Leicester University Press.

Sutcliffe, A (1981) *Towards the Planned City: Germany, Britain, the United States and France, 1780–1914* Oxford, Basil Blackwell.

Topalov, C (ed) (1999) *Laboratoires du Nouveau Siècle: la nébuleuse réformatrice et ses réseaux en France, 1880–1914* Paris, École des Hautes Études en Sciences Sociales.

Weber, AF (1899, repr. 1963) *The Growth of Cities in the Nineteenth Century* Ithaca, NY, Cornell University Press.

White, P (1984) *The Western European City: a social geography* London, Longman.

CHAPTER 1 BARCELONA AND MUNICH

Abrams, L (1992) *Workers' Culture in Imperial Germany: leisure and recreation in the Rhineland and Westphalia* London, Routledge.

Annuaire Estadistico de la Ciudad Barcelona, 1902 and 1903.

Artells, J (1972) *Barca, Barca, Barca* Barcelona, Laia.

Aurin, R "Pere Garcia Fària" in *Contemporary Barcelona, 1856–1999* Catalogue of Exhibition, Centre de Cultura Contemporània de Barcelona, 75–7.

Bianchini, F and Parkinson, M (1993) *Cultural Policy and Urban Regeneration: the West European experience* Manchester, Manchester University Press.

Blackbourn, D (1997) *The Fontana History of Germany 1780–1918* London, HarperCollins.

Bleek, S (1991) *Quarterbildung in der Urbanisierung. Das Münchner Westend, 1890–1933* Munich, R. Oldenbourg.

Boa, E (1987) *The Sexual Circus: Wedekind's Theatre of Subversion* Oxford, Basil Blackwell.

Brooke, MZ (1970) *Le Play: engineer and social scientist: the life and work of Frédéric Le Play* London, Longmans.

Carr, R (1966) *Spain 1808–1939* Oxford, Clarendon Press.

Casassas, J (1994) "Batallas y ambigüedades del catalanismo" in Sánchez, A. (ed) *Barcelona 1888–1929: modernidad, ambición y conflictos de una ciudad soñada* Madrid, Alianza Editorial, 127–40.

Castells, J (1994) "Guía urbana de la diversión" in Sánchez, A. (ed) *Barcelona 1888–1929: modernidad, ambición y conflictos de una ciudad soñada* Madrid, Alianza Editorial, 233–4.

Cipolla, CM (ed) (1973) *Fontana Economic History of Europe*, Vol 3, London, Collins.

Collins, GR (1960) *Antonio Gaudí* London, Mayflower.

Collins GR and Collins CC (1986) *Camillo Sitte: the birth of modern city planning* New York, Rizzoli.

Eisenberg, C (1991) "Football in Germany: beginnings, 1890–1914" in *International Journal of the History of Sport* 8, 2, 205–20.

Estapé, F (1996) "Ildefons Cerdà I Sunyer" in *Contemporary Barcelona, 1856–1999* Catalogue of Exhibition, Centre de Cultura Contemporània de Barcelona.

Fehl, G and Rodríguez-Lores, J (eds) (1983) *Stadterweiterungen 1800–1875: Von den Anfängen des modernen Städtebaues in Deutschland* Hamburg, Christians.

Fehl, G (1994) "Carl Henrici (1842–1927): pour un urbanisme allemand" in Dethier, J and

Guiheux, A (eds) *La Ville, Art et Architecture en Europe 1870–1993* Paris, Editions du Centre Pompidou, 136–7.

Fisch, S (1988) *Stadtplanung in 19. Jahrhundert: Das Beispiel München bis zu Ära Theodor Fischer* Munich, R. Oldenbourg Verlag.

Geary R (1987) "Working Class Culture in Imperial Germany" in Fletcher, R (ed) *From Bernstein to Brandt* London, Edward Arnold.

Geretsegger, H and Peintner, M (1970) *Otto Wagner 1841–1918: the expanding city, the beginning of modern architecture* London, Pall Mall.

Geyer, MH (1993) "Munich in Turmoil: social protest and the revolutionary movement, 1918–9" in Wrigley, CJ (ed) *Challenges of Labour: Central and Western Europe 1917–1920* London, Routledge, 51–71.

Green, M (1974) *The Von Richthoven Sisters: the triumphant and tragic modes of love* London, Weidenfeld & Nicolson.

Guardia y Albert García Espuche, M (1994) "1888 y 1929. Dos exposiciones, una sola ambición" in Sánchez, A (ed) *Barcelona 1888–1929: modernidad, ambición y conflictos de una ciudad soñada* Madrid, Alianza Editorial, 25–43.

Heartle, VK-M (1988) "Münchens 'verdrängte' Industrie" in Prinz, F and Kraus, M (eds) *München: Musenstadt mit Hinterhöfen: Die Prinzregentenzeit 1886–1912* Munich, Verlag CH Beck.

Hughes, R (1996) *Barcelona* 2nd edn, London, Harvill Press.

Kaplan, T (1992) *Red City, Blue Period: social movements in Picasso's Barcelona* Berkeley and LA, University of California Press.

Ladd, B (1990) *Urban Planning and Civic Order in Germany 1860–1914* Cambridge, Mass., Harvard University Press.

Lahuerta, JJ (1994) "Antonio Gaudí: poeta visionario, arquitecto demiurgo" in Sánchez, A (ed) *Barcelona 1888–1929: modernidad, ambición y conflictos de una ciudad soñada* Madrid, Alianza Editorial, 166–81.

Lampugnagi, VM (1996) "Cerdà's Plan or progressive urbanism" in *Contemporary Barcelona, 1856–1999* Catalogue of Exhibition, Centre de Cultura Contemporània de Barcelona.

Large, DC (1997) *Where Ghosts Walked: Munich's road to the Third Reich* New York and London, WW Norton and Co.

Lees, A (1985) *Cities Perceived: urban society in European and American thought 1820–1940* Manchester, Manchester University Press.

Lenman R (1980) 'Politics and Culture: the State and the avant-garde in Munich 1886–1914" in Evans RJ (ed) *Society and Politics in Wilhelmine Germany* London, Croom Helm.

Leviné-Meyer, R (1973) *Leviné: the life of a revolutionary* Farnborough, Saxon House.

Lindauersche, J (1938) *Statistisches Handbuch der Hauptstadt der Bewegung für 1927–37* Munich, Universitäts-Buchhandlung.

Mackay, D (1985) *Modern Architecture in Barcelona 1854–1939* No. 3, Anglo-Catalan Society Occasional Papers, University of Sheffield.

Makela, M (1990) *The Munich Secession: arts and artists in turn of the century Munich* Princeton, NJ, Princeton University Press.

Marfany, J-L (1996) *La Cultura del Catalanisme: el nationalisme catala en els sens inicis* Barcelona, Editorial Empuries.

Mendoza, C y E (1989) *Barcelona Modernista* Barcelona, Editorial Planeta.

Mitchell, A (1965) *Revolution in Bavaria 1918–19: the Eisner régime and the Soviet Republic* Princeton, NJ, Princeton University Press.

Montaner, JM (1997) *Barcelona: a city and its architecture* Cologne, Taschen.

Nerdinger, W (1994) "Theodor Fischer: le plan d'occupation des sols, Munich" in Dethier, J and Guiheux, A (eds) *La Ville, art et architecture en Europe 1870–1993* published on the occasion of the exhibition *La Ville* Feb–May 1994, Paris, Centre Georges Pompidou, 138–9.

Olsen, DJ (1986) *The City as a Work of Art: London, Paris and Vienna* New Haven and London, Yale University Press.

Pérez de Rozas, E (1994) "¡Barc-ça, Bar-ça, Bar-ça!: el catalanismo sentimental" in Sánchez, A (ed) *Barcelona 1888–1929: modernidad, ambición y conflictos de una ciudad soñada* Madrid, Alianza Editorial, 213–25.

Pujadas, X and Santacana, C (1990) *L'Altra Olimpíada. Barcelona '36. Esport, societat i política a Catalunya (1900–36)* Barcelona, Llibres de l'Index.

Ravetllat, PJ (1996) "Future Barcelona" in *Contemporary Barcelona 1856–1999* Catalogue of Exhibition, Centre de Cultura Contemporània de Barcelona, 87–9.

Richardson, J (1992) *A Life of Picasso Vol. I 1886–1906* London, Pimlico.

Roca, F (1994) "Ildefons Cerdà: 'el hombre algebraico'" in Sánchez, A (ed) *Barcelona 1888–1929: modernidad, ambición y conflictos de una ciudad soñada* Madrid, Alianza Editorial, 155–66.

Rosell, J (1996) "'Catalan construction' for modern architecture" in *Contemporary Barcelona 1856–1999* Catalogue of Exhibition, Centre de Cultura Contemporània de Barcelona.

Rudloff, W (1992) "Notjahre. Stadtpolitik in Krieg, Inflation und Weltwirtschaftskrise 1914 bis 1933" in Bauer, R (ed) *Geschichte der Stadt München* Munich, CH Beck.

Sambricio, C (1994) "Arturo Soria y Mata (1844–1920), La Cité linéaire" in Dethier, J and Guiheux, A (eds) *La Ville, art et architecture en Europe 1870–1993* published on the occasion of the exhibition *La Ville* Feb–May 1994, Paris, Centre Georges Pompidou, 162–3.

Soria y Mata, A (1913) *La Ciudad lineal como arquitectura nueva de ciudades* Madrid.

Sutcliffe, A (1981) *Towards the Planned City: Germany, Britain, the United States and France 1780–1914* Oxford, Basil Blackwell.

Teichler, HJ und Hauk, G (1987) *Illustrierte Geschichte des Arbeitersports* JHW Dietz Nachf.

Toutcheff, N (1994) "Léon Jaussely 1875–1932. Les débuts de l'urbanisme scientifique en France" in Dethier, J and Guiheux, A (eds) *La Ville, art et architecture en Europe 1870–1993* published on the occasion of the exhibition *La Ville* Feb–May 1994, Paris, Centre Georges Pompidou, 169.

Weber, AF (1899, repr. 1965) *The Growth of Cities in the Nineteenth Century: a study in statistics* Ithaca, New York, Cornell University.

Weiss, P (1970) *Kandinsky in Munich: the formative Jugendstil years* Princeton, NJ, Princeton University Press.

Zwischau, W (1988) "Heimatstil und Funktionalismus. Fabrikbau in München" in Prinz, F and Kraus, M (eds) *München: Musenstadt mit Hinterhöfen: Die Prinzregentenzeit 1886–1912* Munich: Verlag CH Beck, 114–18.

CHAPTER 2 VIENNA, BUDAPEST AND PRAGUE

Banik-Schwietzer, R (1990) "Vienna" in Daunton, M (ed) *Housing the Workers: a comparative history, 1850–1914* Leicester, Leicester University Press, 107–48.

Bender, T and Schorske, CE (eds) (1994) *Budapest and New York: studies in metropolitan transformation 1870–1930* New York, Russell Sage Foundation.

Berend, IT and Ránki, G (1974) *Economic Development in East-Central Europe in the 19th and 20th Centuries* New York and London, Columbia University Press.

Boyd Rayward, W (1975) *The Universe of Information: the work of Paul Otlet for*

Documentation and International Organisation published for the International Federation for Documentation by the All-Union Institute for Scientific and Technical Information, Moscow.

Cisar, J and Pokorny, F (1922) *The Czechoslovak Republic: a survey of its history and geography, its political and cultural organisation and its economic resources* London, T. Fisher Unwin.

Enyedi, G and Szirmai, V (1992) *Budapest: a Central European capital* (English trans.) London, Belhaven Press.

Freudenberger, H (1977) *The Industrialisation of a Central European City: Brno in the eighteenth century* London, Edington.

Geddes, P (1904) *City Development: a study of parks, gardens and culture institutes. A Report to the Carnegie Dunfermline Trust*, Bournville, the Saint George Press and Edinburgh, Geddes and Company.

Geddes, P (1913–14) "Two Steps in Civics: Cities and Town Planning Exhibition" and "The International Congress of Cities: the Ghent International Exhibition, 1913" both in *The Town Planning Review* IV.

Geddes, P (1915) *Cities in Evolution: an introduction to the town planning movement and to the study of civics* London, Williams and Norgate.

Gyáni, G (1990) "Budapest" in Daunton, MJ (ed) *Housing the Workers: a comparative history* Leicester, Leicester University Press, 149–50.

Gyáni, G (1994) "Uses and Misuses of Public Space in Budapest, 1873–1914" in Bender, J and Schorske, CE (eds) *Budapest and New York: studies in metropolitan transformation 1870–1930* New York, Russell Sage Foundation, 90–2.

Gyáni, G (1995) 'Ethnicity and Acculturation in Budapest at the turn of the century" in Zimmermann, S (ed) *Urban Space and Identity in the European City 1890–1930s* Budapest, Central European University, 107–13.

Hall, T (1997) *Planning Europe's Capital Cities: aspects of nineteenth century urban developments* London, E & FN Spon.

Herman, AH (1975) *A History of the Czechs* London, Allen Lane.

Hobsbawm, E (1994) *Age of Extremes: the short twentieth century 1914–1991* London, Michael Joseph.

Jeszenszky, G (1990) "Hungary through World War I and the End of the Dual Monarchy" in Sugar, P, Hanák, P and Frank, T (eds) *A History of Hungary* Bloomington, Indiana University Press, 274–5.

Kren, J (1996) *Konfliktgemeinschaft: Tschechen und Deutsche 1780–1918* Munich, R. Oldenbourg Verlag.

Lichtenburger, E (1993) *Vienna: bridge between cultures* London, Belhaven Press.

Lukacs, J (1993) *Budapest 1900: a historical portrait of a city and its culture* London, Weidenfeld & Nicolson.

Mamatey VS and Luza, R (eds) (1973) *A History of the Czechoslovak Republic 1918–1948* Princeton, NJ, Princeton University Press.

Melinz, G (1995) ' 'Red' and 'Catholic' Social Integration and Exclusion: municipal welfare policy and social reality in Vienna (1918–1938)" in Zimmermann, S (ed) *Urban Space and Identity in the European City 1890–1930s*, Budapest, Central European University.

Melinz, G and Zimmermann, S (eds) (1993) *Wien, Prag, Budapest: Blütezeit der Habsburgmetropolen: Urbanisierung, Kommunalpolitik gesellschaftliche Konflikte (1867–1918)* Vienna, Promedia.

Meller, H (1990) *Patrick Geddes: social evolutionist and city planner* London, Routledge.

Miklós, H (ed) (1980) *Budapest Története: a Forradalmak Korától a Felszabadulásig* Vol. V, Budapest, Akadémiai Kiadó.

Nagy, ZL (1985) "State Power, Autonomy, and Liberal opposition in Budapest 1919–1945" in *Études historiques Hongroises* Vol. II, Budapest, 73–89.

Nagy, ZL (1994) "Transformations in the City Politics of Budapest: 1873–1941" in Bender, T and Schorske, CE (eds) *Budapest and New York: studies in metropolitan transformation 1870–1930* New York, Russell Sage Foundation, 46–8.

Pollard, S (1973) "Industrialisation and the European Economy" *Economic History Review* Vol. XXVI, 4, 636–48.

Romsics, I (1999) *Hungary in the Twentieth Century* Budapest, Corvina.

Rothschild, J (1974) *East Central Europe between the two World Wars*, Seattle and London, University of Washington Press.

Schorske, CE (1980) *Fin-de-Siècle Vienna: politics and culture* London, Weidenfeld & Nicolson.

Svácha, R (1995) *The Architecture of the New Prague 1895–1945* Cambridge, Mass., MIT Press.

Teichova, A and Matis, H (eds) (1996) *Österreich und die Tschechoslowakei: 1918–1938. Die wirtschaftliche Neuordnung in Zentraleuropa in der Zwischenkriegszeit* Vienna, Böhlau Verlag.

Teplán, I (1994) "St Imre Garden City: an urban community" in Bender, T and Schorske, CE (eds) *Budapest and New York: studies in metropolitan transformation 1870–1930* New York, Russell Sage Foundation.

Timms, E (1989) "Images of the City: Vienna, Prague and the Intellectual avante-garde" in Pynsent, RB (ed) *Decadence and Innovation: Austro-Hungarian life and art at the turn of the century* London, Weidenfeld & Nicolson.

Volet-Seanneret, H (1988) *La Femme Bourgeoise à Prague 1860–1985: de la philanthropie à l'émancipation* Paris, Slatkine.

Wagner-Rieger, R (1969) *Das Kunstwerk im Bild* Vol I of *Die Wiener Ringstrasse: Bild einer Epoche* Vienna, Hermann Böhlaus Nachf.

Wingfield, NM (1992) "Czech, German or Jew: the Jewish Community of Prague during the inter-war period" in Morison, J (ed) *The Czech and Slovak Experience* London, Macmillan.

Wiskemann, E (1938) *Czechs and Germans: a study of the struggle in the historic provinces of Bohemia and Moravia* London, Oxford University Press.

CHAPTER 3 THE GARDEN CITY IDEAL IN EUROPE

Bakule, I (1995) "Riga's Garden Suburb" *Planning History* 17, 2, 6–11.

Bauer, C (1934) *Modern Housing* Boston and New York, Houghton Mifflin.

Beevers, R (1988) *The Garden City Utopia: a critical biography of Ebenezer Howard* Basingstoke, Macmillan.

Bliznakov, M (1976) "Urban Planning in the USSR: Integrative theories" in Hamm, MF (ed) *The City in Russian History* Lexington, University of Kentucky Press.

Brand, D (1992) "Ullvål Hageby: Engelsk inspirert arkitektur i Oslo" (Ullvål Garden City: English-inspired architecture in Oslo) and "Ullvål Hageby i internationalt perspecktiv" (Ullvål Garden City in international perspective) *Byminner* Oslo 3, 7–17.

Brumfield, WC (1991) *The Origins of Modernism in Russian Architecture* Berkeley, CA, University of California Press.

Bullock, N (1978) "Housing in Frankfurt and the new Wöhnkultur" *Architectural Review* 335–44.

Burlen, K (ed) (1987) *La Banlieue Oasis: Henri Sellier et les cités-jardins 1900–1940* Paris, Presses Universitaires de Vincennes.

Calabi, D (1996) "Marcel Poëte: pioneer of 'L'urbanisme' and defender of 'L'histoire des villes'" *Planning Perspectives* 11, 413–36.

Celzota, A (1935) *Zlín, Ville d'Activité Vitale* Zlín, TISK (a multilingual guidebook published in Zlín in the mid-1930s).

Clark, V (1990) "The Struggle for Existence: the professionalisation of German architects" in Cocks, G and Jarausch, KH (eds) *The German Professions* New York, Oxford University Press.

Cohen, Y and Baudoui, R (eds) (1995) *Les Chantiers de la Paix Sociale (1900–1940)* Fontenay-aux-Roses, ENS Editions.

Collins, CC and Swenarton, M (1987) "CIAM, Teige and the Housing Problem in the 1920s" *Habitat International* 11, 153–9.

Cooke, C (1978) "Russian Responses to the Garden City Idea" in "Garden City Legacy" *Architectural Review* 361.

Crew, DF (1979) *Town in the Ruhr: a social history of Bochum 1860–1914* New York, Columbia University Press.

Geary, D (1991) "The Industrial Bourgeoisie and Labour Relations in Germany, 1871–1937" in Blackbourn, D and Evans, RJ (eds) *The German Bourgeoisie: essays in the social history of the German middle class from the late eighteenth to the early twentieth century* London, Routledge.

Giedion, S (1941) *Space, Time and Architecture* Cambridge, Mass., Harvard University Press.

Glogar, A (1995) "The Study Institute in Zlín: example of a multi-purpose cultural institution" in Ševeček, L and Zahrádková *The Cultural Phenomenon of Functionalism* Second Conference Proceedings, Zlín, Státní Galerie Zlín.

Gropius, I (1972) *Walter Gropius, Buildings, Plans, Projects 1906–69* Massachusetts, Catalogue of the International Exhibition Foundation.

Halík, P (1995) "Zlín" in Ševeček, L and Zahrádková *The Cultural Phenomenon of Functionalism* Second Conference Proceedings, Zlín, Státní Galerie Zlín.

Hall, P (1988) *Cities of Tomorrow: an intellectual history of urban planning and design in the twentieth century* Oxford, Basil Blackwell.

Hardy, D (1991) *From Garden City to New Towns: campaigning for town and country planning 1899–1946* 2 vols, London, E & FN Spon.

Hennaut, E and Liesens, L (eds) (1994) *Cités-jardins 1920–1940* Brussels, Archives d'Architecture Moderne.

Howard, E (1898) *Tomorrow: the peaceful path to real reform* London, Swann Sonnenschein.

Kafkoula, K (1996) "An Out-of-Place Utopia? Garden city movement and the planning of capital cities outside the European metropolitan regions" *The Planning of Capital Cities* Proceedings of the 7th International Planning History Conference, Thessaloniki, 160–77.

Karfík, V (1934) "Bat'a Architecture in Zlín" in Šlapeta, V (ed) *Bat'a Architektura a Urbanismus 1910–1950* Zlín, Státní Galerie ve Zlíně.

Lane, BM (1968) *Architecture and Politics in Germany, 1918–1945* Cambridge, Mass., Harvard University Press.

Lebas, E, Magri, S and Topalov, C (1991) "Reconstruction and Popular Housing after the First World War: a comparative study of France, Great Britain, Italy and the United States" *Planning Perspectives* 6, 249–67.

Magri, S and Topalov, C (1987) "De la cité à la ville rationalisée: un tournant du projet réformateur. Étude comparative France, Grande-Bretagne, Italie, États-Unis" *Revue française de sociologie* 28, 3, July–Sept., 417–51.

264

Meacham, S (1994) "Raymond Unwin 1860–1940: designing for democracy in Edwardian England" in Pederson, S and Mandler, P (eds) *After the Victorians* London, Routledge.

Meller, HE (1995) "Philanthropy and public enterprise: international exhibitions and the modern town planning movement, 1889–1913" *Planning Perspectives* 10, 295–310.

Mikuláštík, T (1993) "Kulturaktivitäten in Zlín in der zweiten Hälfte 30-er Jahre" in *Funktionalismus von Zlín* First Conference Proceedings, Zlín, Státní Galerie Zlín.

Mumford, E (1992) "CIAM Urbanism after the Athens Charter" *Planning Perspectives* 7, 391–417.

Nicoulaud, O (1987) "De la cité-jardin à la cité moderne" in Burlen, K (ed) *La Banlieue Oasis: Henri Sellier et les cités-jardins 1900–1940* Paris, Presses Universitaires de Vincennes.

Novak, P (1993) *Zlínská Architektura 1900–1950* Zlín, Vydala Agentura Cas.

Novotný, P (1995) "Kudlov Barn" in Ševecek, L and Zahrádková *The Cultural Phenomenon of Functionalism* Second Conference Proceedings, Zlín, Státní Galerie Zlín.

Phillips, WRF (1996) "The 'German Example' and the Professionalisation of American and British City Planning at the Turn of the Century" *Planning Perspectives* 11, 167–83.

Pokluda, Z (1993) "Die Umwandlung einer Landstadt zu einem Industriezentrum – die Bevölkerungsdichte in Zlín in 1900–1940" in *Funktionalismus von Zlín* First Conference Proceedings, Zlín, Státní Galerie Zlín.

Pokluda, Z (1995) "A Picture of Zlín in the Years between the Wars" in Ševecek, L and Zahrádková *The Cultural Phenomenon of Functionalism* Second Conference Proceedings, Zlín, Státní Galerie Zlín.

Porfyriou, H (1992) "Artistic Urban Design and Cultural Myths: the garden city idea in Nordic countries" *Planning Perspectives* 7, 263–301.

Rapoutov, L and Lang, MH (1991) "Capital City as Garden City: the planning of post-war revolutionary Moscow" in *The Planning of Capital Cities* Conference Proceedings 7th International Planning History Conference, Thessaloniki, 795–812.

Rebérioux, M (1987) "Un milieu socialiste à la veille de la grande guerre: Henri Sellier et le réformisme d'Albert Thomas" in Burlen, K (ed) *La Banlieue Oasis: Henri Sellier et les cités-jardins 1900–1940* Paris, Presses Universitaires de Vincennes.

Schollmeier, A (1990) *Gartenstädte in Deutschland: ihre Geschichte stadtbauliche Entwicklung und Architektur zu Beginn des 20. Jahrhunderts* Münster, Lit.

Sedlák, J (1993) "Die Kleinwohnungfamilienhäuser in Brünn und in Zlín" in *Funktionalismus von Zlín* First Conference Proceedings, Zlín, Státní Galerie Zlín.

Sedlák, J (1995) "The Zlín Architectural Phenomenon" in Ševecek, L and Zahrádková *The Cultural Phenomenon of Functionalism* Second Conference Proceedings, Zlín, Státní Galerie Zlín.

Šlapeta, V (ed) (1991) *Bat'a Architektura a Urbanismus 1910–1950* Zlín, Státní Galerie Zlín.

Šlapeta, V (1995) "Architect Miroslav Lorenc" in Ševecek, L and Zahrádková *The Cultural Phenomenon of Functionalism* Second Conference Proceedings, Zlín, Státní Galerie Zlín.

Smets, M (1977) *L'Avènement de la cité-jardin en Belgique: histoire de l'habitat social en Belgique de 1830 à 1930* Bruxelles, P. Mardaga.

Smets, M (ed) (1985) *Resurgam: La reconstruction en Belgique après 1914* Brussels, Credit Communal de Belgique.

Starr, SF (1976) "The Revival and Schism of Urban Planning inTwentieth Century Russia" in Hamm, MF (ed) *The City in Russian History* Lexington, University of Kentucky Press.

Sutcliffe, A (1981) *Towards the Planned City* Oxford, Basil Blackwell.

Švácha, J (1995) Zlín: Modernism without the avantgarde' in Ševecek, L and Zahrádková *The Cultural Phenomenon of Functionalism* Second Conference Proceedings, Zlín, Státní Galerie Zlín.

Uyttenhove, P (1990) "The Garden city education of Belgian planners around the First World War" *Planning Perspectives* 5, 271–283.

Vašicek, V (1995) "The Zlín School of Art" in Ševecek, L and Zahrádková *The Cultural Phenomenon of Functionalism* Second Conference Proceedings, Zlín, Státní Galerie Zlín.

Von Petz, U (1990) "Margarethenhohe, Essen: Garden City, Workers' Colony or Satellite Town?" unpublished paper at Bournville conference.

Von Petz, U (1995) "Vom Siedlungsverband Ruhrkohlenbezirk zum Kommunalverband Ruhrgebiet – 75 Jahre landsplanung und Regionalpolitik im Revier" in *Kommunalverband – Ruhrgebiet Wege, Spuren: Festschrift zum 75 jährigen Bestehen des Kommunalverbandes Ruhrgebiet* Essen, Kommunalverband, Ruhrgebiet.

Ward, SV (1994) *The Garden City: past, present and future* London, E & FN Spon.

Wilpert, B (1990) "How European is Work and Occupational Psychology?" in Drenth, R and Tobias, RJ (eds) *European Perspectives in Psychology* Chichester, J. Wiley and Sons.

Wingler, HM (ed) (1978) *The Bauhaus, Weimar, Dessau, Berlin, Chicago* Cambridge, Mass., MIT Press.

Zatloukal, P (1995) "Memorial to Tomás Bat'a" in Ševecek, L and Zahrádková *The Cultural Phenomenon of Functionalism* Second Conference Proceedings, Zlín, Státní Galerie Zlín.

CHAPTER 4 HAMBURG AND MARSEILLES

Ashworth, W (1987) *A Short History of the International Economy* 4th edn, London, Longmans.

Bardet, G (1990) *L'Urbanisme* 12th edn, Paris, Presses Universitaires de France.

Barsotti, C (1984) *Le Music Hall Marseillaise, 1815–1950* Arles, Meselun.

Borruey, R (1992) "Réinventer une ville-port? Le cas de Marseille" in Bonillo, J-L, Donzel, A and Fabre, M (eds) *Métropoles portuaires en Europe: Barcelone, Gênes, Hambourg, Liverpool, Marseille, Rotterdam* Bouches-du-Rhône, Éditions Parenthèses, 127–47.

Bosma, K and Hellinga, H (eds) (1997) *Mastering the City: North-European city planning 1900–2000* vol II, Rotterdam, NAI Publishers/The Hague, EFL Publications.

Calabi, D (1996) "Marcel Poëte: pioneer of 'l'urbanisme' and defender of 'l'histoire des villes'" *Planning Perspectives* 11, 4, 413–36.

Camau, E (1905) *Marseille au XXe siècle: tableau historique et statistique* Marseilles, Paul Rivat.

Casciato, M (1996) *The Amsterdam School* Rotterdam, OIO Publishers.

Choay, F (1965) *L'urbanisme, utopies and réalités. Une anthologie* Paris, Seuil.

Choay, F (1983) "Doctrines et Théories d'Urbanisme Non progressistes" in Duby, G (ed) *Histoire de la France urbaine, Vol 4. La Ville de l'âge industrielle* Paris, Seuil.

Christ, O (1997) "Vom Erbe Lichtwarks zum 'Museum einer Weltstadt': die Hamburger Kunsthalle unter Gustav Pauli" in Schneede, M and Leppien, H (eds) *Die Hamburger Kunsthalle: Bauten und Bilder* Leipzig, Seemann.

Comfort, RA (1966) *Revolutionary Hamburg: labor politics in the Early Weimar Republic* Stanford, Stanford University Press.

Dethier, J and Guiheux, A (eds) (1994) *La Ville, art et architecture en Europe 1870–1993* published on the occasion of the exhibition *La Ville* Feb–May 1994, Paris, Centre Georges Pompidou.

Evans, RJ (1987) *Death in Hamburg: society and politics in the cholera years 1830–1910* Oxford, Clarendon Press.

Faux, Cubells and Moy (eds) (1988) *Les Étrangers à Marseille, 1880–1939* Dir. des archives des Bouches-du-Rhône.

Ferguson, N (1995) *Paper and Iron: Hamburg business and politics in the era of inflation 1897–1927* Cambridge, Cambridge University Press.

Frank, H (1994) "Fritz Schumacher 1869–1947: Hambourg et Cologne" in Dethier, J and Guiheux, A (eds) *La Ville, art et architecture en Europe 1870–1993* published on the occasion of the exhibition *La Ville* Feb–May 1994, Paris, Centre Georges Pompidou, 144–5.

Georgel, C (ed) (1994) *La Jeunesse des Musées: les musées de France au XIXe siècle* Paris, Réunion des Musées Nationaux.

Gibbs, CH (1981) *The Great Exhibition of 1851*, 2nd edn, London, HMSO.

Gombrich, EH (1970) *Aby Warburg: an intellectual biography* London, Warburg Institute, University of London.

Greenhalgh, P (1988) *Ephemeral Vistas: Expositions Universelles, Great Exhibitions and the World's Fairs 1851–1939* Manchester, Manchester University Press.

Guide de l'exposition Marseille au XIXe siècle March–July 1993, Paris, Éditions Reuions de Musées Nationaux.

Harouel, J-L (1991) *Histoire de l'urbanisme* 4th edn, Paris, Presses Universitaires de France.

Harouel, J-L (1993) *L'embellissement des villes. L'urbanisme français au XVIIIe siècle.*

Harris, N, de Wit, W, Gilbert, J and Rydell, RW (eds) (1993) *Grand Illusions: Chicago's World Fair of 1893* Chicago, Chicago Historical Society.

King, A (1991) "The Global, the Urban, and the World" in King, AD (ed) *Culture, Globalisation and the World System* Basingstoke, Macmillan.

Ladd, BK (1990) *Urban Planning and Civic Order in Germany 1860–1914* Cambridge, Mass., Harvard University Press.

Lees, A (1985) *Cities Perceived: urban society in European and American thought, 1820–1940* Manchester, Manchester University Press.

Lefebvre, H (1970) *La révolution urbaine* Paris, Gallimard.

Lepetit, B (Eng. trans. 1994) *The Pre-industrial Urban System: France, 1740–1840* Cambridge, Cambridge University Press.

Leppien, H (1997) "Alfred Lichtwark: der erste Direktor der Kuntshalle" in Schneede, U and Leppien, H (eds) *Die Hamburger Kunsthalle: Bauten und Bilder* Leipzig, Seemann.

Lorente, JP (1998) *Cathedrals of Urban Modernity: the first museums of contemporary art 1800–1930* Aldershot, Ashgate.

Lortie, A (1994) "Jacques Gréber: les plans pour Philadelphie, 1917 et Marseille, 1933" in Dethier, J and Guiheux, A (eds) *La Ville, art et architecture en Europe 1870–1993* published on the occasion of the exhibition *La Ville* Feb–May 1994, Paris, Centre Georges Pompidou, 161.

Mandell, RD (1967) *Paris 1900: the great World's Fair* Toronto, University of Toronto Press.

Meller, H (1990) *Patrick Geddes: social evolutionist and city planner* London, Routledge.

Mulder, S (1997) "Cologne 1923: Generalsiedlungsplan" in Bosma, K and Hellinga, H (eds) *Mastering the City: North-European city planning 1900–2000* Vol II, Rotterdam, NAI Publishers/The Hague, EFL Publications, 192–9.

Plagemann, V (1997a) "Die Anfänge der Hamburgischen Kunstsammlungen und die erste Kunsthalle" in Schneede, U and Leppien, H (eds) *Die Hamburger Kunsthalle: Bauten und Bilder* Leipzig, Seemann.

Plagemann, V (1997b) "'Wir wollen nicht ein Museum, das dasteht und wartet': Lichtwark al Kultur politiker" in Schneede, U and Leppien, H (eds) *Die Hamburger Kunsthalle: Bauten und Bilder* Leipzig, Seemann.

Roncayolo, M (1996a) *Les Grammaires d'une ville: essai sur la genèse des structures urbaines à Marseille* Paris, Éditions de l'École des hautes études en sciences sociales.

Roncayolo, M (1996b) "De la croissance libérale aux grands plans d'urbanisme" in J-L Pinol (ed) *Atlas Historique des villes de France* Paris, Hachette Livre.

Schneede, U and Leppien, H (eds) (1997) *Die Hamburger Kunsthalle: Bauten und Bilder* Leipzig, Seemann.

Schumacher, F (1932, repr. 1984) *Das Werden einer Wohnstadt: Bilder aus dem neuen Hamburg* Hamburg, Hamburgische Hausbibliothek.

Schumacher, F (1935) *Stufen des Lebens: Erinnerungen eines Baumeister* Stuttgart, Deutsche Verlags-Anstalt.

Sewell, WH Jr (1985) *Structure and Mobility: the men and women of Marseille 1820–70* Cambridge, Cambridge University Press.

Steenhuis, M (1997) "Paris 1934: Plan d'Aménagement de la Région Parisienne" in Bosma, K and Hellinga, H (eds) *Mastering the City: North-European city planning 1900–2000* Vol II, Rotterdam, NAI Publishers/The Hague, EFL Publications, 226–7.

Ville de Marseille (1935) *L'Œuvre Municipale, 1929–1935* Marseilles, Municipality.

CHAPTER 5 BLACKPOOL AND NICE

Bennett, T (1986) "Hegemony, Ideology, Pleasure: Blackpool" in Wollacott, J (ed) *Popular Culture and Social Relations* Milton Keynes, Open University Press.

Bergamasco, J (1993) "Une Étoile l'éteint sur la Promenade: vie et mort d'Isadora Duncan" *Nice Historique* 96e Année, 71–5.

Bordes, M (ed) (1976) *Histoire de Nice: et du pays niçois* Toulouse, Privat.

Le Breton, G and Nission, A (1993) "Nice 1930: de la Promenade au Palais" *Nice Historique*, 14–29.

Carlin, M (1990) "Nice, Ville Universitaire" *Nice Historique* July–Dec, 83–91.

Catalogue Officielle Illustrée de l'Exposition decennale des beaux arts de 1889 à 1900 (1981) New York, Garland.

Charles, H (1990) "Jean Médecin et le développement de la ville de Nice" *Nice Historique* July–Dec, 47–65.

Cherry, G (ed) *Pioneers in British Planning* London, Architectural Press.

Cross, G (ed.) (1990) *Worktowners at Blackpool: Mass Observation and Popular Leisure in the 1930s* London, Routledge.

Derlange, M (1988) *Les Niçois dans l'histoire* Toulouse, Privat.

Exposition Universelle de 1889: Catalogue illustrée des beaux-arts, 1789–1889 (1981) New York, Garland.

Gilloch, G (1996) *Myth and Metropolis: Walter Benjamin and the city* Cambridge, Polity Press.

Greenhalgh, P (1988) *Ephemeral Vistas: a history of the expositions universelles, the great exhibitions and world's fairs, 1851–1939* Manchester/New York: Manchester University Press/St Martin's Press.

Haug, CJ (1982) *Leisure and Tourism in Nineteenth Century Nice* Kansas, Regents Press.

Hobsbawm, E and Ranger, T (eds) (1983) *The Invention of Tradition* Cambridge, Cambridge University Press.

Lavedan, P (1960) *Les Villes Françaises* Paris, Éditions Vincent.

Mawson, TH (1911) *Civic Art: studies in town planning, parks, boulevards and open spaces* London, BT Batsford.

Mawson, TH (1927) *The Life and Work of an English Landscape Architect* London, BT Batsford.

Jean Médecin. Un homme, une ville. Catalogue of Exhibition, 16th Dec to 19th Feb 1991 Musée d'Art et d'Histoire, Palais Masséna, Nice.

Ousby, I (1990) *The Englishman's England: taste, travel and the rise of tourism* Cambridge: Cambridge University Press.

Pastorelli, E (1964) *Le Tourisme à Nice de 1919 à 1936* Aix-en-Provence, D.E.S. Histoire.

Rouillier, A (1995) "Antoine Sartorio: poète de la pierre" and "Histoire d'un malentendu. La façade du Palais de la Méditerranée" both in *Lou Sourgentin* Vol. 115, Jan–Feb, 16–18 and 19–20.

Schor, R (n.d.) *Nice et Les Alpes-Maritimes de 1914 à 1945* Nice, Publications du Centre Régional de documentation pédagogique de Nice.

Sidro, A (1979) *Le Carnaval de Nice: et ses fous* Nice, Éditions Serre.

Storch, JRD (ed) (1982) *Popular Culture and Custom in Nineteenth Century England* London, Croom Helm.

Thurber, J (1963) "La Grande Ville de Plaisir" in *Vintage Thurber: a collection in 2 vols of the best writings and drawings of James Thurber* London, Hamish Hamilton, 66–71.

Urry, J (1989) "Cultural Change and Contemporary Holiday Making", *Theory, Culture and Society* 5, i, 35–55.

Walton, JK (1975) "Residential Amenity, Respectable Morality and the Rise of the Entertainment Industry: the case of Blackpool, 1860–1914" *Literature and History* 1, 62–78.

Walton, JK (1978) *The Blackpool Landlady: a social history* Manchester: Manchester University Press.

Walton, JK (1983) *The English Seaside Resort: a social history 1750–1914* Leicester, Leicester University Press.

Walton, JK (1988) "The World's First Working Class Seaside Resort: Blackpool Revisited 1840–1974" *Transactions of the Lancashire and Cheshire Antiquarian Society* 88, 1–30.

Walton, JK (1996) "Leisure Towns in Wartime: the impact of the First World War in Blackpool and San Sebastian" *Journal of Contemporary History* 31, 4, 607.

Walton, JK (1998) "Popular entertainment and public order: the Blackpool Carnivals of 1923–4" in *Northern History* Vol XXXIV, 170–88.

Walvin, J (1978) *Beside the Seaside: a social history of the popular seaside holiday* London, Allen and Unwin.

CHAPTER 6 KINGSTANDING AND VILLEURBANNE

Agulhon, M (1993, English edn) *The French Republic 1879–1992* Oxford, Blackwell.

Balfour, M (1985) *Birmingham and Joseph Chamberlain* London, Allen and Unwin.

Bauer, C (1943) *Modern Housing* Boston, Houghton Mifflin.

Bernstein, S (1985) *Edouard Herriot, ou la République en personne* Paris, Presses de la Fondation Nationale des Sciences Politiques.

Bertram, A (1938) *Design* London, Pelican.

Bonneville, M (1978) *Villeurbanne: naissance et métamorphose d'une banlieue-ouvrière: processus et formes d'urbanisation* Lyons, Presses Universitaires de Lyon.

Bouilla, M and Vallat, D (1987) *Les Immeubles d'appartements modernes: Saint-Étienne 1923–1939* St Étienne, École d'Architecture de Saint-Étienne.

Bourgin, J and Delfante, C (1993) *Villeurbanne: une histoire de gratte-ciel* Lyons, Éditions Lyonnaises d'Art et d'Histoire.

Briggs, A (1952) *History of Birmingham: borough and city* Vol II, London, Oxford University Press.

Briggs, A (1963) *Victorian Cities* London, Odhams.

Bullock, N and Read J (1985) *The Movement for Housing Reform in Germany and France 1840–1914* Cambridge, Cambridge University Press.

Chapman, SD (1967) *The Early Factory Masters: the transition to the factory system in the Midland textile industry* Newton Abbot, David and Charles.

Cherry, G (1994) *Birmingham: a study in geography, history and planning* Chichester, J Wiley & Sons.

Chinn, C (1991) *Houses for People: 100 years of council housing in Birmingham* Exeter, Birmingham Books.

Cohen, Y and Baudouï, R (1995) *Les Chantiers de la paix sociale (1900–1940)* Fontenay/St Cloud, ENS Editions.

Daunton, MJ (ed) (1990) *Housing the Workers: a comparative history 1850–1914* Leicester, Leicester University Press.

Davidoff, L, Doolittle, M, Fink, J and Holden, K (1999) *The Family Story: blood, contract and intimacy, 1830–1960* London, Longman.

Fishman, F (1977) *Urban Utopias in the Twentieth Century: Ebenezer Howard, Frank Lloyd Wright and Le Corbusier* New York, Basic Books.

Greatorex, J and Clarke, S (1984) *Looking back at Wythenshawe* Timperley, Willow Publishing.

Green, EHH (1999) "Gentlemanly Capitalism and British Economic Policy, 1880–1914: the debate over bi-metallism and protection" in Dunett, RE (ed) *Gentlemanly Capitalism and British Imperialism* London, Longmans, 52–4.

Guerrand, RH (1987) *Propriètaires et Locataires: les origins du logement social en France (1850–1914)* 2nd edn, Paris, Quintette.

Hardy, D (1991) *From Garden Cities to New Towns: campaigning for Town and Country Planning, 1899–1946* Vol I, London, E & FN Spon.

Harrison, M (2000) *Bournville: model village to garden suburb* Chichester, Phillimore.

Hopkins, E (1998) *The Rise of the Manufacturing Town: Birmingham and the Industrial Revolution* Stroud, Sutton.

Jennings, H (1962) *Societies in the Making: a study of development and redevelopment within a country borough* London, Routledge and Kegan Paul.

Jullian, R (1989) *Tony Garnier: constructeur et utopiste* Paris, Philippe Sers Editeur.

Lagier, A (1989) "Les Gratte-ciels de Villeurbanne" in Gages, P (ed) *L'Avenir Enterprise Coopérative 70 ans de l'histoire d'une métropole* Liège, Pierre Mardaga, 63–75.

Marrey, B (ed) (1998) *Henri Sellier: une cité pour tous* Paris, Édition du Linteau.

Mearns, A (1883) *The Bitter Cry of Outcast London* London, Frank Cass, reprint 1970.

Meller, HE (1976) *Leisure and the Changing City 1870–1914* London, Routledge and Kegan Paul.

Meurat, B (1980) *Croix Luizet: quartier de Villeurbanne* Lyon CNRS, Centre Régional de Publication de Lyon.

Meurat, B (1982) *Le Socialisme municipal: Villeurbanne 1880–1962 – une histoire d'une différenciation* Lyon, Presses Universitaires de Lyon.

Morton, J (1991) "The 1890 Act Housing Act and its aftermath: the era of the 'model dwellings'" in Lowe, S and Hughes, D (eds) *A New Century of Social Housing* Leicester, Leicester University Press, 13–32.

Musée Urbain Tony Garnier (1991) *La Cité de la création* Lyons, Centre de Recherche Esthétique et Cités.

Nettlefold, JS (1908) *Practical Housing* Letchworth, Letchworth Garden Press.

Pawlowsky, C (1967) *Tony Garnier et les débuts de l'urbanisme fonctionnel en France* Paris, Centre de Recherche d'Urbanisme.

Pierrou, N (1989) "Tony Garnier et l'école lyonnaise" in Gages, P (ed) *L'Avenir Enterprise Cooperative: 70 ans de l'histoire d'une métropole* Liège, Pierre Mardaga.

270

Pinol, J-L (1980) *Espace Sociale, espace politique: Lyon à l'époque dy Front Populaire* Lyons, Presses Universitaires de Lyon.

Pinol, J-L (ed) (1996) *Atlas Historique des Villes de France* Barcelona and Paris, Hachette Livre.

Pollard, S (1965) *The Genesis of Modern Management: a study of the industrial revolution in Great Britain* London, Edward Arnold.

Pooley, CG (ed) (1992) *Housing Strategies in Europe 1880–1930* Leicester, Leicester University Press.

Power, A (1993) *Hovels to High Rise: state housing in Europe since 1850* London and New York, Routledge.

Rapaport, A (1981) "Identity and Environment: a cross-cultural perspective" in Duncan, JS (ed) *Housing and Identity: cross-cultural perspectives* London, Croom Helm.

Ravetz, A with Turkington, R (1995) *The Place of Home: English domestic environments 1914–2000* London, E & FN Spon.

Rodger, R (1995) "Scottish Housing and English cultural imperialism c 1880–1940" in Zimmermann, S (ed) *Urban Space and Identity in the European City 1890–1930s* Budapest, CEU History Dept, Working Paper Series 3, 73–94.

Ruby, M (1979) *Le Résistance à Lyon: 19 Juin 1940–3 Septembre 1944* Lyon, L'Hèrmes.

Savage, M and Miles, A (1994) *The Remaking of the British Working Class 1840–1940* London, Routledge.

Sutcliffe, A (1974) "A Century of Flats in Birmingham 1875–1973" in Sutcliffe, A (ed) *Multi-Storey Living: the British working class experience* London, Croom Helm.

Sutcliffe, A and Smith, R (1974) *Birmingham 1939–1970: History of Birmingham* Vol III, London, Oxford University Press.

Swenarton, M (1981) *Homes for Heroes: the politics and architecture of early state housing in Britain* London, Heinemann Educational.

Tarn, J (1973) *5% Philanthropy: an account of housing in urban areas between 1840–1914* Cambridge, Cambridge University Press.

Tinkler, P (1995) "Women and Popular Literature" in Purvis, J (ed) *Women's History: Britain 1850–1914* London, UCL Press.

Travis, AS (1977) *The Evolution of Town Planning in France 1900–1919, with Special Reference to Tony Garnier and Planning in Lyon* Birmingham, University of Birmingham, Centre for Urban and Regional Studies.

Wiebensen, D (1969) *Tony Garnier: the Cité Industrielle* London and New York, Studia Vista.

Wohl, AS (1977) *The Eternal Slum: housing and social policy in Victorian London* London, Edward Arnold.

Yelling, JA (1990) "The Metropolitan Slum: London 1918–51" in Gaskell, SM (ed) *Slums* Leicester, Leicester University Press, 186–223.

Yelling, JA (1992) *Slums and Redevelopment Policy and Practice in England, 1918–45 with Particular Reference to London* London, UCL Press.

Young, M and Willmott, P (1957) *Family and Kinship in East London* London, Routledge and Kegan Paul.

LIST OF ILLUSTRATIONS

Acknowledgements

I would have found it impossible to complete a study of European cities without much help, both material and scholarly. I would like to express my thanks to the Leverhulme Trust for an institutional research grant from 1994–6, which made the whole project possible. My part-time secretary, Linda Howell, and my research assistant, David Pomfret, made an invaluable contribution in those first two years. David's ability to find his way around libraries and archives all over Europe became legendary! I would also like to acknowledge the substantial help I have received from the University of Nottingham in terms of grants and study leave; and to the Arts and Humanities Research Board for a grant under the extended study leave scheme, which enabled me to finish the manuscript and collect the illustrations.

I tried out many of my ideas in conference papers over the past five years at the conferences of the European Urban History Association, the International Planning History Society and the British Urban History Group. Attending these conferences in Budapest, Venice and Berlin; in Hong Kong, Thessaloniki, Seattle, Sydney and Helsinki; and in different cities in the UK, has been an education in itself. It has also brought me friends and much scholarly help with this book. I would like to thank the following for their encouragement and advice: Heleni Porfyriou, Donatella Calabi, Bob Morris, Richard Rodger, Dick Geary, John Walton, Anthony Sutcliffe, Karl Ditt, Thomas Hall, Pedro Lorente, Xavier Monclus and Geneviève Massard-Guilbaud. It is with much gratitude that I would like to acknowledge the help of Ilona Sármány-Parsons who gave unstintingly of her time to guide me on the history and culture of Central Europe; the help of Elizabeth Boa who made sure I understood my German sources; and Maria Bailey, who translated much on Barcelona for my benefit. So many people helped me to overcome language barriers. I would particularly like to thank Mme Hana Rosiková, the librarian in the Muzeum Jihovýchodní Moravy ve Zlíné, who made my study of this town possible. Of course, all remaining errors are my responsibility.

I would like to express my thanks for permission to reproduce illustrations to the following:

Introduction: Professor Dr Winfried Nerdinger, Professor of Architecture at the Technical University of Munich; the Stadtarchiv München; the Biblioteca, Palau de la Música Catalana, Barcelona; Arxiu Fotogràfic, Arxiu Històric de la Ciutat, Barcelona; and the Houghton Library, Harvard University.

278

Chapter 1	Budapest Archives; Professor Rostislav Švácha of the Institute of the History of Art, Prague; and Dr Ilona Sármány-Parsons.
Chapter 2	Archives d'Architecture Moderne, Bruxelles; Muzeum Jihový-chodni Moravy ve Zlíné; and Mr Pavel Novak.
Chapter 3	The Warburg Institute, London University; Chambre de Commerce et d'Industrie Marseille-Provence; Musée d'Histoire de Marseille.
Chapter 4	Cultural Services, Blackpool Borough Council; Musée d'Art et d'Histoire, Bibliothèque de Cessole, Palais de Masséna, Nice.

I would like to record my warm thanks to Glyn Halls, Photographic Technician of the Institute of Architecture, University of Nottingham, who has reproduced the photographs with such skill. I would also like to give special thanks to Chris Lewis, Head Cartographer, Department of Geography, University of Nottingham for all his really superb work on the sketch maps. I would also like to extend my thanks to the publishers, John Wiley and Sons, and to the editors, from Iain Stevenson who commissioned this work, to Maggie Toy and her assistant, Abigail Grater, who saw it through the press, who have been unfailingly helpful and supportive.

Finally, it gives me much pleasure to acknowledge more personal debts. Nick Hewitt has given support and help, and much practical assistance throughout this project. I dedicate this volume to him, he has truly earned it! And also thanks to my daughter, Meesha, who not only gave much emotional support but used her linguistic skills in Spanish on my behalf.

Helen Meller
January 2001,
Nottingham

INDEX

Page numbers in italics refer to illustrations

Index compiled by Caroline Wilding